MINI

MINI

RESTORATION / PREPARATION / MAINTENANCE

JIM TYLER

OSPREY
AUTOMOTIVE

Published in 1992 by Osprey Publishing Ltd
59 Grosvenor Street, London W1X 9DA

A catalogue record for this book is available on request
from the British Library.

ISBN 1-85532-229-3

Page design: Paul Kime
Editor: Shaun Barrington
Phototypeset by Tradespools Ltd., Frome, Somerset
Printed in Great Britain by BAS Printers Limited,
Over Wallop, Hampshire

CONTENTS

ACKNOWLEDGEMENTS

The author gratefully acknowledges the help and assistance given by companies and individuals in the preparation of this book.

SIP Holdings provided the excellent Handymig gasless MIG welder and the Tornado compressor which are used by the author. Sykes Pickavant were helpful in providing photographs of their renowned range of hand tools.

Alan Gosling of Central Garage, Martley, kindly trusted the author to use his hydraulic flywheel remover, without which the engine of the project car could not have been stripped.

Graham Hickman and the staff of Rolling Road Auto Tune (RATS) of Martley kindly gave the benefit of their many years of experience in performance preparation.

Dennis Baldry kindly supplied the photographs reproduced in Chapter One. With thanks to the Mini Centre, Eckington.

In particular, Autodata kindly gave permission for illustrations from their car manual to be reproduced. Without their cooperation, this book would not be possible.

Thanks are due to the staff of Which Kit? and Kit Car magazines for supplying up to date information on Mini-based kit cars.

Lastly but by no means least, the author gives his grateful thanks to the many friends who, over the years, have contributed to his knowledge of the maintenance, repair and restoration of the Mini.

INTRODUCTION

There has never been another car quite like the Mini. From humble beginnings as a cheap runaround for the petrol-starved late 1950s, the Mini quickly became a cult car for the swinging sixties and a motorsports car with an outstanding competition success history. It became a van, a pickup and an estate. Throughout the 1970s and 1980s the Mini continued in production whilst many more recently designed cars were discontinued. Today, more than thirty years after its launch, the Mini has been named as Britain's best-selling export car!

At the time of writing, the Mini is one of the commonest cars on the roads of the UK, despite the relatively low production figures in recent years. This is due to the innumerable examples of 1980s, '70s and '60s Minis which have somehow survived the ravages of time whilst the majority of their contemporaries succumbed to body rot and were consigned to the scrap heap.

Yet the days of any Mini which is approaching or has passed its tenth birthday will be numbered, unless action is taken to find and rectify the developing body and mechanical faults which would otherwise one day degenerate to the point at which restoration costs far exceed resultant market value. People are happy to lavish large sums of money on the complete restoration of a genuine Cooper or a very early Mini, because they can quite properly (unless classic car values plummet from today's fairly sensible starting point, which is not likely) view that outlay as something of an investment: and an investment which will give the owner untold pleasure.

Minis with substantial collector's values are of course very much in the minority. For every 1960s classic Mini which survives there may well be many 1970s and a number of 1980s examples which are just clinging on to roadworthiness. The costs of professional restoration, which would be fully justified for a 1275 Cooper S, bear no relation to the final values of most 1970s or 1980s Minis, so that the only financially viable option for the owners of such cars is DIY.

This book is intended to help the Mini owner to bring his or her car to roadworthy condition at the lowest cost, then to keep it there with proper mechanical and bodywork maintenance. It is not a full workshop manual, nor is it a general guide to the arts of classic car restoration. The author recommends that the book is used in conjunction with a good workshop manual, such as the one published in the Autodata series. If the reader seeks more in-depth information on any aspect of restoration, then Osprey Automotive publish an excellent range of guides to the individual elements of restoration.

This book has been designed so that irrespective of whether you wish to deal with a particular mechanical fault or bodywork problem, or whether you wish to carry out a full 'bare shell' restoration, the information you need is easily accessed and presented in a sensible order. The text is based on the experiences of the author in working on poorer examples of the car, and so highlights many special problems which some workshop manuals might miss. A good general example is the typical simple advice one might find in a workshop manual to 'remove the large nut', which fails to point out that in the case of an older example of the car, the said nut will be well and truly seized up and require the use of an unburstable hexagonal impact socket, at least a two foot long lever and a hefty swipe with a lump hammer to budge it!

The author has endeavoured as far as possible to

avoid continual cross-referencing between chapters, which can force the reader to flip backwards and forwards through a manual in order to piece together what should otherwise be a straightforward and commonplace working sequence. In order to avoid too much duplication of information, some cross references are, however, unavoidable.

Before embarking on the restoration of a Mini variant which has low or no classic car value, the reader is advised to produce, as accurately as possible, a costings forecast. In some instances it may prove far more economical to purchase a bodyshell in better condition than the original (the Mini Owner's Club magazine usually includes advertisements for shells in addition to all other Mini spares). In other cases you may discover the most sensible route to be restoring the existing shell but using a majority of mechanical components from another car whose body is on the way out.

There is always the kit car option for those cars whose restoration cannot be financially justified. Some enthusiasts will undoubtedly frown on the inclusion of kit cars in a book largely dedicated to the production Mini, but the kit car offers owners of some low value 1970s and early 1980s Minis the option to build themselves a car which can provide as much pleasure as the Mini itself from a car which common sense would otherwise consign to the scrap heap.

1 · A SHORT HISTORY

The Mini was launched (badged as both the Austin Seven and the Morris Mini Minor) during August of 1959. The car represented several departures from contemporary automotive design conventions, because it had actually been designed specifically to offer advantages in the economic climate of a few years before. At the time of the conception of the car, petrol had been strictly rationed in the UK. Due to the petrol shortage, many motorists were leaving their larger 1950s cars (which generally had high fuel consumption) in the garage and instead using an economical moped, scooter or one of the European bubble cars as daily transport.

The majority of vehicles of the time were either larger saloon cars which offered passenger comfort but were expensive to run, or small cars such as the Austin A35 which offered reasonable economy but which could not seat four adults in anything approaching comfort. There was an obvious niche for a more economical small car which could nevertheless carry four adults in reasonable comfort, and the British Motor Corporation Chairman, Leonard Lord, gave the resultant design brief to the brilliant Sir Alec Issigonis.

The BMC small cars of the 1950s included the A30/35 and the Morris Minor series, both of which were based around the 'traditional' geometry of an in-line engine at the front of the car and driving wheels at the rear. This arrangement naturally gave the cars relatively long bonnets for their overall size, a quite long engine bay being necessary to house the engine, fan and radiator. It also restricted the internal passenger volume due to the intrusion of the transmission tunnel down the centre of the car and the bulge necessary to give clearance for the differential and rear suspension. Short vehicles of the day, such as the A35, thus offered little in the way of

passenger comfort, being especially cramped for those sitting in the back (the rear seat was often more suitable for children than adults).

The revolutionary element within the design of the Mini was to turn the engine through ninety degrees and to situate the gearbox essentially within the sump (it is housed in an aluminium casing which bolts directly onto the lower face of the engine) to drive the front wheels. This arrangement allowed sufficient passenger space for four adults to be built into a car which had an overall length of just ten feet (3.05 metres).

Initially, the Mini was to have been fitted with a two cylinder engine, but the greater smoothness offered by a four cylinder unit (probably added to the fact that BMC already possessed a suitable engine in their 'A' series unit) resulted in the fitting of the four cylinder unit. Engine capacity was reduced by 100cc from 948cc to 848 cc and a single SU carburettor was fitted in place of the Zenith unit used on the A35. The resultant power output of the Mini engine equalled that of the larger 948cc A35 unit at 34bhp.

The engine, transmission and suspension components were mounted on two subframes, one front and one rear. In monocoque cars of the time it was usual for these components to be mounted on fixed chassis members which were built into the bodyshell, but the Mini's subframes could both be removed. This can make restoration of the Mini slightly easier than that of most monocoque cars.

The original rubber suspension possessed limited travel and gave the car taut handling qualities which, allied to the natural characteristics of the front engined, front wheel drive configuration, made the car very easy and forgiving to drive in a sporty fashion. Having a wheel 'at each corner' gave the car the maximum wheeltrack, which also contributed to

The standard Clubman is not a good prospect for the restorer, but an example like this could be turned into a reliable workhorse.

roadholding. The roadholding of the car was in fact so marked an improvement over that of all contemporary comparable small cars that it is not an exaggeration to state that it set new standards.

By the time of the Earl's Court Motor Show in October 1959, two other British manufacturers were launching small cars to compete with the Mini. Ford introduced the Anglia, a monocoque-bodied front engined rear wheel drive car with sharp (American influenced) styling but little in the way of innovation: Triumph launched their Herald, which possessed a separate chassis and also retained the standard engine-drive layout. The Anglia had a production life of just eight years and the Herald lasted until 1979, whereas the Mini at the time of writing is still in production in little-changed form over thirty years after its launch! There can be little doubt that the Mini is not only the most revolutionary auto design of all time but that it has proven the most lasting and successful of all truly 'revolutionary' cars.

Although sales were initally slightly disappointing, home market sales quickly picked up as the practical advantages of the new car became apparent and as the car went on to become almost a fashion item in the UK of the 1960s. The Mini became the first truly 'classless' car insofar as it was affordable to any motorist yet at the same time coveted and enjoyed by the rich and famous.

Perhaps encouraged by the early commercial success of its new car, BMC introduced the Mini Van in 1960, which was followed by the estate version (the Austin badged version called the 'Countryman' and the Morris car the 'Traveller'). Both estate versions had wood body trimmings in the style of the earlier and much-loved Morris Minor Traveller, although the wood became optional from 1962. The pickup version was introduced in 1961 and, like the van, proved very popular with small businesses, farmers and those in the building and service industries. Also in 1961, the first of the Mini Coopers appeared.

It was perhaps inevitable that a 'sports' version of the Mini would appear; the ability of this little car to easily take corners at speeds which would have

The Mini Van quickly became established as the most economical and practical vehicle for the small businessman and tradesman. These diminutive vans found favour with farmers due to their off-road abilities, and many examples finally expired on the fields of England!

defeated most if not all other small saloon cars of the day showed the car's potential for rallying.

The original Mini Cooper (developed by John Cooper) was fitted with a 997cc version of the 'A' series engine which delivered 55bhp at 6000rpm and cut the 0-60mph time from just over 20 seconds for the 848cc standard car to a creditable 15 seconds, in addition to raising the top speed from 75mph to 90mph. This variant almost immediately began to win rallies and awoke the motorsport world to the fact that this audacious little car could quite easily be turned into a competition winner. Few people at that stage, however, could have foreseen that the car would soon come to dominate the most prestigious rally event in the world.

A 'Super' and a 'De Luxe' version were introduced, both to be replaced by the 'Super De Luxe' in 1962. Before that, two other luxury versions of the car – the Wolseley Hornet and the Riley Elf – were launched. These cars offered increased boot luggage space by incorporating a boot which protruded between two 'normal' if short rear wings. They also possessed far more luxurious interior trim and larger, more efficient brakes. From 1963, the Mk.2 versions of both the Hornet and the Elf were fitted with a 998cc engine developing 38bhp.

The 998cc Cooper replaced the 997cc version in early 1964. From 1963 to 1964 the 1071cc Cooper S – now a very rare and expensive classic – was sold. In 1964 Paddy Hopkirk drove the 1071cc Cooper S to an outright win in the Monte Carlo. This version was superseded by the 1275cc Cooper S, which won the Monte Carlo rally outright in 1965 and 1967. In 1966, the car took 1st, 2nd and 3rd places in this rally, which must have greatly upset some people because scrutineers disqualified all three Coopers (plus the Lotus Cortina which came 4th) on a technicality which some might consider 'trumped-up' and which (surprise) permitted a French car to officially come first. The problem concerned the British cars' front lights, which were held to differ from those of the standard production vehicles. It is now generally believed that this complaint was without foundation. The 970 Cooper S was also introduced to be campaigned (successfully) in sub-1 litre competitions.

The Mini Moke was also launched in 1964. During its four years of production, the majority of examples appear to have been exported and few original BMC cars remain in the UK. Manufacture of the Moke switched to Australia and subsequently to

YBY 444G

The Wolseley Hornet was positively luxurious compared to the Minis of the time, sporting leather-faced seats, walnut dash and fitted carpet.

Portugal. There are, however, many very creditable imitations available as kit cars even into the 1990s. Those who crave the Mini Moke experience are able to build themselves a vehicle which matches the original in everything save collector's values. At the time of writing, the Portugese manufactured Moke is being imported into the UK in limited numbers and at attractive prices. In 1965 an automatic gearbox produced by Automotive Products was added, and these cars are usually denoted in advertisements today by the letters AP.

The Mini 1000 (fitted with the 998cc engine from the Wolseley Hornet/Riley Elf which were to be discontinued in 1969) appeared as an option in 1967, as the Mk.2 Mini. The bodyshell was altered to accept a larger rear window. Two years later the 'Clubman' bodyshell, with a longer bonnet which allowed better engine access, appeared in 998cc and 1275GT versions. The standard bodyshell was again altered the following year to accept larger doors.

The majority of Mini variants manufactured between 1964 and 1970 (1971 in the case of the Clubman) ran on Hydrolastic suspension, a fluid-based system which gave a softer ride than the earlier rubber alternative but which is disliked by some enthusiasts of the car who believe the rubber suspension to be superior. It is in fact not too difficult a job to convert a Hydrolastic car back to rubber suspension, the components being widely available at any scrap yard! Mini vans and estates continued to be manufactured with rubber cone suspension throughout.

Numerous minor design changes have occurred from the 1970s to date. The 850cc engine was phased out in 1980 when the 998cc engine became the only option, and the Clubman was also discontinued. An 'E' (Economy) and an HLE saloon were introduced in 1982, with the 998cc engine and raised compression (from 8.3:1 to 10.3:1) plus higher gearing for overall greater economy.

In 1984 a special limited edition (5000) 'Silver Jubilee 25' was produced to celebrate the 25th anniversary of the car's launch. A number of limited edition cars followed including the Ritz, Chelsea, Piccadilly, Park Lane and Advantage.

During the late 1980s there were many rumours that the car was to be discontinued. From the manufacturer's viewpoint, the Mini must have been

Mini Clubman Estate.

seen to be taking a share of the sale which might otherwise have gone to the Metro, the successor to the earlier British Leyland Allegro and BMC 1100/1300 cars, both of which were similarly front engined, front wheel drive cars which the Mini has seen come and go during its long production life. Also, the fact that the production methods employed in the manufacture of the Mini are out of keeping with the modern trend towards greater automation must weigh against the car.

Despite the above considerations, the Mini continues to sell in such high numbers that the manufacturers are loathe to discontinue it. The modern buyer of a Mini is choosing this thirty-year-old car in preference to alternatives which offer greater comfort, speed and which, because they embrace all the advantages of modern technology, are on paper arguably superior in every department. Thus the single greatest advantage which the Mini can offer against its modern rivals is a character which makes motoring a pleasure in a world where the alternatives are bland. In March 1991 it was reported that the Mini had become the best selling British car in Japan. The production figures for the Mini have now topped 5 million and, with the car still in production by the original manufacturer, there appears to be no end in sight!

Into the Nineties

The cylinder heads fitted to all Minis prior to 1989 were manufactured from cast iron and should on no account be used with unleaded fuel, because this burns the valve seats in a very short time. Cars supplied from mid-1989 have cylinder heads fitted with special hardened valve seats able to withstand the higher temperatures and lack of lead protection associated with unleaded fuel, and are fully compatible with its use. If you are in any doubt that your car might not be compatible with unleaded fuel then use only leaded petrol until you are able to

The Mini Traveller was a viable alternative for those who might otherwise have opted for the larger and much-loved, though dated Morris Minor traveller. Like the Mini Van, the Traveller gave a comparatively huge carrying volume for the size of the vehicle, and it was also a favourite of the small businessman.

confirm with your nearest Rover Group dealer or representative whether the car is suitable for unleaded petrol. Cylinder heads fitted with hardened exhaust valve seats and valves are available on an exchange basis for most Minis and these will permit the use of unleaded fuel.

During the early part of 1991, it was announced that the Mini had become Britain's best selling car in export markets. Whether this indicates the excellence of or fondness for the Mini, or whether it is a sad indictment on the state of the rest of the British motor manufacturing trade, will probably be a subject for hot debate. The author is inclined to accept the former reason.

LIVING WITH A MINI

That a car should not only remain in production for thirty years but also retain its popularity should in itself serve as more than adequate comment on its fitness for the intended purpose; yet at the time of writing there are those (in the main motoring journalists) who would pronounce their own, unfavourable, judgement on the car and publish it for all to see. Anyone contemplating the purchase of a new Mini could easily be influenced by various published comparison reports into opting instead for an alternative of more modern design. The offending articles which criticise the Mini are inevitably based on direct comparisons between today's Mini and today's hatchback 'supermini', including the now ubiquitous 'Hot Hatch'. It is therefore politic to begin this part of the book by reviewing and re-appraising those comparisons.

Mini or 'SuperMini'?

The Mini was conceived and designed essentially as a 'town' car, able to show great manoeuvrability in congested traffic areas and to park in the smallest of spaces. This role it has fulfilled admirably and

The Clubman was available with 998cc and 1100cc engines. The shell was used for the sporty 1275GT.

without equal for over thirty years. The Mini was also designed to be capable of transporting four adults in reasonable comfort and in an economical manner – in these roles it is still very creditable but has arguably been surpassed by some examples of the modern so-called 'supermini'.

It seems as though whenever motoring journalists nowadays turn their attentions to the Mini (except in those articles which treat the Mini only as a classic car) it is inevitably to compare it with the very best of today's supermini hatchback cars which, of course, have the advantage of being designed to enjoy the fruits of the technological advances of the past thirty years. It can hardly be considered surprising that, in such comparisons, the Mini is often criticised for its lack of interior space, for its level of comfort and refinement. Yet the Mini is 14″ (35.5 cms) shorter in overall length than its nearest supermini rival, and 37″ (94 cms) shorter than the longest of the superminis. Inch for inch, the Mini still appears to offer more interior passenger space than any of the modern rivals. In terms of its abilities as a town car which may be parked in the smallest of spaces, the Mini is only rivalled by the diminutive Fiat 126 – a car over which it is in the author's opinion superior in every other way.

In overall economy, the Mini is still to all intents and purposes the equal of the very best which modern technology can offer, substantially surpassed – as are all petrol cars – only by the better examples of diesel cars. The frugal fuel consumption (which averages around 40 mpg) is bettered by some modern petrol cars, but when the costs of maintenance, repair and insurance are also taken into consideration, then the Mini remains in the first division of economical cars.

The 'refinement' offered by the Mini – for which it is often criticised in comparisons with modern cars – is determined only by the marketing policies of its manufacturer. If required, the Mini could be given a degree of interior luxury to match or exceed that of its modern rivals – but those who buy new Minis obviously do not attach too much importance to such refinement. Instead, they are buying a car which after thirty years is still doing the job it was originally

The sheer numbers of Minis in various guises that were produced means that there are often rich pickings around for the restorer, even from a sorry sight such as this.

MINI BRITISH OPEN

ASSIC

designed to do. The manufacturers could also give the Mini more 'refined' handling qualities simply by softening the suspension or reverting to a hydraulic system or alternatively a pneumatic suspension system. Neither would really fit in with the character of the car. The manufacturers have of course previously tried softening the suspension with their 'Hydrolastic' suspension, but went back to the harder rubber cone suspension which most Mini enthusiasts seem to prefer.

Thus, every criticism of the Mini – comfort, economy and refinement – by the modern motoring journalist can be answered very satisfactorily. The Mini remains an excellent new car and will undoubtedly continue to be so for as long as the Rover Group continue its manufacture.

It is worth mentioning that the Mini appears to be the only car which has been in continuous production since the 1960s which is directly compared with rivals of more modern design in test reports published in periodicals.

The Versatile Mini

Whether you are looking for an economical small car for utilitarian reasons, whether you relish pleasurable motoring with surefooted and sporty handling or whether you desire the satisfaction of driving a truly classic car then the right example of the Mini is unlikely to disappoint you. The nature of the car depends on what you ask of it and what you give to it.

Take one 848cc Mini. You have a shopping car able to hold a surprising quantity of groceries split between the boot and the back seat (the author used to carry a full drum kit around in an 850 Mini saloon and later in a Wolsey Hornet), able to nimbly weave through the traffic, able to park in spaces which are so small that they are in effect automatically 'reserved' for Minis because so few other cars can use them. You have a car in which two people and their luggage can travel to a holiday, in which four adults can travel at legal maximum motorway speeds. You have a car which can be driven with confidence over snow and ice or mud, which can even be driven off the road more surely than most other 2WD cars. Take the same 848cc Mini, fit an 1100cc or

Rover press release picture for the latest special edition with power operated fabric sunroof.

1275cc engine and the mildest of performance modifications and you have a surprisingly fast road car with vast potential for further performance modifications to turn it into a capable competition car for a range of events. And the self-same 848cc Mini can be a classic car when it has aged sufficiently. The car is whatever you make of it.

Driving the Mini

The roadholding of the Mini was considered nothing short of astounding to those lucky enough to savour it in the early years. The experience of being pulled around bends is usually taken for granted by those younger motorists who have always driven front wheel drive cars, but when the Mini was new, the vast majority of drivers were used to rear wheel drive and found this a strange but very pleasing sensation.

The front wheel drive of the Mini allowed a new rally driving technique; that of engaging the handbrake whilst applying power to the front wheels to make the rear end break and swing smartly into line on sharp corners. Rally drivers will also have appreciated the ability of the Mini to make progress up snow-covered hills when rear wheel drive cars simply lost traction and the rear end of the cars started to slide sideways. If the Mini driving wheels slid sideways, the drivers simply turned the wheels against the direction of the slide to pull the front end back into line. Drivers of rear wheel drive cars can do no more than turn into the direction of a side which, to say the least, makes life very difficult on a snow-covered narrow mountain road.

Although the roadholding of the most basic Mini is in the sports car class, the engines fitted to the cars (Coopers excepted) have in general been anything but sporty in character.

An 850 Mini can take just over 20 seconds to reach 60mph, so that rapid progress is possible only by virtue of the car's great roadholding, and as long as a reasonable overall speed can be maintained. The car is not so good if progress is hindered by slower-moving traffic, due to its sluggish overtaking abilities. Having said that, a properly set-up 850 in good order actually feels quite lively – certainly some seem to be

The famous monocoque body and little else left. The fact that the Mini body is small does not, of course, mean that restoration is easier than for a larger car.

much quicker than published performance figures indicate. However, the 850 engine was phased out in 1980, and owners of such elderley cars are likely to covet them as classics and cast a blind eye to any deficiencies in the 30-50mph acceleration times.

The 1000 Mini is far more satisfactory. Although early examples still took 20 seconds to reach 60mph, the higher torque (52 ft lbs against 44 for the 850) made overtaking far safer. Published figures for recent 1000cc Minis shave the 0-60mph time down to just over 17 seconds, which makes them better still. Again, it is imperative that the cars are properly set up.

The 1100 Mini Clubman had a performance very similar to that of more recent Mini 1000s; the larger 1275GT offered considerably more power (60 bhp, 84 ft lbs of torque) and was and still is a very capable road car which allows quite high average speeds to be maintained on ordinary roads. The top speed of the 1275GT was 90 mph and this, coupled with its 0-60 mph time of 13.5 seconds, makes the 1275GT a quite creditable performer even today. The early 997/998 Mini Coopers were not so fast as the far later 1275GT, although the 'S' Coopers could all show the 1275GT a clean pair of heels.

In early 1990 the Rover Group launched a performance conversion for the 1000cc Mini, dubbed the 'John Cooper Conversion' because it was substantially the same conversion which had been selling in great quantities when marketed by John Cooper Garage. Offering a 0-60mph time of just over 12 seconds and a 90 mph top speed, this is hardly competition for the 1980s 'Hot Hatchback' and GTi's, but rather recreates the kind of performance level of which the Cooper variants of the 1960s were capable. This is but one of many alternative performance increasing packages which are available for the Mini; some packages turn the car into real competition for the 16 valve GTi's.

At the time of writing, Janspeed are developing an eight port cross-flow cylinder head which, in conjunction with a fuel injection system and other mods, will ensure that the car will actually 'see off' the GTi pack! Several other companies are also continuously developing performance modifications for the Mini.

The vast majority of Mini owners, however, are more than content with the performance, with the driver and passenger comfort, with the carrying capacities and the driving pleasure offered by the standard car, be it a 1275S Cooper or, indeed, the humble 850.

2 · BUYING A MINI

Few cars enjoy a production life as long as the Mini's, and so few cars can be found on the second-hand market (particularly in the UK) in such abundance as the Mini. This does not, unfortunately, make the business of locating the right Mini any easier, because a great many of the older examples on offer will require extensive and expensive bodywork repair; others are so rotten as to be downright dangerous.

The correct way to go about buying a Mini (especially an earlier example) is to learn all that it is possible to learn about bodywork faults, how to discover them and how to uncover attempts at disguising them, before beginning to view potential cars. All too often, would-be Mini buyers (as buyers of all types of second-hand car) set out to adjudge the vehicle merely by the condition of the paintwork and the cleanliness of the carpets!

The sad fact is that very few cars of any make or model survive much beyond their tenth birthday without some fairly substantial bodywork repair becoming necessary. Even cars which remain locked in garages deteriorate unless the garage is air conditioned and de-humidified, because moisture in the air condenses out onto bodywork due to temperature changes, and the rusting process begins, often hidden within box sections.

In viewing any car over five or so years of age it is necessary to assume that there will be some degree of surface rust or bodyrot and to try and establish the extent and rectification costs of the rust. Equally important are finding disguised bodyrot and finding evidence of uncorrected crash damage which might have distorted the body. There is a lot to learn.

The first question to be addressed is usually 'which Mini?'. No other single car can fulfil so many roles as the Mini. It is at once a collector's car, a sports car and a competition car; it is equally a small business 'workhorse', a runabout, a shopping car, a family transport car yet also (at the time of writing) a new car.

The apparently simple decision to buy a Mini is thus anything but straightforward. One buyer might desire a classic 1959 Austin Seven whilst another seeks the reliability of a brand new Mini 1000; one buyer might require a 1275S Mini Cooper to campaign in classic rallies whilst another seeks a well-used Mini Van or Pickup for transporting sheep around a farm. No buyer's guide could cater comprehensively for such a wide range of interests.

This chapter will concentrate on the interests of two specific groups of buyers but, in doing so, will hopefully offer much to anyone who wishes to buy a Mini for whatever reason. The two groups are those who see the Mini as a classic (collector's) car, and those who wish to buy a used example of the car for normal road use – those who simply want an economical car.

Before considering the question of which Mini to buy it is as well to consider where to buy the car from. There are several sources of used Minis.

Private Sale

The majority of Minis which change hands in the UK pass from one private individual to another. The economical motoring which the Mini offers ensures that the car is rarely difficult to sell second-hand (in comparison with other cars) if in good condition and so there is often no need for the vendor to take the car to a dealer in part-exchange against a newer car; which might be described as the traditional way to dispose of a car for which there is low demand. Of these privately sold cars, those variants which are widely regarded as classics may be advertised nationally within the established classic car press; others may be advertised within a region, or even within a very small locality.

Those seeking a very rare variant will almost certainly have to look within the national press and be prepared to travel some distance in order to view cars. A car like the Cooper S or the British-made Mini Moke will usually be owned by an enthusiast and only advertised within the classic car press. The less rare variants also appear in the classic car press but are also to be found in regional and sometimes local media. A Mark 1 Morris Mini Minor, 997/998 Cooper or 'woody' traveller can be advertised anywhere from the most prestigious classic car magazine to the local shop window.

If a more ubiquitous variant is sought then there is no need and no justification for travelling long distances in order to view cars, because there should be a good choice closer to home. The great problem with travelling long distances to view cars is that many of the descriptions of the cars given in advertisements are, to put it mildly, misleading. You might drive 100 miles to view a car which has been advertised as being in concours condition only to discover that the bases of the roof pillars consist largely of body filler. Such wasted journeys are costly in terms both of time and money.

Local cars may be found through 'word of mouth' if you let it be known amongst friends and neighbours that you are looking for a Mini. Alternatively, a classified 'Wanted' advertisement in the local press can produce results and is especially useful for finding 'restoration project' cars which may be languishing in their owner's garage and which the owner never quite 'gets around' to advertising for sale or restoring himself. The advantage of going out and finding cars rather than answering advertisements is that you will not be in competition with other buyers.

Buying from a private vendor is not without risk. Most private vendors assume that all responsibility for the car they sell to you ceases the moment you drive away, and if a subframe detaches itself from the body twenty yards down the road, the vendor will not wish to make a refund and will not consider him or herself liable. Some private vendors are rogues and will sell a car which has serious but camouflaged bodyrot; others might sell such a car in good faith, being genuinely unaware of the problems. In most cases, it is very difficult to gain compensation.

Another pitfall when buying from a private vendor is the car on which a Hire Purchase debt is outstanding. The vehicle is in effect hired from the finance company and is the property of that company, and it is only after the full payment period that it becomes the property of the person named in the HP agreement. If you buy a car on which there is the smallest outstanding HP debt then the HP company will quite legally repossess the car as soon as they discover what has happened. You will lose both your money and the car. For this reason, you must insist on seeing a receipt for the purchase of the car.

Buying privately also increases the chances of unwittingly buying a stolen vehicle. As the values of classic cars rise they become more attractive targets for thieves, and there are a number of ways in which a stolen vehicle may be sold. The most common method of disposing of a stolen vehicle is to make it a 'ringer'; that is, it is given a registration, engine and chassis number from another example of the car of the same year and colour. A 'replacement' registration document is applied for and the apparently legitimate car then offered for sale.

There is no certain safeguard against buying a car which is a ringer. However, in addition to a registration document, the vendor should be able to show you a road fund licence disc, an MOT certificate (or its local equivilent outside the UK) and insurance documents, (none of which need be current) as well as a sale receipt from the previous owner of the car. If you unwittingly buy a stolen vehicle and its true identity is subsequently discovered then you will lose the car and most probably your money as well. Take every precaution in this respect, especially when buying a newish car or one which is considered a classic and which possesses classic car value.

In the UK and in several other countries, there are clubs devoted to the Mini, and the members of these clubs are arguably the best people to buy a Mini from, because they will probably have themselves checked the car's legality in the past.

In the case of the classic Minis, authenticity is also an important consideration. There is nowadays a great temptation for unscrupulous people to alter a standard 1960s Mini so that it resembles a Cooper S worth many times the value of the standard car. The best safeguard against buying such a vehicle is to contact the British Motor Industry Heritage Trust (Castle Road, Studley, Warwickshire B80 7AJ, England tel. 052785 4014). For a fee, the BMIHT will check the details of any UK-manufactured Mini against their records of the car when it was manufactured. If a standard car has been altered then this check should reveal that fact. Be warned, however, that no manufacturers' records appear to exist for Minis manufactured after 1969; certainly the BMIHT possess none.

In favour of buying a Mini from a private vendor is the possibility of buying a car at a bargain price. Against this must be weighed the foregoing considerations.

Trade Sales

More recent cars are often sold by mainstream car trade dealers. Buying from a reputable dealer has certain advantages in that serious structural problems and also more minor mechanical faults may be dealt with under the terms of the dealer's guarantee. Also, if the car you buy turns out to be stolen then you have a great chance of obtaining a refund from the dealer. Not all used car dealers, however, are honest.

Consumer protection laws in many countries have become much stronger in recent years and have forced many 'cowboy' used-car dealers out of the trade, although a number of unscrupulous dealers remain in business. The best way to avoid buying from a questionable business source is to buy only from those which possess workshop and bodyshop facilities, so that if any serious faults are discovered with the car then they may be put right at the dealer's own premises. The large business which not only sells but also repairs and rebuilds cars will be very keen to maintain its reputation and will usually be willing to rectify any faults which appear on cars it has sold.

Classic car dealers have appeared in great numbers in recent years and, like mainstream used car dealers, there are both good and bad amongst them. Minis are starting to appear in the advertisements of classic dealers, but, in the main, these are mainly Coopers and freshly-restored very early cars. Again, the best business to deal with is one which not only sells, but also repairs and restores its cars. The worst business to deal with is that owned by a former classic car enthusiast who trades from private household premises, because such businesses have no means of repairing faults and, importantly, no reputation to uphold.

A reputable mainstream or classic car dealer can be an excellent source of a Mini, although you will not find cars being offered at 'bargain' prices. If you buy from a good classic car dealer then you will be taking advantage of his knowledge of the car, for he is unlikely to buy in a car which has serious problems. The prices asked by reputable dealers will reflect the actual market worth of the vehicles in question.

If you are buying a Mini to restore and intend to (as is recommended) have some of the restoration work carried out professionally, then you could consider asking the restoration company to locate a suitable car on your behalf. In practice, the company will usually wish to buy the car and then sell it on to you, taking a small profit in the process. There are advantages to finding a Mini in this way. For a relatively small fee, you gain the benefit of the knowledge and experience of someone who is truly expert in buying good examples for restoration, and who will probably arrange transportation into the bargain. A professional will probably negotiate a rather better price for the purchase than you, so that, even after his profit has been added on, you may pay very little less than you would have by buying the car directly yourself.

Any restoration company should be able to help you locate a suitable car, although some companies may be reluctant to become involved unless they are to carry out all of the restoration work themselves. Export Services of Redditch are a good example of the type of company to seek out. Originally, the company sourced, restored and shipped Minis to Japan, sometimes finding rare or particular individual cars to order. Although the demand from this market is now far less than in its heyday, the company still deals with the restoration of Minis ranging from classic one-off specials and cars with particular historical importance to more modern cars suitable for day to day use. No matter what Mini you are seeking, a competent and helpful company should be able to help you.

Auctions

There are two types of car auction. The classic car auction at which you will find Minis is a relatively modern phenomenon and, if you become adept at appraising cars very quickly, it can be a reasonable place to buy a classic Mini. In favour of this type of auction is the fact that many potential buyers will be present, and by eavesdropping on other conversations you can take advantage of their experience! If you see a person kick a tyre and make a pronouncement on the car then do not place too much faith in his or her opinion; the person who lifts carpets and who shines a torch beam into crevices is the one whose opinion matters.

At the classic car auction you are unlikely to be able to take a test drive, and so many mechanical problems could exist unseen. Furthermore, you will have very little time to make up your mind as to whether the car really suits your needs. These are necessary gambles.

The general (as opposed to the 'classic') car auction in the UK is usually the place where 'difficult to sell' cars are sold. There is no legitimate reason why a good condition classic Mini variant should ever appear at such an event, and little reason for anyone to dispose of a saleable recent Mini there, either. However, such events as company liquidations, estate disposal and so on do provide reasonable vehicles from time to time at general car auctions. By and large they are places best avoided, given the tremendous selection of privately-owned Minis which may be found on the open market at any time.

Irrespective of where you look for a car, bear in mind that the Mini is one of the most prolific cars on offer. If you have any cause to suspect the car or the vendor then you can afford to walk away in the knowledge that other examples will be available. Do not be pressurised into making a hasty decision, even if the car in question is a particularly rare variant (too much selling pressure could indicate that the car is counterfeit) or is offered at an apparently 'bargain' price. Those who buy in haste usually repent at leisure.

WHICH MINI?

Classic Minis

The vast majority of cars which are considered 'classic' insofar as they are sought after by collectors, are no longer manufactured and, in most instances, they will not have been manufactured for many years. Often, it is the very fact that a car is obsolete which creates its classic value and those cars which

were not commercially successful (and which were consequently only manufactured in small numbers for a limited number of years) are often the most coveted of classics! The Mini is one of the most successful cars of all time, so that while it is undeniably a classic car it is also available in large numbers and may be acquired at more reasonable prices than almost any other classic car.

Which model and year of Mini is a classic car? Is there a particular year of manufacture, a 'cut-off' point, at which a Mini ceases to be considered a classic? There cannot be. There is no strict definition of what exactly constitutes a classic and differentiates it from any other aged car: it is a decision which must and which can only be taken by the individual and, if you choose to call a brand-new Mini 1000 a 'classic' then no-one can really argue that it is not.

There is only one practical guide to the classic status of a car and this should be considered before a car restoration is commissioned. When the purchase price plus professional restoration costs of a car are little or no higher than its eventual worth following restoration, then it is incontestably a valuable classic.

The Mini which is most coveted as a classic car (excepting individual vehicles with historic importance, such as those which belonged to very famous people or which won prestigious events) is the 970cc Cooper S. Because less than 1000 examples of this car were built in 1964 and 1965 it is today very rare. Thus rarity value is added to the intrinsic value of the 970S as a sports/competition classic car, and the prices at which examples change hands can be very high.

All Mini Coopers and especially the Cooper S models are highly coveted as collector's cars; the 1071S which was also manufactured for just two years (4000 were produced) is followed in value by the 1275S which is most widely rembered as the model which dominated the Monte Carlo Rally, and the values of which probably reflect this – almost cult – status. The 998 and 997 models (Cooper Mark 1,2 and 3) will generally be the most reasonably priced, although an example of any Mini Cooper which is in original condition (not restored or re-bodied) will continue to fetch ever-higher prices.

The Mini Coopers are not, by today's standards, particularly fast cars, in fact their performance in both top speed and acceleration is exceeded comfortably by many higher-performance variants of modern cars. Despite this, the cars are all capable of faster progress than the majority of drivers can handle in safety on the open roads and, in practical terms, the cars will all take a driver from A to B along typical roads as quickly as would the modern performance car.

Few people, however, would wish to drive a valuable classic car to its limit on public roads. The last Mini Cooper (the 1275S) was manufactured during 1971 and is today an old car with a majority of old components. To drive such a car to its limit is to invite many components to fail unless the car is used in classic competitions, in which case it will usually have been extensively if not completely rebuilt to withstand the unavoidable stresses of competition. Those who buy Mini Coopers usually covet them as classic cars rather than as sports cars.

The value of all older Minis but especially Mini Coopers is dictated primarily by authenticity, by originality. Like many cars, the Mini is the subject of counterfeiting, whereby a standard 848cc car is rebuilt disguised as a Mini Cooper and sold at an inflated price. A seemingly original 1960s car might contain many components from a far more recent car, or might even possess a more recent bodyshell. It is important to establish authenticity if rarity value influences the asking price of a Mini. An example which retains its original bodyshell (perhaps with some evidence of rust repair) its original interior and engine will sometimes be worth more than an example which looks better but which is heavily restored.

The Mini Cooper is a sporty yet quite economical little car, though few are now used as daily transport due to their appreciating value. Of all Minis, the Coopers are the most likely to have been driven very hard over the years and consequently they are the most likely to have seen extensive mechanical (and crash) repair.

Following the Mini Cooper cars in value comes the Mk.1 Mini manufactured between 1959 and 1967. Of the standard cars, this is the most outstanding simply because few examples have survived the years and, the earlier the example, the more collectable it becomes.

Like a Mini Cooper, a Mk.1 Mini should be authenticated. As these early cars become more coveted as classic cars, there is a temptation for unscrupulous people to build counterfeit examples using later components but the registration documents, badges, engine and chassis plates from an early but scrapped car. Like many classic British cars, some of the original trim from a Mk.1 Mini is being

remanufactured, and a side effect of this could be to encourage counterfeiters in their efforts.

Originality is also important for an early Mini. Very few Mk.1 or Cooper Minis remain which have not at some time undergone at least a partial and usually an extensive body restoration. This is only to be expected, and on its own need not have a detrimental effect on the value of the car. When such work is undertaken, however, very often the upholstery and the external trim of the car will be replaced. Whilst modern reproductions of early components can be very accurate, the purist will usually prefer a genuinely original Mini in poor to average condition to a nice looking car which is filled with reproduction components.

It would be unfair to expect either the Mk.1 (and to some extent all Minis over the age of ten years) and the Cooper variants to withstand the rigours of daily use in anything but the driest of climates without at some stage a restoration becoming necessary. These early cars are best suited to the collector or to the enthusiast who will restrict their use to kinder weather conditions, who will leave them in the garage during the winter when corrosive salt might be spread on icy roads.

The other 'performance' Mini variant is the 1275GT which has the Clubman bodyshell and was manufactured between 1969 and 1980. For many years, purist enthusiasts derided this variant but more recently it is starting to become recognized as possessing classic car value. The engine as fitted to the 1275GT developed 60 bhp, which makes the car slower than the Coopers 1275S, 1071S, 970S, but faster than the 'non-S' Coopers with 997 and 998 engines.

The 1275GT is a car which falls between two stools. It is much slower than the more recent performance variants of small saloon cars (the GTi's and similar) and cannot be considered a 'performance' car; it is too recent and too ubiquitous to be a highly desirable classic car. The Clubman body style also, in many people's opinion' detracts from the car's value as a classic. Yet the 1275GT combines a degree of performance with a degree of 'collectability' at prices which are often so low that, within its price range, the car is truly unique.

The Clubman bodyshell has a longer bonnet than the standard Mini design and offers far better and easier access to the engine bay for maintenance and repair. It may or may not offer more passenger protection in a front-end collision but certainly offers a greater feeling of safety and security than the short standard Mini bonnet. Many enthusiasts still prefer the classic styling of the standard Mini bodyshell despite the cramped engine bay.

The 1275GT is actually a very useful 'everyday' car with at least latent classic value and a reasonable turn of performance. It is at a peculiar stage in the life of a classic car (a stage which will last many years), at which the car is too common to possess a high enough classic value to warrant expensive restoration, yet at the same time it is constantly becoming rarer because older examples are being allowed to rot away. There will come a time when enough examples have gone for the remaining few to be considered highly desirable classic cars. At this stage they will assume rather higher values. Be aware, though, when buying a 1275GT, that no production records for this car are believed to exist. No car (known competition cars excepted) can therefore be verified as being a genuine 1275GT. Because of this, the car can never be expected to realise a really high price.

The Clubman bodyshell was also used for an 1100 (1098cc) version which was manufactured between 1975 and 1980. This particular variant lacks the performance of the 1275GT and shares its drawbacks in styling; it is probably the least 'collectable' of Minis.

The real 'luxury' version of the Mini was that badged as the Wolseley Hornet and Riley Elf. The basic Mini dashboard and trim was replaced in part with burr walnut and the seats were leather faced. Today, both of these cars are relatively rare. Like the Mk.1 Mini and the Coopers, it can be argued that they are really too collectable to be treated as everyday cars, and deserve to be treated in the gentle manner befitting classic cars.

The automatic Mini with the Automotive Products gearbox is, like many automatic versions of classic cars, not so sought-after as manual gearbox versions, despite having greatly increased rarity. This remains, however, an historically important car, because automatic transmission was very rare on so small a car in 1965 at the time of its introduction. (Indeed, the author remembers how many first-time drivers in the 1960s selected the automatic Mini as the car in which to take their driving test!)

The automatic transmission presents few problems even today. True, refurbishing is beyond the amateur and should be left to a professional, although the costs of rebuilding an automatic gearbox should be little, if any, greater than those for the rebuilding of a manual unit.

The earlier Mini van and pickup models are not only very useful vehicles in their own right but are also quite collectable, because most suffered rigorous working lives in unforgiving environments and consequently, relatively few are left today. Some of the body panels of each (and this is also true of the Wolseley Hornet/Riley Elf) will not be so easily acquired (some appear not to be available at all) as those of the standard Mini or the Clubman bodyshells. The early estate, especially examples with wood trim, is also becoming quite sought after.

Unusual Variants

Both the Mini Moke and the Innocenti (standard and hatchback) Mini are rarely seen or offered for sale in the UK, very few having been sold originally on this market. The Moke was generally exported to more suitable (hot) climes, and many examples overseas will not have suffered bodyrot to the extent that it strikes cars in the UK. Like the Austin Healey, E-Type Jaguar and MGBs, some examples will almost certainly be re-imported because the collector's value of the car in the UK exceeds by a wide margin that of examples in other countries.

Those who wish to own a car in order to enjoy the Mini Moke *experience* however, will find a wide range of very similar vehicles being sold in kit form. Usually comprising either a GRP or commonly a galvanised steel bodyshell which is mounted on a tubular chassis, these kits can be quite straightforward to build and utilise (almost 100%) widely available standard Mini components. This is, however, a digression, because no kit of this ilk can be seriously considered a 'classic' for many years. A genuine UK-manufactured Mini Moke today commands a high price, and examples manufactured in Australia until 1978 and thereafter in Portugal will also be increasingly sought-after (at the time of writing, the Moke is in current manufacture, and must qualify for the title of 'a classic in its own lifetime').

All elderly classic variants of the Mini will be encountered from time to time, advertised as being recently restored. The costs of a professional restoration to most variants and years will be above the resultant value of the car, so it is difficult to see why someone would go to the trouble and expense of commissioning a restoration only to immediately sell the car afterwards at a loss.

Such cases must be treated with caution. True, many people overspend during a car restoration and have to sell the car due to financial pressure. Often, though, the restoration will not have been of a very high standard.

Usable Minis

The distinction between 'classic' and 'usable' Minis is by no means clear; a sixties Mini is without doubt a classic car which may be used as everyday transport if desired and a late eighties Mini is an eminently usable car with classic status to look forward to in some year's time. In between these two extremes there are untold opportunities to acquire cars which combine a degree of classic appeal with usability, yet often at prices which do not reflect the true values of either.

It being impossible to define the collectability of a Mini according to its year of manufacture, it might be suggested that any example which is over ten years of age possesses a degree of classic car status provided that its condition does not fully reflect its age. For instance, a 1979 Mini in need of total restoration will be practically worthless except if broken up for spares, because the restoration costs will by many times exceed the eventual worth of the vehicle. The same car in well-above average condition, on the other hand, will have a financial value which exceeds the motor trade depreciation 'book' price and hence has a certain classic car value.

Yet who is to say that a 1990 Mini is not, in its own way, a classic car? Who could argue that the many limited edition variants produced in the 1980s are not now classic cars?

When considering classic Minis we began with the earliest of cars and worked forwards in time, in looking at usable cars we shall begin with the new car and work backwards.

A brand new Mini can be assisted towards longevity and perhaps classic status by offering it protection against the usual ravages of the ageing process; rusting bodywork, deteriorating trim and other obvious problems. Thorough use of a proprietary rust-retarding compound in those areas of the bodywork which are prone to rusting can increase the useful life of the car by a considerable length of time, perhaps doubling it. The regular and thorough cleaning of the underside of the car, especially during the winter months, also helps greatly to slow the rusting process.

The interior of the car could be protected by the use of covers on the upholstery, by refraining from smoking in the car and by using sacrificial foot mats to soak up the water from shoes. Regular waxing helps to retain the paintwork in good condition, and regular inspection for and rectification of stone chips in the paintwork can prevent rust from becoming established underneath, where it might spread. As a new car, the Mini will depreciate in value for a period of several years until such time as its 'book' value falls to a point under its collector's value. When this point has been reached the depreciation should stop and perhaps reverse. The period of maximum depreciation can be bypassed by purchasing an example which is a few years old, for the depreciation of a car, of all cars, if shown as a graph, would be a very steep curve which increasingly levels out. In other words, the depreciation, year on year, slows.

At the time of writing, a car of four or perhaps five years of age could cost less than half the price of a new one, and its depreciation over the following twelve months as a percentage of its purchase price would be a fraction of that of a new car; the actual amount of the older car's depreciation could be a quarter of that of the new car.

At such an age the car would probably either have recently been fitted with or would imminently require certain consumables, such as a battery, exhaust system, tyres and so on. In other mechanical and structural respects the car should be both sound and clean; still able to benefit from the care and attention against rusting and ageing outlined previously.

A car of eight to ten years of age will have depreciated to the point at which the annual depreciation is negligible, but it will obviously require a certain amount of repair and replacement of components, in addition to rectification of bodywork rust damage. At this point the car may well be eminently usable; its value will have depreciated to the point from which it cannot show further reductions.

Limited edition cars from the 'Advantage' of 1987 back to the '1000 S' of 1979 can all become to a degree collectable before their age might otherwise indicate, and they should all have a greater worth by virtue of their enhanced specifications over the standard production cars of the same years.

APPRAISING THE MINI – BODYWORK

When appraising the bodywork of an older car there are a number of very useful tools which you should take along with you. A screwdriver can be poked into suspect metal to reveal the presence of bodyrot. A magnet will reveal the presence of body filler and GRP. A torch will enable you to closely examine nooks and crannies. You will also need a sturdy (preferably a trolley) jack and axle stands, a tape measure and a notepad and pencil.

Always try to take along a companion. Obviously, an experienced person will be a great asset, although even a complete novice might spot a problem so obvious that it escapes your attention! Make a list of work which needs doing to the car, because this might serve as a negotiating point if you decide to haggle over the price. A list of faults will also give you an all-round picture of the car's condition and be a great aid when making up your mind whether to buy or to leave it, as well as giving you a strong bargaining position.

The most expensive mistake which the potential Mini buyer could make would be to buy one with a rotten or, even worse, an accident-damaged and distorted body. All mechanical faults pale into insignificance compared to such major bodywork repairs. It is thus important to learn how to recognize bodywork faults before starting to view cars. In order to understand the importance of the structural integrity of certain bodywork components, a knowledge of how the Mini is put together is needed.

There are two general methods of car construction. For many years, car bodies were attached to a chassis, which is a strong framework onto which the engine, drive train and suspension components were fitted, and onto which the separate body of the car would then be mounted. More recently, the separate chassis has been largely replaced by strong 'chassis rail' sections which are built into the pressed steel bodyshell of a car, and this method of construction – called 'monocoque' or 'unitary' – is used for the vast majority of cars on the market today. The Mini, however, possesses characteristics of both types of construction.

Basically, the Mini could be thought of as possessing two separate 'chassis', called the subframes – one each front and rear – on which the engine, transmission, suspension/brakes and body are mounted. The subframes therefore absorb many of the stresses imposed on the car when it is on the move.

Because both subframes are bolted to the body, it is the body which holds the two in the correct positions relative to each other. Bodyrot which weakens this 'bridge' between the subframes (and allows the body to become distorted) or uncorrected accident damage can result in one or both subframes moving out of the correct alignment. When this happens, the front and rear wheels will be out of alignment, giving very peculiar and often dangerous handling characteristics, such as a tendency for the car to jump to one side when driven over a bump in the road, or a general crab-like sideways movement.

Checking the alignment of the subframe mounting points can reveal whether the body is distorted, and this is a messy but absolutely vital check to make. Measure, each side of the car, the distance between the rear and front subframe mounting points, then check the measurements of the diagonals between rear offside/front nearside and vice versa. The two diagonal measurements must be the same, and the two front to back measurements must also be the same. If there is the slightest discrepancy then the car should be rejected, because rectification of such body distortion is a job for professionals, and will cost so much that only the highest-value variants of the Mini will justify the expenditure.

There are two ways of making these measurements. The first is to park the car on a flat, even, surface and take the perpendicular from each point and make marks on the ground, drive the car forwards and then carry out the measurements. The second method is to make up a special measuring jig, like the example in the photographs. This is made from a 6-foot-long piece of softwood, and has two 13″ uprights attached. The end upright is glued into position to keep it firm, and the other, held by small nails, may be repositioned in order that different measurements may be taken.

This check will not, however, give 100% assurance that the two subframes are perfectly aligned, for the body could be twisted in such a way that the subframe mounting point measurements, by sheer chance, are still equal. To check for twisting, raise the car and support it on axle stands so that the two subframes are parallel with the ground, then take vertical measurements from the subframe mounting points.

ABOVE *This very simple measuring device allows distances between the front and rear subframe mounting points to be accurately compared. If the two front to back or the two diagonal measurements differ in the slightest then the body is probably twisted and will need straightening on a jig, although the individual mounting points (rubber mounted subframe cars) can sometimes become distorted following accident damage, which can be more easily corrected.*

RIGHT *The measurements for comparison. Merely taking the front to back measurements will not be sufficient, because the car could have been involved in a collision which shunted one side of the car further backwards than the other, or which could have pushed either the front or the rear end of the car sideways, in both cases, giving a trapezoid instead of a rectangular shape. Taking the diagonals as shown will show such problems up.*

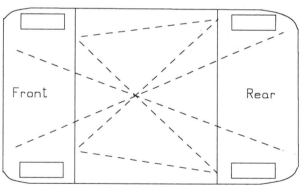

Checking the sill measurements

Lines converge at single point

These should be the same either side of the car. The author prefers to raise one subframe onto axle stands, so that the subframes themselves are level, then to check the height of the sills above the ground. As with the other checks listed, the car needs to be on firm, level ground.

Even if this careful checking appears to show up no problems, the body could be distorted. You may make a mistake when measuring or a very weak body could be flexing back into alignment as it is raised onto axle stands. Look at the car from all angles and from a few yards away and try to assess whether the car sits level to the ground from all angles. Using a long straight edge, check the relative alignments of the 'C' roof pillar, 'B' pillar and front screen pillar. You may discover that one side of the car is slightly bowed or concave from side impact damage.

Alternatively, take along a length of string. Attach one end to the boot handle and lead the string around the side of the car then pull it taut so that it just touches the (B post) roof support pillars. A companion can take comparative measurements of the distances from the string to the front roof support and even to the front wing (it is far from unknown for a Mini front end to be welded on at an angle!).

If any doubt exists after these checks have been made then it is usually best to reject the car unless a full restoration which includes a visit to a bodyshop with jigging facilities is planned.

Body distortion which has been badly repaired can sometimes be witnessed simply by visual checks along the sides, roof and underside of the car. Rivelling (corrugation-like unevenness), dents or any sort of misalignment can reveal that the car has suffered poor body rebuilding practices.

Check that the wheels are central within each wheelarch, or at least that they are in the same relative position each side of the car. On the author's 1275GT the offside tyre had a good clearance from the front of the wheelarch, whilst the nearside tyre was very close to the front of the wheelarch. Trying to find the source of the ½" difference proved very difficult. Originally, it appeared that the difference was due to different width 'A' panels, yet, on removal of the offending wing and A panel, discrepancies were discovered in other dimensions.

The author took a series of comparative measurements from the front subframe mounting points to various points on the body. Some were even on both sides whilst others differed by amounts ranging from ⅛" to ⅝"! In the end, the problem

was found to have a number of causes. The 'A' panel was indeed partly to blame, in addition to a misshapen inner flitch panel, a dented and badly straightened toe board panel (on which the subframe is mounted) and minor discrepancies in the suspension. The body was also distorted, and a number of panels had been replaced onto the distorted areas. So, if you discover an apparent reason for a fault, do not automatically assume that it is the sole reason!

Lift the carpet or mat from the toe board and examine this panel to see whether it has suffered impact at any time. If it is crumpled then it has been bent and poorly straightened. The rear mounting for the front subframe is situated on this panel, and if it is bent on a car with the rubber mounted subframe then this can put the subframe slightly but disastrously out of alignment.

A distorted toe board on an older Mini can indicate that the car has been driven off-road and that it has 'grounded' at speed. Sadly, Minis seem to be very prone to having suffered collisions over the years. Obviously, all Coopers stand a chance of having been driven hard and suffering accident damage as a result. Less obviously, the humble 850 cc Mini has always found favour as a learners' car and as a 'first' car for the young driver. As any insurance company will tell you, younger drivers are more prone to drive into things . . .

Check the gaps around the bonnet, boot lid and doors. The gaps should be fairly even all around. If the bonnet does not fit squarely, then one wing is obviously higher than the other, or the two are out of alignment.

Look at the flitch panels (inner front wings), because these are often the only remaining visible casualties of a front-end collision. When such cars are badly repaired, all of the front end panels excepting the flitch panels are usually replaced, and the result will be corrugated flitch panels. Even mild undulations in the flitch panels indicate a front-end collision, and a car which has all of the front end except the flitch panels rebuilt will often prove to have serious subframe mis-alignment.

Check for distortion in the roof by firstly measuring the height of the pillars each side then by looking along the roof from an acute angle, which will reveal undulations. The author's car had a vinyl roof covering, with obvious unevenness underneath which could have indicated serious problems. After removal of the vinyl (and a day spent cleaning

On rubber mounted subframe variants, the front subframe could be mounted out of true. In the event of a front-end collision, the subframe may be pushed rearwards and distort the toe board to which it is attached. The top mountings have sufficient 'give' to allow the subframe to be attached at the toe board and top mountings, and if the front end of the car is rebuilt using the subframe as a guide, it will be out of true. Here, the author is measuring from the front edge of the sill to a point on the suspension, which highlighted a discrepancy either side of the car due to one toe board mounting being ⅛" further forwards than the other. It is important to measure to a point on the suspension which is fixed. The nut on the bottom end of the swivel axle assembly is fixed, whilst, for instance, the hub assembly itself is not. The ⅛" at the toe board mounting pushed the suspension ⅓" further forwards. Moral? Measure everything!

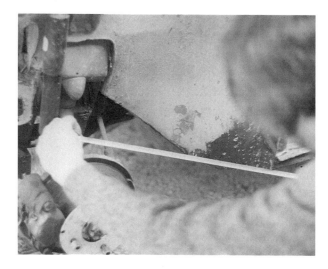

Every dent tells a story. A very bumpy area was apparent in the edge of the roof (which was covered in vinyl) of this 1275GT. This indicated that the car had been rolled on to its side at some time, but the bumps did not have the hard edges which one would normally expect when metal is crumpled in this way. Removing the vinyl covering revealed a poorly applied large lump of body filler which had been crudely slapped on to the still painted surface of the crumpled zone.

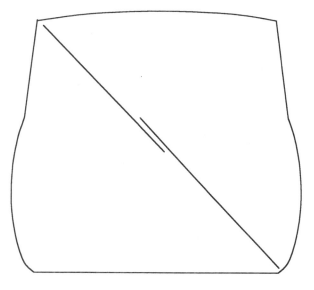

If you hold two pieces of wood as shown in the diagram and mark a line across both then reassemble them on the opposite diagonal, you can check for side impact damage. If the car is hit in the side then the sill can be distorted inwards, if the car is rolled then the roof edge can be pushed inwards. In both instances the door should be a poor fit and give the game away, although if the damage was partially corrected the door could still be made to appear to fit well and close properly.

The Mini Sill

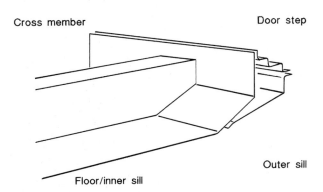

Cross member

Door step

Outer sill

Floor/inner sill

A cross section through the sill structure. None of the individual components possesses any great strength, but when all three are strongly welded into a box section, a very rigid structure results. The outer sill section is the one which usually suffers the most from rot, and happily, it is not too difficult a task to replace this. Some people, however, find the correct procedures too much trouble, and instead of cutting away the rotten old sill, they hammer it inwards and weld on another to cover up their shoddy workmanship. Counting the layers of metal – there should only be two – in the door frame (door step to inner sill join) and at the side seam (outer sill to door step join) will reveal whether this has happened.

rubberised glue off the underlying paintwork), the cause of the unevenness was apparent. A dent above the central pillar had been crudely filled with bodyfiller (so crudely that the dents could be seen even through the vinyl covering). This filler had been applied directly over the surface of the paint, and had consequently broken free. The roof had been scored (to key the glue), and a few hour's work with an orbital sander and a cup brush in the angle grinder prepared the roof for dressing then filling properly.

If doubt remains regarding whether the body is distorted or not, there are a couple of quick checks which will instantly reveal any distortion. Take two lengths of wood, aluminium extrusion or steel bar which are each roughly three feet long. You can use these as a crude but effective internal measuring device to check the shell from the inside. Lift the seats forwards, then check the diagonals from the inner sill corners to the opposite door frame top. (See illustration). If you hold the seats inclined forwards at an angle then it will also just be possible to measure from the front subframe rear mountings back to the heelboard panel, which is under the rear seat and immediately ahead of the front edge of the rear subframe. These two checks should show up any body distortion.

Following body distortion, the next most important check is for bodyrot. Begin by looking at the roof pillars. The bases of the front pillars (including the ends of the top shroud panel) often rot and are 'repaired' (meaning that the rot is disguised or hidden) with bodyfiller or crude welding of steel plate. Check for the presence of body filler by placing a magnet onto the metal in the vicinity. If the magnet is not strongly attracted then the surface is obviously

not steel! On many cars (the Mini included) the roof can play a significant role in maintaining the rigidity of the body, and a weak roof structure can place extra stresses on the floor pans and sills which are the main strength of the body.

If rot is discovered in any part of the roof structure (including the roof pillars) then repairs can be very expensive, and are really the province of the professional.

The sills run under each side of the body, and comprise a compound box-section which possesses great rigidity. They are absolutely fundamental to the strength of the body. They rot, both from the outside and from the inside, and are often 'repaired' with steel covers which lack the necessary strength to prevent the whole body flexing (which can make the handling of the car downright dangerous) and which are often fitted over the original rotten sections with the result that the new covers rot through in record time. It can be difficult to assess the true condition of the sills, especially when metal cover sections have been recently welded on and covered with underseal. Possibly the best guide to the condition of the sills is to look at surrounding bodywork, because it is not possible to weld new sills strongly onto really rotten metal. If the condition of the sills appears much better than that of adjacent metal, then unless some proof (preferably photographic) can be offered that the sills were properly replaced then the advice must be to reject the car or to adjust your offer to account for sill replacement costs.

Be especially thorough when checking the sill ends, because this is where the need for strength is the greatest and the potential for rot the greatest. Use a magnet to check for bodyfiller (honestly!) and probe

This badly dented A panel had been covered with a thick layer of body filler when it would have taken a matter of minutes to straighten it out using a hammer and dolly and then to smooth the surface with a thin layer of filler. The problem with using body filler in thick layers is that it is very prone to break free if the panel flexes, whereas a thin layer will flex with the panel. Again, this filler had been applied over paint and rust alike, and would have been destined to drop out sooner or later irrespective of whether the panel flexed or not! A magnet would reveal such misuse of body filler, although merely feeling the inside and outside of the panel would have sufficed in this instance.

With the carpets lifted, the areas to concentrate attention on are the toe board (dents could indicate a heavy enough collision to move the lower subframe mounting points) the inner wing base (which can rot out completely) the join between the floor and toe board and the floor itself.

This is the kind of rot which can be hidden with body filler. Quite a large area had rusted very thin, and the filler was used to build it up to a respectable thickness as well as to cover up the small area which had rusted right through. This serves to illustrate exactly what sort of tricks the prospective Mini buyer must look out for.

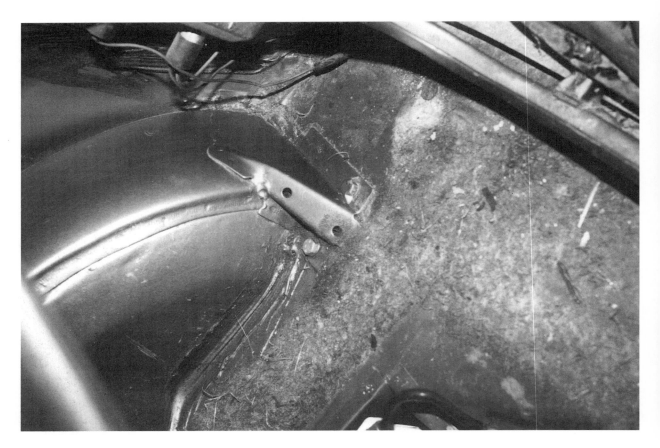

vigorously with a sharp screwdriver to check for rot.

Look closely for signs of side impact damage in the 'A' panels (just ahead of each door) and the B posts, and at the doorstep and the floorpans adjacent to the sill sections. Side impact damage is easy to reveal, simply by feeling the thickness of the 'A' panel; if it is thicker in some places then others, then the difference is bodyfiller. Side impact damage here could have affected the front suspension, so check this carefully.

From inside the car, lift the carpets from the bulkhead and examine the floors, especially the seam between the floor and the toe board panel. Rot here is quite common, and is too close to both the front jacking reinforcing points and the front subframe rear mounts for comfort. If serious rot is discovered here, then check again for subframe mis-alignment. Remove the trim from the floors of the small 'pockets' either side of the rear seat. The metal which is exposed should be sound and clean, especially the vertical panel at the rear of the compartment, because this area is adjacent to the front mounting for the rear subframe, and it often rots seriously.

The metal surrounding the rear subframe mounting points should not have rusted except on the oldest examples of the car. However, in the case of cars which are kept in a hostile environment (such as a coastal location) or cars on which scratches to the topside of the panel and underseal damage to the underside have been left unattended for years, check more recent cars thoroughly. Pay particular attention to the seam between the boot floor and the rear of the wheelarch. Those mountings which are covered by the fuel tank can be checked from underneath the car.

Under the rear seat ledge, the continuation of this panel (called the 'heelboard') can be found and examined, using a torch for better illumination.

Inside the boot of the car there are several likely rust areas. Remove any carpeting or other covering and closely examine the visible inner wheel arch pressing (one will be covered by the fuel tank and both will be thus covered in the case of the Cooper S) and especially the welded seams for signs of rot or badly-repaired rot. A favourite trick of the cowboy

The flitch panel metal in the area of the top damper mounting bracket is prone to rusting and although it is not structurally vital (the damper bracket takes huge forces but it is bolted through onto the heavy main cross member) it is a difficult area to repair. Furthermore, rust spreads, and untreated rusting here will find its way into the cross member and surrounding panels.

bodyshop here is to weld 20 swg steel plates into the wheelarch, rather than to replace them. The usual finishing method for such work is to flush over with bodyfiller, and so the magnet will reveal the quality of any repair work in this vicinity. Always check the wheel arches from the outside, by firstly raising the rear of the car and removing the rear road wheels. The area around the top damper mounting is especially noteworthy.

The battery box bottom also rots badly, especially at its base, where battery acid attacks it from above and water and mud from the road splashes onto the underside, and this may be checked from underneath the car or by removal of the battery. Although the

battery box is not structurally important, it is a UK MOT test failure point. Beware of shoddy pop-riveted repairs to the battery box floor.

Still within the boot, there are four bolt heads (only two of which are visible) which belong to the important bolts which hold the subframe rear mountings. Using the torch, look at the underside of this area and poke it with the screwdriver to test for rot. If the visible bolt heads within the boot are surrounded by rotting metal then expect the other side to be at least as bad if not worse. On the Cooper S, all four bolt heads will be obscured by the twin fuel tanks, and in this case the metal should be thoroughly probed from the underside.

Lift the bonnet and visually inspect the state of the heavy section bulkhead crossmember and the flitch panels. The crossmember holds the main subframe mountings and the top damper mountings. Although serious rot is unlikely, it obviously pays to check. Some surface rusting of the flitch panels is common, especially on the nearside flitch panel which houses the radiator surround and air intake. Check also for distortion of the flitch panels which

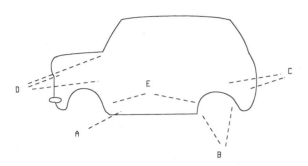

Mini rust areas. A; The sills. B; Rear subframe mounting points. C; From inside boot. Rear inner wings, battery box and rear subframe mounting points. D; A posts and panels, flitch panels, top shroud and roof pillars. E; Toe board and heelboard.

could indicate a badly-repaired front end collision. On the Clubman, examine the brackets between the front panel, flitch panel and front subframe mounting. These will very often be thoroughly rotten, so also bear this area in mind when undertaking bodywork preventative maintenance!

From inside the front wings, poke vigorously with the screwdriver at the metal around the upper damper mounting bracket, and even more vigorously at the metal around the front subframe rear mounting points on the toe board panel, to test for rot. The subframe mountings should also be checked from the inside of the car.

The 'A' post is prone to rot at its base and top and, because this is not one of the more straightforward of repairs and because the panel is structurally important, test also for filler 'repair' with the magnet.

Examine all welded seams very carefully for rot. You will be able to tell how well any previous repairs to the wings/flitch or front panels were carried out by examining the state of the welds. If repairs are needed to the wings, flitch or 'A' panels, beware the car which has been badly MIG 'spot' or 'plug' welded. Unlike normal spot welds, which may be easily drilled out, MIG plug welds can be very difficult to deal with. The problem is that the welding process can easily burn away the edges of the drilled hole and enlarge it, so that instead of having a neat ⅜″ circle to deal with, you are faced with an oval area of unknown

size. To give you a taster of what is to come further on in this book, they must be ground down to surface level (access is sometimes impossible), then either the actual weld must be found and ground out, or the weld (and the underlying panel) must be drilled. In both cases it is often necessary to part the repair using a sharpened bolster chisel. It can be almost impossible to part these joins without seriously damaging one or both panels.

Of the external panels, the front wings are cheap enough and relatively easy to fit, so that rust is not too great a problem. You can cut out either a front wing or an 'A' panel without distorting adjacent panels. The panels at the side and rear of the car are not so easily dealt with, so it pays to examine these rather more closely.

The area between the rear of the door and the front of the rear wheelarch rots and is often poorly dealt with using body filler and GRP. The magnet will reveal either, and looking along the panels at an acute angle will reveal welding heat distortion as well as the presence of bodyfiller. Filler here could be due to side impact damage, so also examine the 'B' post for distortion, because if the damage is extensive then the entire side of the car will have to be replaced.

The roof guttering and the roof itself in the vicinity of the guttering are both prone to rot. The guttering is often covered by a plastic moulding, which has to be eased off for proper inspection. Because removing the guttering trim can destroy it, the vendor may be understandably reluctant to allow this. Use the magnet to check for filler or GRP roof 'repair'. Neither are acceptable.

MECHANICAL/ELECTRICAL INSPECTION

In the UK, the Mini is so prolific a car that almost any spare part may be obtained cheaply from almost any breaker's yard, and even brand-new spares are reasonably inexpensive and widely available. The consequences of buying a Mini with mechanical faults are therefore not nearly so great as with many other classic or even current vehicles.

Nevertheless, some mechanical and electrical faults are potentially very dangerous. Corroded brake pipes could split and you could find yourself with no brakes, a fuel line could split with obvious dangers or an area of insulation could break down and start an

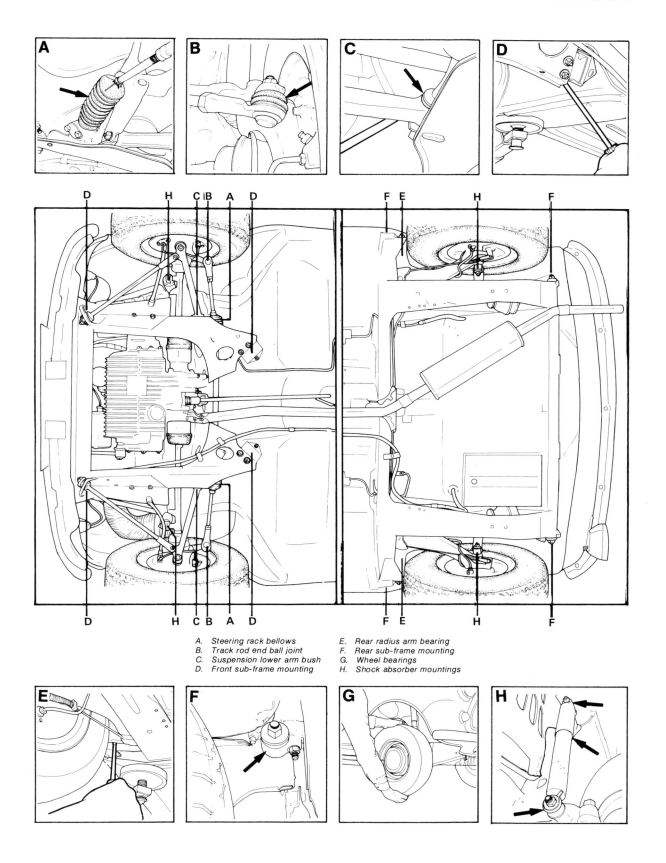

A. Steering rack bellows
B. Track rod end ball joint
C. Suspension lower arm bush
D. Front sub-frame mounting
E. Rear radius arm bearing
F. Rear sub-frame mounting
G. Wheel bearings
H. Shock absorber mountings

PREVIOUS PAGE *These are the main UK MoT test underbody checking points, worth checking before buying a car. Check A: the steering rack bellows for splits. B: track rod end for condition. C: condition of suspension arm lower bushes. D: strength of front subframe mountings. E: Rear radius arm bearing for excess sideways movement. F: strength of metal around rear subframe mounting points. G: Wheel bearings, H: damper (shock absorber) mountings for strength and damper for leakage. (Courtesy Autodata)*

ABOVE RIGHT *Pull and push the steering wheel to reveal excess play in the steering column universal joint, and try to lift and lower column to reveal looseness of fittings. (Courtesy Autodata)*

RIGHT *Splits in the driveshaft boots are MoT test failure points; they also allow the ingress of dirt and water – accelerating wear in the joint.*

BELOW *Checking the tyre tread can tell you a lot about how the car has been maintained and driven, and can reveal certain suspension faults. Be warned, however, that some people will rotate tyres to try and spread the wear more evenly over the tread pattern. (Courtesy Autodata)*

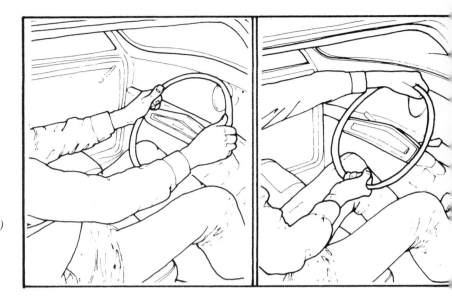

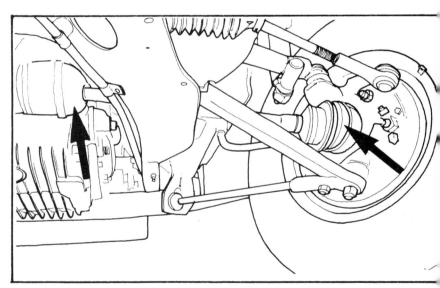

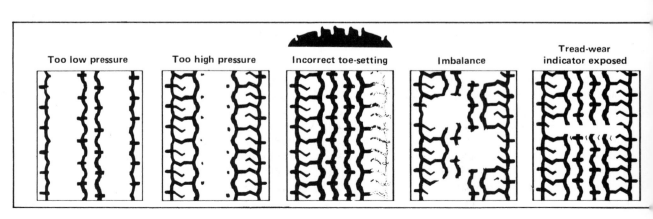

| Too low pressure | Too high pressure | Incorrect toe-setting | Imbalance | Tread-wear indicator exposed |

electrical fire. The mechanical and electrical inspection should be very thorough, both from the restoration/repair costs viewpoint and the safety viewpoint.

You will need a notepad and pen to list the faults, both minor and major, which you discover. The finished list will give you an opportunity to take an overall view of the car's condition and to properly appraise its true worth. Being able to confidently list the cars problems to the vendor may prove an excellent bargaining tool. The list should especially highlight any safety-related faults, which must be marked for immediate attention.

Engine

The 'A' series engine is an extremely robust and long-lived unit which should give little trouble if correctly maintained. However, uncorrected minor faults, such as running the car for any length of time with too rich a mixture, neglecting oil changes or incorrectly setting the ignition timing, can cause more serious problems in the long term.

Refer to the photographs and illustrations in Chapter 4. Firstly, take a general look at the engine, the ancillaries and the engine bay. If everything is covered with a mixture of oil and dirt then obviously maintenance has been skimped in the past. Look especially at the state of the distributor and the oil filter. If these components are covered with dirt then they have not received any attention for a long time and the car could have been run with badly set ignition timing or without the oil and filter having been changed.

If the entire engine unit is covered with oil then obviously there is an oil leak somewhere high up on the engine. Sometimes the rocker box cover seal will allow oil to leak (easily and cheaply corrected) but unless proven to the contrary, the leak should be assumed to emanate from the cylinder head gasket, which could be an indication of expensive repairs.

Inspect all visible nuts, bolt heads and screw slots. These give an excellent indication of the competence of the people who have worked on the engine in the past. Rounded nuts and bolt heads, damaged screw slots all point to a slipshod attitude and, worse, the use of a very poor toolkit. If any work has been carried out on the engine internals by the person responsible, then you can expect the engine internal components to be in a similar mess.

Examine the state of the insulation of visible wiring, check that all spade connectors are insulated and be on the lookout for loose wires which go nowhere. If you discover a length of wire with burnt insulation then there is a chance that wires within the loom also have damaged insulation, which means that a new loom should be fitted to make the car safe.

Inspect the hoses for signs of perishing or splitting, and the radiator for staining on the fins which indicates a coolant leak. Check the tightness of the fan belt, the coolant and oil levels, again as an indication of the level of maintenance which the car has received.

The engine must be cold before you start it up. Many vendors will warm up engines which are difficult to start before you arrive and, if this is so, let the engine become cold before re-starting it. Ask the vendor how much choke the engine likes; if it will fire up from cold without choke in cool temperatures then it is probably running too richly, which could indicate future problems. Start the engine yourself, and listen for problems with the starter dog/starter ring, and for rumblings within the engine in the first two seconds or so of it firing up (indicating a worn oil pump and consequently mains and/or big end bearings which are on the way out). Replacing the starter ring is a difficult task with the engine in or out of the car because it is heat-shrunk on to the flywheel. Although replacing the starter bendix drive is not too difficult a task, the replacement unit is quite expensive. Rumblings within the engine immediately on firing up indicate worn bearings, and an engine rebuild could be not too far away.

As the engine fires, look in the rear view mirror for a cloud of blue smoke, which can indicate that oil has leaked past the worn valve guides while the engine has been idle. Constant blue smoke from the exhaust, even after the engine is at normal operating temperature, indicates worn or damaged bores and piston rings, and is particularly common on the 1275GT. Feel the temperature of the top hose and if it begins to warm up as soon as the engine starts then the thermostat has been removed, probably to hide an overheating problem.

Allow the engine to come to normal operating temperature, and watch around the cylinder head gasket for oil or water leaks. Watch the exhaust gas. Steam could indicate cylinder head problems, either a blown gasket or a cracked cylinder head, blue smoke worn bores or damaged piston rings and black smoke indicates an over-rich fuel/air mixture.

Listen to the noises made by the engine at idle and when it is revved. Some noises, such as timing chain tinkle, idler gear howl and tappet rattle, will be obvious to all but the least experienced DIY mechanic, so if you do not think that you could recognize these sounds then you should have brought along a person who can! Some noises can be difficult to trace, in which case placing the end of a large screwdriver on various parts of the engine unit and holding the other end to your ear can help track their sources down. If you have a compression tester, then use it at this stage; if you do not possess one, do not worry.

Stop the engine and let the pressure subside from the top hose (this can be felt by squeezing the hose). Carefully remove the radiator cap, then look at the surface of the coolant for oil droplets or an oil film, which indicate cylinder head problems. If no coolant is visible, either top up the system with hot water or let the engine cool then top up with cold water and repeat the exercise to see whether coolant is being lost continuously.

Take out the oil dipstick and look for water droplets, then remove the oil filler cap and look inside the rocker box cover for water droplets or the typical emulsified mess which indicates established mixing of water and oil, and an engine in need of extensive attention.

Road Test

If the car has passed all of the tests so far, then a road test will enable you to discover many of the potential drive/suspension faults without dirtying your hands.

The author and publishers can assume no responsibility for the consequences of any of the following advice. It is up to the individual to ensure that the car is driven in a safe manner with full regard to the safety of other road users.

If you are to drive the car then ensure that you will be not inadvertently break any motoring laws in the process.

This means that the car must be roadworthy and taxed and that you must be properly insured.

If the vendor is to drive, ensure that he or she is acting within the law, because you could be regarded as an accomplice if the vendor is stopped and charged of an offence by the police during the test drive.

Note throughout whether there appear to be any problems in engaging gears, or with the car jumping

out of gear, either of which indicate a worn selector mechanism (if the vendor drives and keeps one hand firmly on the gearchange lever, then this may be to stop the car from jumping out of gear).

Note whether the steering tries to return to the straight-ahead position after cornering.

If the car shows signs of 'floating' at speed then the dampers are worn; if the front of the car nose-dives as the brakes are applied, if the bonnet pitches up and down as the car moves away from a standstill, expect to find worn or leaking dampers.

From 30mph, brake to a standstill and note whether the car pulls to one side (worn or contaminated brakes). If the brakes have to be 'pumped' before they will operate properly then there is air in the system.

A clonk on braking could indicate suspension problems or a loose brake caliper (disc braked models only).

If a clonk can only be heard when the car is first braked when travelling either forwards or in reverse, the caliper pistons could be sticking.

In all gears, accelerate and decelerate sharply to see whether the car can be encouraged (under provocation) to jump out of gear! Reverse the car a short distance and again brake to a halt, listening for clonks which could indicate suspension problems or a loose brake caliper.

If at any stage in these tests any doubts emerge regarding the brakes or suspension of the car then it is best to discontinue the road test on the grounds of safety.

Increase speed to normal road speeds and repeat the braking and gearchange tests, when any deficiencies in the engine, transmission or suspension not previously noted will be accentuated.

Stop somewhere off the public highway. Engage the handbrake, then slowly let the clutch out, depressing it again immediately the engine begins to labour. If the car begins to creep forwards then the handbrake is out of adjustment or the rear brakes are worn or contaminated. If the engine does not labour appreciably then the clutch is slipping and in need of attention.

Drive slowly in a tight circle and listen for a clicking noise which indicates that the universal joints are in need of replacement.

If at any point during the road test you feel that there is something not quite right about the handling or roadholding, the brakes, steering or electrical system, them terminate the test immediately.

Suspension/steering/brakes

Chock the rear wheels, raise the front of the car and support it on axle stands placed under the subframe or the reinforced sections at the front ends of the sills.

With an assistant holding the steering wheel firmly, grasp each front wheel in turn and rock it from side to side. Play here could indicate a worn wheel bearing or problems with the steering rack or track rod end. Grasp the top and bottom of the wheel and rock it to show worn wheel bearings or play in the swivels. Grasp each track rod end and feel for play in the steering rack (a horrible item to have to replace unless the engine is removed first), then grasp the end of the rack and feel for looseness (it is easily tightened) or worn bushes. Check the condition of the brake pipes and hoses.

Turn the steering wheel from lock to lock, feeling for any roughness or resistance, which indicates the need for a new steering rack. Replacing the Mini steering rack is a horrendous job for the amateur, because the entire engine/subframe assembly has to be moved before the steering rack can be accessed. Before lowering the front of the car, check the visible bodywork. Examine the brake backplates (drum brakes) for brake fluid leakage or the discs for scoring or corrosion.

Lower the front end of the car, chock the front wheels then raise the rear of the car and support it on axle stands placed under the subframe. Try rocking the rear wheels to indicate worn wheel bearings. Place a lever between the outer end of the radius arm and the subframe and try to move the radius arm outwards. If it will move, this indicates a worn radius arm bearing bush.

Examine the rear bodywork (and especially the subframe) for rot whilst the car is raised, and look for patches of dark staining on the fuel tank (vans and estates) which indicate leakage. Inspect the brake backplates for fluid leakage and the brake pipes for corrosion or damage. Check the handbrake moving sectors to ensure that they can move freely. Inspect the brake pipes, and see whether the brake adjusters (including those on front drum brakes) will turn freely.

Electrical

When examining the engine bay, the underside and the interior of the vehicle, take time to find and inspect any wiring in the vicinity. Note any poor in-line connectors for immediate replacement should you decide to buy the car. Look for signs of insulation breaking down or damage, either of which could be the cause of an electrical fire.

Look in the fuse box. If the slip of paper inside a fuse is browned then the fuse is operating at or very near to its limit, and this may be due to electrical leakage or to too many appliances being attached to the circuit: for example, a radio or extra internal lights could have been added to an existing circuit. In such circumstances, a new fused circuit should be created for the extra appliances.

Whilst the car is raised, examine the main power feed from the battery. If this has even the slightest insulation defects then it should be replaced, because a full discharge from this wire will cause an electrical fire.

Interior

Most items of interior trim are now being re-manufactured by specialists, although many enthusiasts still prefer to see worn but original trim rather than smart but not quite 'right' reproductions. Expect to pay a premium if an early car in good overall condition still has original trim in the correct colours.

All instruments are now available either new or reconditioned and, although non-functioning instruments pose no problems in themselves, they do indicate a slipshod attitude to maintenance by the vendor. Check all visible wiring for damage and to ensure that any accessories have been correctly fused.

QUICK REFERENCE CHECK LIST

Super-quick check

The person looking for a car which will not require extensive bodywork can rule out many cars by firstly checking the rear heelboard from inside the car. Look underneath the rear seats, probing for rot and using a magnet to check for body filler (yes, it has been known), and remove the trim from the small luggage compartments either end of the rear seat and make the same checks. If any rusting other than the slightest surface rust is discovered in the heelboard, the chances are that extensive body restoration will be needed.

Lift the carpets. Check the inner sills, cross member, toe board and floor sections for rust and for poor repair of rust and collision damage.

Lift the bonnet and examine the flitch panels for any distortion.

If these areas appear sound, then check for body distortion by measuring from the toe board front subframe mounting points to the heelboard, and checking the internal diagonals – in both cases, use two lengths of wood as previously described.

With your eye two or three inches above the panel in question, look along all external body panels for rivelling or other unevenness.

Main checklist

1. Bodywork.
Check visually:
    gaps around doors, bonnet;
    external panels for rivelling:
    overspray.
Check visually and with magnet:
    'A' panels:
    door bottoms and adjacent lower portions of rear wings;
    top shroud and all roof pillars;
    roof.
Check visually, with magnet and probe with screwdriver:
    inner wings front/rear;
    toe board, floor, cross member;
    subframes;
    boot floor, battery box;
    sills.

2. Engine/transmission.

Check visually:
    state (clean, dirty, oily);
    general condition of hoses/electrics;
    state of coolant;
    oil level and condition;
    state of bolt heads, nuts, screw slots;
    fan belt, fan blades;
    oil/coolant leaks;
    non-standard components;
    worn engine restraint bushes.
Audible/visual checks:
    starter motor/ring gear noise;
    blue smoke or steam from exhaust on starting;
    tappet noise;
    idler gear howl;
    timing chain tinkle;
    bottom-end rumble;
    temperature;
    oil/coolant loss under car.
Electrics:
    battery condition, security, electrolyte level;
    battery leads;
    under-dash and engine compartment wiring;
    all lights and equipment;
    instrumentation.
Steering/suspension:
    steering rack/track rod ends;
    wheel bearings;
    radius arms;
    dampers;
    all bushes.

3. On the road

    tendency to float or pull;
    steering self-correction out of bend;
    straight-line acceleration/braking;
    wheel 'wobble';
    temperature/oil gauges;
    gears – noise in, jumping out of, synchromesh;
    transmission clonks, universal joint clicks;
    engine – missing, pinking, knocking;
    handbrake;
    footbrake;
    clutch.

3 · MAINTENANCE

Even if you intend to always have your own car serviced professionally, this chapter will give you an insight into what work a service centre or garage should actually carry out during the various services.

The basic maintenance of the whole range of Minis is within the abilities of the majority of owners, because the mechanicals of the cars are relatively simple and straightforward, the spares and consumables low cost and widely available. An advantage of the mechanical simplicity of the Mini for those who have servicing and repair work carried out professionally as that the work is within the scope of any garage – even one specialising in other makes of car.

Carrying out your own servicing brings great savings; most modern garages allow their mechanics set amounts of time for servicing different cars, and irrespective of the actual time taken servicing an individual car, the cost to the customer is based on the time allowance in full. The garage owner will base his hourly charges not only on the wages of the mechanic, but also on his general overheads such as rent, electricity and so on, plus depreciation on the garage equipment, and a profit for the business. The savings to be made by carrying out your own maintenance are obvious.

Some garages carry out work which is not strictly necessary but which may be recommended for the particular service. For instance, a car which has covered 10,000 miles since its last service might be fitted with new brake shoes when in fact the existing shoes would be quite safe for another 5,000 miles. Some unscrupulous garages might charge for replacement of the brake shoes but not carry out the work; in the UK, Government Trading Standards Officers constantly discover garages with such practices. Those who have their cars serviced professionally should hopefully be able to spot such malpractices after reading this chapter.

There is another, greater, advantage to carrying out your own servicing in that you will know that the job has been carried out properly, and that every necessary task has been done.

Different service routines are recommended for all cars at appropriate time intervals, or after the car has travelled a set number of miles. The recommended routines described in this chapter include a series of checks which should be carried out on a weekly basis. It would obviously prove very expensive to have this work carried out professionally at such regular intervals, and so it is recommended that the individual owner – irrespective of whether he or she feels mechanically inept – does the checks.

Premises

It is perfectly feasible to carry out a large service with the car parked at the roadside; however, at the very least a hard and level surface, such as concrete, is necessary if the car is to be raised safely with a jack and supported with axle stands.

It is better to find a garage building in which to carry out servicing, so that work need not stop due to bad weather or failing light. An electricity supply for lighting or power tools is a great help.

SAFETY FOR MAINTENANCE AND REPAIR

The price of ignoring safety recommendations can be severe. Never ignore them. If in doubt – do not proceed with the job but seek further advice.

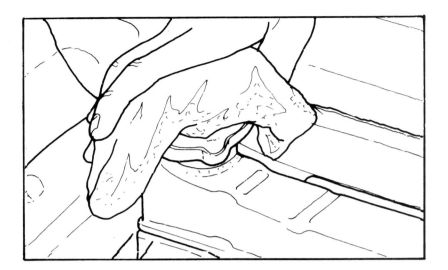

Even after you have checked that there remains no pressure within the cooling system, it is advisable to use a cloth as shown when removing the radiator cap if the engine is hot. (Courtesy Autodata)

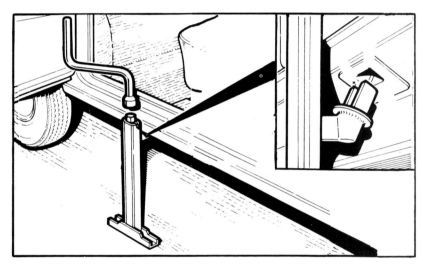

The correct method of raising the Mini, using the appropriate jack. However, on some Minis you may find that a shoddy sill 'repair' has covered up the jacking point hole shown – not a good recommendation when buying a Mini. (Courtesy Autodata)

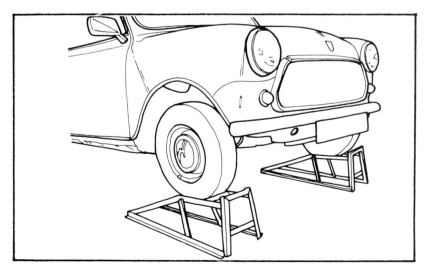

Wheel ramps are very useful when carrying out certain maintenance tasks, but are limited in their usefulness by the fact that the roadwheels must remain attached to the car! Beware cheaply made ramps; these can sometimes easily topple sideways. For this reason, only use ramps on level and firm surfaces. (Courtesy Autodata)

The correct method of raising and supporting the front of the Mini. Always use plenty of packing to prevent damage to the sump and, of course, two axle stands (only one shown here). Never rely on a jack to support any weight, even if the burden is shared with other devices. (Courtesy Autodata)

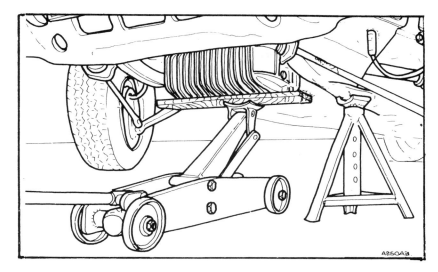

The suggested method of raising the rear of the car. (Courtesy Autodata)

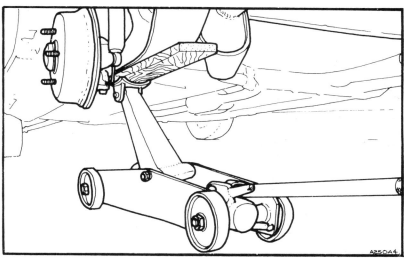

When supporting the rear of the car for most work, place the axle stands underneath the subframe as shown; if the subframe is to be removed, use the two reinforced areas at the rear of the body, just ahead of the heelboard/subframe mountings. (Courtesy Autodata)

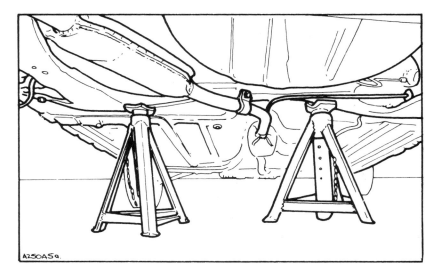

Never work under the car while it is supported only by a jack, but ensure that it is firmly supported on axle stands or solid ramps which themselves are on a solid surface. Even a relatively lightweight car such as the Mini can do you serious injury or even crush you to death if it falls whilst you are working underneath.

Always disconnect the battery (disconnecting the earth strap alone is acceptable, and when you disconnect both leads always remove the earth lead first) before starting work on the fuel or electrical systems and before starting any major repair. An electrical fire caused by a short circuit to earth is easily accidentally started and at best will wreck the wiring loom, at worst the car.

Remove the fuel tank and, where fitted, the electric fuel pump, before carrying out any welding to the rear or the underside of the car. When welding, always keep a proper fire extinguisher to hand. Stop welding frequently to check that nothing is about to catch fire and to let the surrounding metal cool, because the quite thin metal sheets used in car construction transmit heat very efficiently, and unseen soundproofing material, paint or underseal could come into contact with red-hot metal.

Beware of inhaling possibly toxic fumes which can be given off by fuel and by many of the products used in car repair. Bear in mind that many such fumes can also be explosive and, being heavier than air, will 'fall' into and fill an inspection pit. Never have a naked flame near the pit or under any circumstances when fumes might be present. Even in winter, allow the maximum workshop ventilation.

Whenever possible, make the fullest use of protective barrier creams and clothing such as goggles, respiratory masks and heavy leather gloves to avoid injury. Avoid any apparel such as ties and watches which could become entangled with moving components.

MECHANICAL MAINTENANCE

With an older example of the Mini there can be no hard and fast recommended 'service intervals' because there are too many variables involved. Not only does the Mini possess thousands of individual components ranging from those which are as good as new to others which are nearing the end of their

useful life and which could fail at any time, but also so much depends on the way the individual car is driven. An old car which is driven hard or in adverse conditions will obviously require more attention more regularly than one which is gently driven only on dry and warm days.

Adhering to certain service routines, however, will help to ensure that the car remains roadworthy. The recommended weekly maintenance routines are all checks which are centred around safety considerations. Parts of the other recommended services listed below are also primarily safety orientated.

The recommended intervals relating to lubrication err on the side of caution for the average car operated in average conditions, but should be taken as minimum requirements for a car which is used in very hot and/or dusty climates, or one which is driven hard.

Whenever you drive the car

Listen to the sounds of the engine and gearbox and take note of and investigate at the earliest opportunity any additional sounds. Constantly monitor the oil pressure gauge (if fitted) or oil warning light and water temperature gauge; if oil pressure drops then stop the engine the moment it is safe to do so, if water temperature suddenly rises then stop as soon as possible, and in both cases thoroughly investigate: do not run the engine again until the cause of the problem has been found and dealt with.

Remember that no mechanical fault nor electrical fault can 'cure' itself. If a loud noise suddenly stops then it is more ominous than a new one starting. If the lights suddenly go off and then come back on then the fault will re-occur, probably when you least expect it.

Weekly maintenance

The primary object of weekly maintenance procedures is to reveal potential problems, especially any which can affect the safety of the car, at the earliest opportunity. A minor fault, if left untreated, can quickly develop into a major problem or cause another much more and expensive secondary fault.

The only tools which may be necessary are a good jack to raise the car, axle stands to support it, a

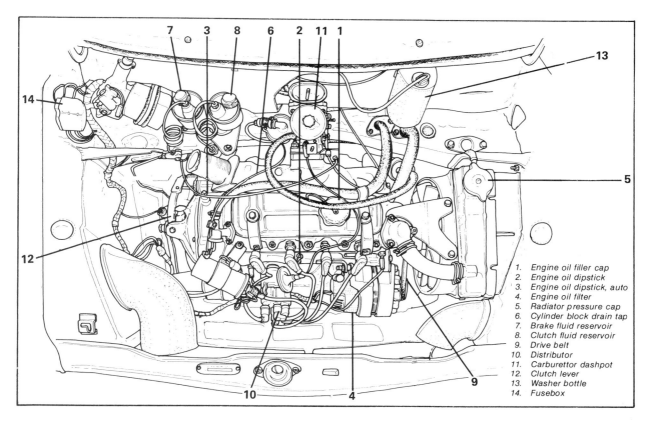

1. Engine oil filler cap
2. Engine oil dipstick
3. Engine oil dipstick, auto
4. Engine oil filter
5. Radiator pressure cap
6. Cylinder block drain tap
7. Brake fluid reservoir
8. Clutch fluid reservoir
9. Drive belt
10. Distributor
11. Carburettor dashpot
12. Clutch lever
13. Washer bottle
14. Fusebox

Engine compartment service points (air filter not shown). (courtesy Autodata)

tyre pressure gauge and pump, a selection of screwdrivers and some spanners if any work proves necessary.

If you intend to carry out your own servicing then you should keep a stock of certain consumables. You will require distilled water for the battery, good quality motor oil, brake/clutch fluid, grease and anti-freeze. This list will grow at each service interval, but the foregoing is sufficient for day to day maintenance.

Check the level of the battery electrolyte and the security of the terminal fittings. If the electrolyte is low then top up using distilled water. Remember to wash your hands afterwards and keep battery acid off your clothing! If a terminal fitting is loose then the opportunity to remove and clean both terminal and fitting should be taken before reassembling and covering lightly with petroleum jelly. Be sure to re-fit the insulation cap on the non-earthed terminal.

Jack up and support in turn the front and rear ends of the car, placing chocks on the other set of

wheels. Check the tyres for bulges, cuts, abrasions and stones/nails. Check the tread depth and look for the first signs of uneven wear. The legal minimum tyre tread depth will differ according to the country in which the car is to be driven, and it is up to the individual to seek out the relevent details – any service centre or law officer should be able to tell you. Lower the car to the ground and check the tyre pressures and the tightness of the wheel nuts. Avoid the common mistake of over-tightening the wheel nuts beyond the recommended 45 foot pounds, because you may find it impossible to subsequently remove them in the case of a roadside puncture. Check the pressure of the spare wheel tyre.

Lift the bonnet. The engine may be warm but should not have run for a few minutes. (When the engine has recently been running then oil will not have had sufficient time to drain down into the sump). Check the oil level and top up if necessary with fresh motor oil. Pour a small quantity of oil through the filler hole in the rocker box cover, then check the level again. If you over-fill then the excess will have to be drained (this procedure is described later in the chapter). Carefully remove the caps from

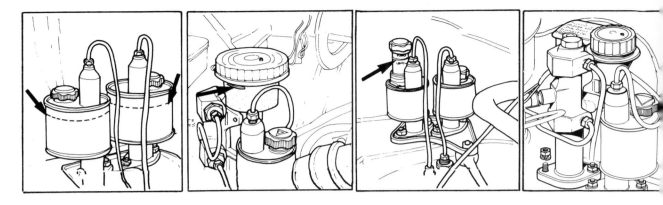

the brake and clutch reservoirs and check the levels of each. Top up if necessary, taking great care not to splash the fluid onto paintwork because it is a very effective paint stripper! If either level has dropped substantially since the last check then the reason for this should be investigated (see chapter 4 dealing with clutch and braking system).

Ensuring that the coolant system is not pressurised by feeling the top hose (you should not feel pressure if you gently squeeze it), carefully remove the radiator cap and check the coolant level. If this has dropped substantially then investigate the reason. Top up if necessary, remembering during cold weather to include anti-freeze. Check the level of the windscreen washer bottle. Check the windscreen wiper blades for damage and replace if necessary.

Test the lights, preferably by operating the switches and brake pedal while another person watches the lights coming on. Check all other electrical equipment. Start the engine and listen closely for any noises which were not previously apparent.

2-3 MONTHS OR 3-4000 MILES

Although a normal toolkit and a warm, dry and well-lit place of work will suffice, many of the jobs will be made so much easier with a pit or a hydraulic lift available that if you anticipate extensive work underneath the car then it is worth seeking out one of the modern DIY service centres and paying the not unreasonable charges levied for the use of such facilities. Alternatively, enrolling in a car maintenance course at the nearest college with facilities is an excellent idea for the novice. In

The types of clutch and brake fluid reservoirs will vary according to the year and model in question. The fluid used is highly corrosive and is a very effective paint stripper, so be careful not to allow any to spill on to paintwork. The fluid can also be highly flammable, and is rumoured to be more prone to combustion than petrol, so no smoking! (courtesy Autodata)

addition to gaining the use of good tools, those who do enrol on such a course will naturally benefit from the expert advice and assistance from the lecturer.

From the following recommended toolkit list, you will see that if you are starting from scratch and have to buy a full toolkit then the cost benefits of doing your own servicing will only become apparent in the longer term! Good tools are never cheap and it is recommended that you buy the very best quality tools which you can afford, because in the long run they will save you time and trouble, expense and possible injury. A cheap spanner, for instance, can quickly become 'cow-mouthed' (the jaws open up). If you subsequently try to use it on a stubborn nut then you will find that it can 'round' the nut, so that more drastic measures may have to be taken to get the now useless nut off. Even worse, a badly fitting spanner can suddenly break free whilst you are applying pressure.

TOOLKIT:

1. Essential.
A selection of open ended and ring spanners. The imperial sizes (earlier cars) ¼", ⁵⁄₁₆", ⅜", ⁷⁄₁₆", ½", ⁹⁄₁₆", ⅝" and ¹¹⁄₁₆" and/or metric (depending on year) sizes 7mm-21mm which must be in excellent condition.

Imperial and metric socket set, preferably with ½" and ⅜" drive, with 5" and 10" extension bars and speed brace. (Special spark plug socket if not included).

Selection of engineer's screwdrivers (parallel bladed – not carpenter's/electrician's screwdrivers which have tapered blades).

Car jack, preferably trolley jack with 2 ton capacity (for safety). Big bottle jack acceptable – scissor jack unacceptable. Axle stands.

   Wire brush.
   Emery cloth.
   Grease gun and grease.
   Pliers, long-nosed pliers and side cutters.
   Brake adjusting and bleeding tools.
   Feeler gauges, tyre pressure gauge and pump.
   Oil and oilcan.
   Light/medium weight soft face hammer.
   Small and large ball pein hammers.

2. Equipment you will wish you had!
   12 volt inspection light.
   Hacksaw and junior hacksaw.
   Mole wrench.
   Allen keys.
   'Strobe' timing light.
   Thick leather gloves.
   Overalls.
   Goggles.
   Impact driver.
   Fire extinguisher.
   Vice.

3. Non-specific Consumables.
   Selection of self-tapping screws.
   Selection of nuts, washers, bolts and set screws.
   Selection of electrical terminals, fuses and wire.
   Insulating tape
   Sticking plasters!
   Set of appropriate lightbulbs for car.
   Freeing agent (WD40 or similar).

When buying spares and consumables, remember that the quality of both can vary. Genuine Rover Group spares and those of the factory third-party component suppliers such as Lucas or SU will usually be of higher quality than 'pattern' components from external suppliers. This is especially true of body panels. Consumables such as oil and filters, spark plugs and brake shoes also vary in quality. It is in the

interests of the longevity of your car to invest in the appropriate quality consumables.

Preliminary considerations

Before rendering your car immobile do ensure that you possess all the parts necessary in order to get it back on the road! Before starting any mechanical work, examine every nut, bolt, stud, circlip and split pin which may have to be undone/removed, and if they show signs of corrosion or thread damage then order spares just in case you render them useless during removal. Most of the consumables required for even a major service will be widely available not only from Rover Group dealers but also from many motor factors. If you happen to live in an isolated small village with only a small general garage for a local source of supply, remember that most can order spares on your behalf early in the morning for delivery the same afternoon.

   Like many older cars, the Mini is liable to have many stubborn and totally seized nuts and bolts. Attacking these with too much gusto can not only risk damaging them but also the components they are fastening. A 'war of attrition' in which you soak the stubborn fitting in a freeing agent, then move it (however slightly), and leave it to soak in freeing agent again for a while before repeating the exercise is often the only solution. The use of heat where appropriate (and safe) can often help, but outright force is normally counter-productive. Before starting the service, carry out the jobs and checks recommended in the previous service.

Test Drive

Take the car for a short test drive, listening carefully for any 'new' noises. Park on a slope and check that the handbrake will hold the car. Making sure that the road ahead and behind is clear, gently apply the handbrake at about 30mph (keeping the release button depressed) and see whether the car pulls to either side. Brake normally (with the foot brake) to a halt, again checking for any tendency for the car to pull to either side. (See Chapter 4 – Brakes).

   Accelerate hard and judge whether the car pulls to either side. From 30mph in fourth gear, accelerate and listen for 'pinking'. If any of these fault manifest themselves then either seek professional assistance or read chapter 4 of this book and judge whether you can undertake the repair work yourself. This book is not a full workshop manual, and it will pay you to obtain a good one before starting ambitious repairs. If no obvious faults are apparent, then proceed as follows.

Service

Check the travel of the brake pedal and of the handbrake lever. If either seem excessive then adjust the drum brakes. On most Minis there are drum brakes front and rear which have a square adjuster situated on the brake backplates. Use the correct tool to adjust them. Screw the adjuster in until it will turn no more, then back it off one notch (which can be clearly felt) and check that the wheel turns freely. If not, apply the brakes to centre the brake shoes and try turning the wheel again. If the wheel will still not turn, back off the adjuster one more notch. Repeat for each drum brake. (See Chapter 4 for more details).

Check the headlight alignment. It is a good idea to have this set correctly by professionals and, on your return, to place the car in your garage and mark both the positions of the tyres on the floor and of the dipped and full beams on the wall. This will give you a set of marks to aim for in the future, and will prove quite accurate provided that the car is similarly loaded and has the same tyre pressures when you re-test.

Examine all pipes in the braking and clutch hydraulic systems for damage, and similarly check the fuel pipes. In the case of Hydrolastic cars, also check all suspension pipes and the displacer units for leakage. Whilst under the car, check the exhaust for signs of blowing (carbon deposits visible on the outside) and for its security. Check the deflection of the fan belt (See Chapter 4) and adjust if necessary.

Chock the rear wheels, raise the front of the car and place on axle stands. Referring to Chapter 4, check the steering and suspension systems.

Oil

If the car has been used extensively since the last oil change, take the opportunity to change it now. Under normal conditions, change it as part of the six month service. If the car has been standing overnight, the oil will have all had time to drain to the sump. If the

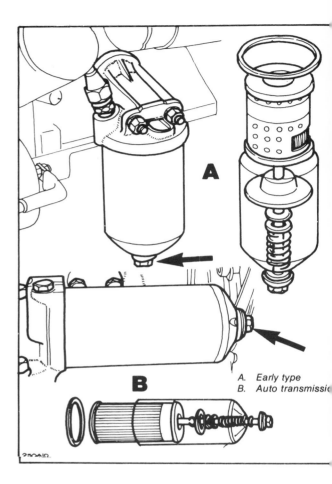

The oil filter cannisters fitted to early cars and to automatics are both rather more trouble to change than the cartridge filters fitted to later cars. (courtesy Autodata)

engine has been run recently, leave it until it has cooled slightly so that the oil has time to drain to the sump. Some people prefer to warm the engine before draining the oil, because this thins the oil which helps to clear more of it from the engine.

The oil and the oil filter must be changed at the same time. Begin by draining the oil. You will need a suitable container for the oil to drain into, and happily an old five gallon oil can with one side cut out is ideal and very cheap. Place this underneath the sump (raising the car to gain clearance where necessary) and remove the sump plug. Then remove the oil filler cap, which will allow the oil to drain more quickly. Allow 20-30 minutes so that all of the old oil has time to drain.

Whilst the oil is draining, change the filter. On early cars, this will be a paper element type which is housed in a canister at the front of the engine. Undo the bolt at the bottom of the unit and lift the canister clear of the engine. Remove the filter element and the old seals, wash the canister out with neat petrol, dry it, then refit the new oil seals and filter element. Fill the unit with oil before fitting it to the car.

Later cars have a cartridge-type filter, which simply unscrews from its mounting. A strap wrench may be needed to start the filter on its thread, although if it cannot be turned by hand (try wrapping rubber around it to gain better purchase) and a strap wrench is unavailable, hammering an old screwdriver through the cartridge will give sufficient leverage to start it turning, although this practice is hardly ideal.

After fitting the oil filter, replace the oil sump plug then refill the engine with the recommended amount of oil. Because the gearbox unit is integral with the engine, they share the same oil and are both automatically replenished at the same time.

EVERY 6 MONTHS OR 5-6000 MILES

Carry out all of the checks and adjustments listed previously, including all of those which were optional.

Some of the more complicated jobs or those which require specialised equipment may be best entrusted to a professional. Most garages are pleased to carry out specific tasks rather than a full 'service'.

In addition to the previously suggested toolkit you will require the following.
Strobe timing light.
Feeler gauges.
Torque wrench.
Carburettor balancing equipment (Cooper S only).
Wheel alignment device. (This is optional, because wheel alignment is normally carried out professionally).

Engine and ancilliaries

If the engine oil and filter were not changed during the previous service then it is essential that they are changed as a part of this service. (See 3 month service).

Check all cooling system hoses for condition and renew any which show signs of perishing, splitting or abrasion. Check the tightness of jubilee clips.

Ignition

It is often cheaper in the long run to buy a complete 'ignition service kit' from a Rover Group dealer than it is to buy certain of the ignition components separately from local garages. Buying a complete kit means that you have all the likely spares to hand; any which are not needed in this service should be used as a matter of course during the next 3 monthly or the annual service.

Check the spark plug leads. Remove the spark plugs, clean and reset them to the correct gap. If they show signs of old age (excessive wear of the electrode) then it is best to replace them. The state of the spark plugs can reveal problems with the ignition, the carburation or the engine itself. If they are badly carbonned (covered with a dry sooty layer) then the mixture has been too rich. This could be due to the carbs being set badly, or to worn jets, a sticking choke cable or clogged air filters (see chapter 4, fuel). If the spark plugs are covered with an oily black layer then oil is getting into the cylinders past the valve guide/ stem or the piston rings (see chapter 4 – engine repair). Carbonned or oiled plugs may be cleaned and re-used.

If the electrodes are burning away, if the core nose is damaged or white (the electrodes will have a glazed appearance) then the plug is overheating for one or more of a range of reasons. Assuming that the correct plugs are fitted, the problem could lie with pre-ignition, too weak a fuel mixture or too low a grade of fuel. The fault in any instance should be traced and rectified before the engine is run again, because serious damage could otherwise result. The spark plugs should in this instance be replaced.

To set the spark plug gap, firstly clean the electrodes thoroughly using a wire brush. Find the appropriate feeler gauge (or use two which add up to the correct thickness of 0.025″) and gently push it into the electrode gap. As electrodes slowly waste away, the gap will normally be slack and should be adjusted using the correct tool (usually attached to the feeler gauge) until the gauge can be moved within the electrode gap and slight resistance felt.

Check that the screw barrel fittings on the ends of the plugs are tight. If they are loose then electrical losses will occur to the detriment of the spark efficiency.

Remove the distributor cap by pressing onto the centre of each fixing spring and lifting away the end. Examine the cap for cracks or burning, if any cracks are found then renew the cap, because any moisture here (such as condensation) will cause a short to earth and prevent the engine from starting! Examine the four metal contacts for signs of damage and the plug lead ends for tightness.

Remove the rotor arm and examine the blade for fouling. Gently clean using fine emery paper if necessary, or replace if the blade is loose.

Examine the contact breaker points for wear and cleanliness. The contacting surfaces should be unpitted, level and clean. If a little light cleaning with an emery cloth will not repair the surfaces then it is best to replace the points. Lubricate the advance/retard mechanism, the cam and the contact breaker pivot.

Re-fit the points. With the engine in fourth gear, the handbrake off and the ignition switch 'off' push the car slowly backwards or forwards until the contact breaker arm is positioned on one of the cam lobes. Check the points gap using a feeler gauge, and if the gap is too large or too small then slacken off the screw which holds the plate and adjust the gap by levering the plate with a small screwdriver inserted into the notch adjacent to it.

If the points gap has to be altered then the ignition timing should be re-set. This may be carried out either with the engine running (dynamic timing) or with the engine idle (static timing).

Static timing

The distributor cap must be removed. The number one cylinder (nearest the radiator) should be on its compression stroke. This may be found by removing the spark plugs and turning the engine over by hand until the cylinder shows compression, or by removal of the rocker box cover and noting when number four cylinder's valves are open (rocker down) and number one cylinder's valves are closed (rocker in uppermost part of travel). Slacken the distributor clamp pinch bolt.

The points at this stage should be starting to open. This can be checked by switching on the ignition (do not leave it turned on for too long, because you can eventually burn the coil out) and fitting a 12V test bulb across the low tension lead and earth, and the bulb will light as the points separate. Ensure that the timing marks are correctly aligned. The timing marks are in different positions according to the year and model.

On later models they are on the timing cover next to the crankshaft pulley, on early models they are under the inspection cover plate in the clutch housing.

Rotate the distributor until the bulb lights and fix in that position by tightening the clamp bolt.

Turn the crankshaft through a complete revolution and check that the bulb lights at the correct moment. If it lights too early then the ignition is advanced, too late and it is retarded. Small adjustments may be made using the vernier adjuster (where fitted).

Dynamic timing

This is preferable to static timing, and requires a stroboscopic timing light. A bottle of typist's correction fluid is also very useful for marking the crankshaft pulley notch and relevant timing mark to aid visibility. Connect the stroboscopic timing light to the number one spark plug and its lead, disconnect the vacuum advance pipe and place a small piece of tape over the hole at the end of the pipe to prevent carburettor air induction.

Start the engine and shine the flashing timing light onto the rotating crankshaft pulley via a mirror. The flashing of the light will apparently arrest the motion of the pulley, and the two marks should appear static. If the marks are out of alignment, turn the ignition off and adjust the distributor as in static timing, to advance or retard the ignition timing. Re-test and readjust until they align. Use the vernier adjuster for fine adjustments.

If the engine speed is increased, the timing mark should appear to drift to the left due to the mechanical (centrifugal) timing advance gear. Reconnect the vacuum advance pipe, again increase engine revs. There should be a further, smaller advance.

A road test can be a useful final check on timing. Warm the engine, and accelerate from around 30mph in top. If the engine pinks then retard the ignition slightly using the vernier adjuster.

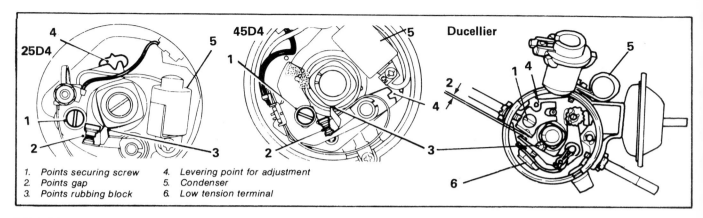

1. Points securing screw	4. Levering point for adjustment
2. Points gap	5. Condenser
3. Points rubbing block	6. Low tension terminal

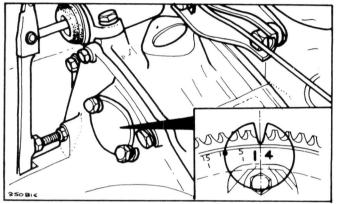

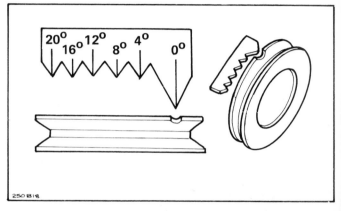

TOP *Three types of distributor have been fitted to the Mini. Most common are the Lucas 25D4 and 45D4. Adjustment is covered in the text, although a special tool is available for easier adjustment of the Ducellier type. (courtesy Autodata)*

ABOVE *The timing marks on early cars are situated underneath a plate which is bolted to the clutch cover, and they are very difficult to see. Try using a mirror and a torch to illuminate them if you have difficulty. When dynamic timing the engine, it can prove rather difficult to make typists' correction fluid marks when you are looking at a mirror image! (courtesy Autodata)*

ABOVE RIGHT *The timing marks on later cars are situated on the crankshaft pulley. The tight engine bay of the Mini can make these almost difficult to see as those of earlier cars. (courtesy Autodata)*

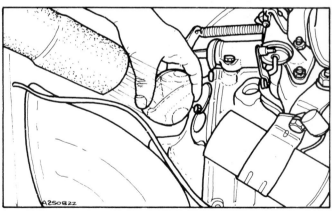

ABOVE *Nobody said that this was going to be easy. Shine the stroboscope light onto the mirror, and angle the mirror so that the light is reflected into the clutch cover and on to the timing marks. Many stroboscope's light output seems too dim for this to be carried out in daylight or even inside a garage with windows, and so you may have to drape a blanket over the raised bonnet in order to shut out other light. (courtesy Autodata)*

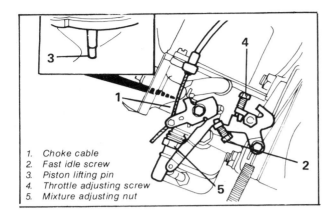

1. Choke cable
2. Fast idle screw
3. Piston lifting pin
4. Throttle adjusting screw
5. Mixture adjusting nut

The smaller HS2 carburettor is fitted to the majority of Minis. When setting the mixture, ensure that the choke is not actuated. (courtesy Autodata)

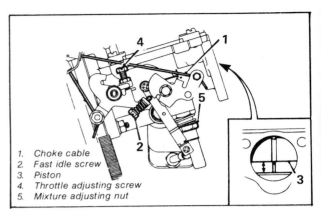

1. Choke cable
2. Fast idle screw
3. Piston
4. Throttle adjusting screw
5. Mixture adjusting nut

The larger HS4 carburettor fitted to early higher performance and automatic Minis and to all Minis from 1974. (courtesy Autodata)

Carburation

Remove the bell housing from the carburettor, withdraw the piston and examine the needle for ridges. Replace if necessary, along with the jet. Check that the jet is centered (see chapter 4, fuel).

Check the mixture. There are special kits available at reasonable cost which enable this to be carried out more accurately, although the following can give fairly accurate settings.

Firstly, examine the exhaust tail pipe. If the inside is blackened then the car is probably running rich, if it is a light grey then the carburation could be too lean. This may be checked by lifting the carburettor piston (using the lifting pin) while the (warmed) engine is at tickover. It will be necessary to remove the air filter housing to gain access for this. If the carburettor is too rich then the revs will pick up and remain higher when the piston is lifted, if it is too lean then the revs will immediately die away. If correctly set, the revs will pick up momentarily and settle back to the norm.

To richen the mixture, the jet adjusting nut should be turned clockwise (looking from the top) to pull the jet downwards, and vice versa. Only turn the jet adjusting nut by a single flat at a time, and on the twin carburettor Cooper S work firstly on one carburettor, then the other, then the first and so on until the correct effect is achieved by lifting either piston.

Even the most avid DIY enthusiast would be well advised to have the twin carburettors of the Cooper S professionally balanced and set.

For more details of setting carburation, see chapter 4 describing the fuel system.

Valve Clearances

Remove any fitments from the rocker box cover and remove the cover itself. Because the engine will have to be turned over by hand, the car may be left in gear and the car 'rocked' backwards and forwards, or the sparking plugs may be removed, the car taken out of gear and the engine turned over by hand. Alternatively, raise one of the front wheels from the ground, remove the sparking plugs and turn the engine by turning the lifted wheel.

Turn the engine until valve number 8 is fully open, that is, the stem has been depressed to its maximum by the rocker gear. When valve 8 is fully open then the gap at valve 1 should be set. Note that the sum of the valve numbers is 8+1 (9). The sum of the valve to be checked and that which is fully open always equals nine with the four cylinder engine. Turn the engine until valve 6 is open, and check valve 3. The remaining sequence is (first number open valve, second number valve to be adjusted) 4+5, 7+2, 1+8, 3+6, 5+4, 2+7.

To adjust a valve if the clearance is not as recommended in the specifications, lock the ball end screw using a screwdriver and loosen the locknut with a ring spanner. With the feeler gauge in position, gently tighten the adjuster until the gauge

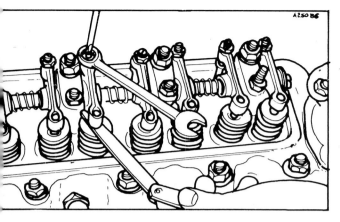

Special tools are available for setting valve clearances, and are very easy to use. However, a cranked ½" ring spanner and a screwdriver will accomplish the same task. Try to find and use a parallel bladed screwdriver which accurately fits the rocker adjuster slot. If you use a carpenter's or electrician's screwdriver then the blade will not bear properly against the slot, and it will in time become distorted. When this happens, it will not be possible to accurately set the clearance, because the rocker adjuster screw will tend to turn whilst the locking nut is tightened. (courtesy Autodata)

can just be moved and offers just a little resistance, and then tighten the locknut (keeping the ball end screw stationary) and recheck the gap (·12").

Front Wheel Alignment

If the front wheels are out of alignment they will 'toe' in or out, that is, they will point either too far inwards or outwards, giving exceptionally high tyre wear on the outside or the inside of the tread respectively. Special kits are available which enable the DIY owner to carry out the measurement and set the alignment, although because this is only an occasional task and a fifteen minute job for a garage or tyre fitting business, the costs of having it done professionally are low.

Do not attempt to realign the front wheels 'by eye' because this is always a mistake. If very severe wear has taken place on one rim of the tyres do not be tempted to over-adjust the alignment to correct this, but rotate the tyres provided, of course, that the front ones are still legal.

Lubrication and Brakes

If the engine/gearbox oil was not changed as a part of the 3-month service routine, then do so now.

While the car is raised, clean and lubricate the handbrake cables and compensating lever. Remove the rear wheels. Slacken off the brake adjusters and remove the brake drums. Check the condition of the shoes (replace if worn; see Chapter 4, brakes) and the drums (clean). The fine dust which is found in the drums is asbestos and very hazardous to health, so wear a dust mark whilst cleaning the drums. If the

shoes have been allowed to wear too far then the drums may be scored, in which case they too should be replaced. Reassemble the brakes and adjust correctly using the proper tool. Screw in the adjuster until the shoes lock the brakes, and then turn the adjuster back by one notch. Check for drag and turn the adjuster back one further notch if necessary. Re-fit the road wheels. Refer to Chapter 4 for photographs and full details of the braking system. Check the condition of brake pipes, and renew any which show signs of corrosion.

Lower the car to the ground and transfer the wheel chocks to the rear wheels, apply the handbrake. Loosen the front wheel nuts, lift the front of the car and support on axle stands. Remove the road wheels and check the condition of the front brake drums and shoes.

Check that the amount of friction material on each shoe is greater than the minimum allowable 0.08". If not, replace (See Chapter 4, brakes). Examine the drums for pitting or scoring. For cars fitted with disc front brakes, check the pad thickness (the minimum allowable is 0.125") and the disc for signs of scoring. To remove the brake pads, simply remove the two split pins from the back of the caliper unit, and the two retaining springs and pads can be lifted away.

Annual Service

The annual service includes all jobs listed under weekly, 3 and 6 month services.

If not previously done in an earlier service, renew the distributor cap and spark plug leads. Drain the coolant from the radiator and the engine block. If the radiator does not have a drain plug then remove the

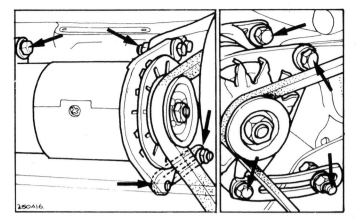

If the fan belt can be deflected by more than ½" on its longest run, slacken off the bolts arrowed to allow the dynamo or alternator to move. Apply pressure to the dynamo/alternator until the fan belt is suitably tensioned, then tighten the bolts on the adjuster bracket then the pivot bolts. Re-test the deflection and adjust again if necessary. It will help to gain some leverage by using a large screwdriver to apply pressure to the dynamo/alternator.

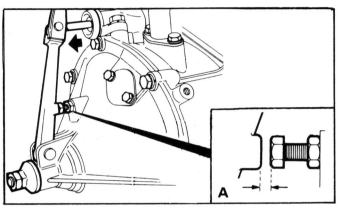

Wear between the clutch release bearing and the thrust ring must be compensated for by adjusting the gap between the moveable stop bolt and the clutch operating lever. Remove the return spring before trying to insert feeler gauges.

bottom hose. Drain the block via the drain plug (if fitted). Flush the system using a proprietary product if desired, or plain water as an alternative. Re-fill the system using the recommended quantity of new anti-freeze (not alcohol based). For temperatures down to −13 degrees celsius use 25% anti-freeze, for temperatures down to −19 degrees celsius use 33% and for temperatures down to −36 degrees celsius use a 50% concentration.

Slacken the bolts which hold the dynamo or alternator and remove the fan belt. Fit a new replacement and tension it so that there is a maximum deflection in the centre of the longest run of ½".

Check all rubber hoses in the coolant system and renew if necessary, check hoses and seals in the hydraulic brake operating system and renew if necessary. Check the crankcase breather hose for blockage and clear if necessary with stiff wire or an air compressor.

Disconnect the battery. Jack up each side of the car in turn and support with axle stands. Visually check the hydrolastic system (if fitted) for damage to pipes or displacement units; otherwise, visually check the hydraulic dampers for signs of leakage. Whilst the car is raised, check the condition of the driveshaft gaiters and replace if they are cracked or split. This is an MOT test failure point in the UK, furthermore, the ingress of dirt will cause rapid wear unless the gaiters are in good condition.

Examine the petrol tank, pump and fuel line for signs of leakage. Check the steering and suspension for play as outlined in Chapter 2. Check that the gaiters on the steering rack are undamaged, and replace if necessary.

Check the clutch lever to stop bolt gap by removing the return spring and inserting feeler gauges into the gap. To adjust, slacken the lock nut and screw the bolt in or out until the correct clearance is obtained, then tighten the lock nut. On early cars the clearance should be .06", on later cars fitted with Borg & Beck clutches .02", and on cars fitted with the Verto clutch .26".

BODYWORK PREVENTATIVE MAINTENANCE

Having read this far, no-one should be in any doubt that the most lethal malady which can strike the Mini is bodyrot! Whilst it is true to say that no matter how badly rotted a car becomes, it can still be rebuilt (albeit at considerable cost), there can be no doubting that prevention is always less expensive and traumatic than cure, and this section of the book looks at ways of extending the life of the bodywork in order to put off that time when extensive bodywork rebuilding will be required.

General care

In order for metal to rust it needs only to be exposed to the slightest amount of moisture (including moisture in humid air). Paint scratches and chips which expose bare metal will obviously permit this to happen, and so any such breaches of the paintwork should receive immediate attention, preferably before any moisture which comes into contact with the metal has sufficient time to let rust gain a foothold.

Very shallow scratches which do not go through to the metal may be gently cleaned out and hand painted with a small brush. If bare metal has been exposed (to all intents and purposes corrosion begins the moment metal comes into contact with air which contains moisture) then it is usually best to take a small area of the surrounding paintwork down with wet 'n' dry (used wet) to reveal a little more metal than was originally exposed. The existing paint at the edges should be 'feathered', that is, there should not be a discernible shoulder around the area. This should be dried and thoroughly de-greased before being treated with Finnegan's 'Number One' primer or Bondaglass Voss 'Bonda Prima'. Either of these products should stop any tiny traces of rust which remain on the surface of the metal from spreading. If necessary, high-build primer can then be applied and flatted down before top coating. Before applying any paint or rust-resistant product, check that it is compatible with the existing surrounding paintwork of the car. DO NOT use cellulose-based products on other types of paint, because the powerful thinners will lift them.

All original Mini paint colours are readily available from any car paint shop with mixing facilities. Do not expect the shop to guarantee to supply the correct colour by name alone, but find the manufacturer's code and quote that as well.

Old paintwork will usually be faded, so that the new paint stands out from the surrounding area. If this is the case then cutting the old and new paint (allowing a suitable period for the new paint to harden first, which varies according to the type of paint used) with a proprietary mild cutting compound will remove accumulated road dirt and take a very thin layer off the old paint to lessen the difference, as well as improving the surface of the new paint. It is best to leave any new paint to harden for at least a fortnight before cutting it back.

Underneath the car, particularly within the wheel arches but also along the run of the sill outer sections and around the sub frames, mud accumulates and should be cleaned off at regular intervals. Mud not only holds moisture in contact with the car body for long periods but it holds the salt which is used on roads in the UK in winter. Little accelerates rusting faster than salt.

Steam cleaning is the very best way in which to remove mud from the underside of the car, although most people make do with a powerful jet of water. High pressure cleaners can also remove underseal which no longer adheres to the metal due to the spread of rust underneath. Far from being a problem, this is a great help because it gives you a fighting chance of dealing with the rust at the earliest opportunity. You can hire such washers by the hour or day from many DIY and equipment hire businesses. If you do use one then firstly make sure you have rust-arresting primer and some underseal to deal with the rusted areas which will be exposed.

Washing the car regularly not only keeps it looking good but also helps to show up any scratches or minor dents which could, if left untreated, lead to the onset of corrosion. It is a good idea to begin by washing the underside of the car and the wheels, since the use of a hose or high-pressure water device can splatter mud all over the place, including onto the paintwork you have just washed if you did things in the wrong order. The head of a stiff broom can be a help in removing mud from under the sill sections, where it can be difficult to direct a jet of water. After cleaning the underside, switch your attentions to the roof and then work downwards.

Never use ordinary washing-up liquid to wash the car, because many liquids contain industrial salts! (Do not use them in the windscreen washer bottle, either, because some of this soapy water will find its way onto the paintwork). It is always safest to use a proper car shampoo. Begin by hosing the car down with fresh water to get as much dirt as possible into suspension and off the body. If you take the wash leather or even a sponge to bodywork covered in gritty dirt then the dirt will grind at the surface of the paint. Begin with the roof, work along the bonnet, down the back and sides and lastly do the valances.

After this initial hosing or washing down it is as well to use a chamois leather and proper car shampoo, gently helping dirt from the surface with the leather.

At this stage you should thoroughly inspect the paintwork for any signs of damage and attend to these before polishing. If the paintwork is very dull then you might consider cutting it back before you polish it, using one of the several products for the purpose which are widely available from motor factors. Finally, polish the paintwork. Car polish repels water, so that water which is kicked up from the road (and which contains dirt) will wash away before the majority of the dirt has an opportunity to come out of suspension and stick to the paint.

Dealing with rust

Whenever a replacement panel which is a part of a box section has to be welded into position, the opportunity should be taken to give as much protection first to the side which will end up inside the section. Obviously, the area of metal which is to be the actual join will have to be cleaned bright and de-greased, but most of the panel can be treated to several layers of primer. Some of this paint protection will probably burn off during the welding process, but any protection is better than none.

The maximum protection against rusting will be gained by using one of the better 'rust arresting' primers rather than normal primer. The two rust-arresting products previously mentioned also perform very well on clean metal, better, in fact, than normal primers.

The Mini, depending as it does on combinations of metal panels welded together for its strength, has a number of box sections, most of which can (and usually do) rust from the inside. When a panel or panels from a box section is repaired the opportunity to give further protection to the metal should not be missed. As soon as the welding is finished and the metal has cooled, Waxoyl or a similar substance

The Waxoyl kit complete with pistol applicator and extension tube for feeding into box sections. It is normally necessary (except on the hottest of days) to have to stand the tin in hot water to warm and thin the Waxoyl for spraying.

should be applied. This will often entail drilling a ⅜" hole in order to gain access to the enclosed section, and the hole should afterwards be sealed with a rubber grommet.

The Waxoyl is applied either with one of the hand pumps supplied by the manufacturer or via a compressor-driven 'parafin' or underseal spray gun. When cold, Waxoyl is of too thick a consistency to spray properly, and so it should be warmed until it becomes thin enough by standing the tin in a bowl of hot water. A cheap alternative to Waxoyl is old sump oil, which will have to be thinned in order to get a fine spray.

Underneath the car, not only the bodywork but also items from the suspension benefit from protection against corrosion. There are various ways in which the suspension and associated components may be protected.

If the underside of the car is steam cleaned, then components previously covered in a layer of mud will be revealed to possess a covering of rust underneath. It is not always practical to clean and repaint such components nor to partially clean and then use a proprietary rust arrester. Many people slow the corrosive process in such cases by spraying or painting on old engine oil.

When oil is applied to a ferrous surface, it spreads to form a thin protective layer which offers the considerable advantage of remaining 'self healing' for a period of time insofar as if the layer is breeched by a scratch then the oil will again spread to re-cover it as long as it remains thin enough to do so. In time, the oil not only thickens of its own accord but also because it is absorbed by dirt, so that in order to work consistently the process should be repeated from time to time. If oil is used thus then be very careful not to let any come into contact with the brakes.

Proprietary wax products such as Waxoyl are used by many in place of oil (which can be very messy to apply), mainly in the protection of the underbody. Waxes remain reasonably fluid during the summer months and so can be self-healing, but in colder winter climates this will not happen.

Underseal is the usual product utilised for underbody protection. It is a very thick substance which can go some way towards absorbing the impact of stones kicked up by the road wheels which would otherwise expose bare metal to the elements. Underseal forms a thick and hard 'skin' over the metal, and here lies its greatest drawback. Any rust which exists before the application of underseal or rust which forms afterwards can spread rapidly and virtually unopposed, unseen under the surface of the underseal.

Underseal works best on new panels which already have some form of rust protection, and is best considered a form of protection for the actual anti-rust protection.

Arresting rust

When rust is discovered on thin body metal or even on sturdy chassis or suspension components there are two options for dealing with it. Preferable is the complete removal of all traces of rust from the surface of the metal, followed by priming and top-coating. This can be a time-consuming process, however, and many people prefer to utilise rust arresting products.

Sometimes, the body panel metal can be so badly rusted and thin that completely removing the rust might result in a hole. In such circumstances a good rust arresting product can help to prolong the life of the metal, provided that it is not a structurally important panel.

The car accessory market usually offers a wide range of chemical treatments which are all 'guaranteed' to arrest existing rust and ensure that the metal never rusts again. Not all appear to actually work in the experience of the author and also according to various published reports of independent testing. Rather than list the many products which do not reportedly work, the two which in the author's experience do work and which he uses are, as already stated, Finnegan's 'Number One' primer and Bondaglass Gloss 'Bondaprima'.

Unlike many other products, Bondaprima is not claimed to chemically alter the composition of rust. The manufacturers state that it works by infiltrating and encapsulating rust particles in a resin. Finnegan's Number One, on the other hand, is claimed to convert rust into 'black mangenite' and to contain particles of glass which give the primer function a tough and smooth finish. Both certainly work.

In order to work properly, rust arresters should be applied only to flake-free, grease-free and dry surfaces, which should ideally have no more than a thin coating of corrosion. Finnegan's Number One is available either in a spray can or a tin, and the former is recommended for most car bodywork because it is much thinner than the paint contained in the tin, which is best suited for use on heavier sections.

It is useless, incidentally, to use any rust arresting primer on metal which is to be filled. If you are straightening out a dent, for instance, then you have to remove all traces of rust before applying the filler straight onto clean metal, because if you were to apply a rust-resistant primer first then the filler will adhere strongly only to the primer, which does not itself possess sufficient adhesion to the metal, and both filler and paint will drop off in next to no time. If you apply filler over rusted metal, the rust will rapidly spread underneath the filler, which will eventually drop out.

To arrest rust, you should begin by thoroughly cleaning and de-greasing the section in question. When it has dried then it may be firstly wire-brushed and finally rubbed with emery cloth or paper in order to remove any loose rust and to key the surface.

Follow the instructions with whichever product you choose to the letter. In the case of Number One, this entails applying two separate coats with a two hour drying interval in between. The work should be carried out in a warm, dust-free and dry building if possible; otherwise on a hot and dry day outside. Bondaprima also comes in a spray can or a tin for brushing or spraying with a compressor. After treatment, cellulose should be applied either within 6 to 24 hours or after seven days; other paints may be applied after four hours.

Areas which can really benefit from rust arresting maintenance are those body panels on the underside of the car, such as the sills and the floor. If underseal on such panels shows any signs of lifting then the following can greatly increase their lifespan (assuming that they have not rusted right through).

Firstly, all traces of old underseal and paint have to be removed. The easiest way in which to achieve this is to use an electric drill (or an air drill powered by a compressor) fitted with one of a selection of wire brushes and 'flap wheels'. An angle grinder fitted with a cup brush is even better, but beware the lengths of wire which become detached from the cup (which rotates at 10,000 or more rpm) and fly off at high speed! Protective clothing, especially goggles, must be worn to avoid personal injury from flying rust flakes and the aforementioned lengths of wire from cup brushes. If the panel being treated is anywhere near the petrol tank then this should firstly be removed.

Next, as much rust as possible should be removed using emery cloth or paper (to work right into corners) in addition to the drill and wire brushes and flap wheels. No more than a very thin coating of rust should remain. Apply the rust arrester, followed by a second coat and a topcoat at the recommended intervals. Underseal may then be re-applied if desired to finish the job.

General bodywork preventative maintenance

On the hottest, driest day of the summer it is a good idea to remove the seats, carpets and interior trim from the car, and to give as much of the newly exposed metal as possible anti-corrosion protection. A thin coating of a moisture-inhibiting wax or oil may be applied under footwell rubber mats to protect the floor and inner sill sections. Even with this protection, if the carpets (where fitted) get wet then they should immediately be removed and dried out. Chromework presents special problems. The tiniest pin-hole will enable rust to become established under the surface of the chrome, and it spreads unseen until large areas begin to 'bubble' and eventually to flake off. New chromework can be polished to provide some protection, but because the bumpers and other items with a chrome finish are vulnerable to stone chipping, there remains very little which can be done in the way of long term protection. The non-chromed side of such fittings does benefit from either wax or oil protection.

Where small chrome fittings meet painted bodywork, problems with rusting can arise. The chrome light surrounds and other fittings are all able to trap and hold water in contact with the bodywork, and furthermore, the bodywork paint is often breached as the pieces of trim are fitted into place. Wax or oil may be used to help prevent this if care is taken not to allow either to run onto surrounding paintwork.

4 · REPAIR AND RESTORATION

A Mini which is professionally restored to truly concours condition could cost the owner as much as if not considerably more than the price of a brand new Mini. It is little wonder that the tens of thousands of owners of restoration-ripe Minis often seek cheaper alternatives.

The DIY restoration is the cheapest route to ownership of a first-class Mini, provided that the person doing the work already possesses not only a full range of tools (and the skills to use them) but also a suitable premises and, not least, the commitment to see the job through.

Many people opt for a semi-DIY restoration, tackling the simple but tedious (and often back-breaking) tasks themselves (which make up a major part of the costs of a complete restoration) and bringing in skilled freelance craftsmen for the more demanding jobs such as welding and spraying. This will be a more expensive exercise than the true DIY restoration but it will still be an economical solution.

The next pricing level is to commission the Mini specialist to carry out (on his own premises) specific work, such as floor, roof and sill replacement and so on. The car may then be brought back home for paint preparation before being returned to the professional for final finishing. The mechanical components are then built back into the 'as new' shell.

Many professional restorers are happy to let (and some encourage) the owner of the car undertake quite a large proportion of the less skilled work themselves, such as stripping off all inner and outside trim and divesting the car of all mechanical and electrical components prior to body rebuilding. Following the actual body rebuilding work, the amateur can then save a lot by stripping the old paintwork himself. Doing just these two jobs can save the owner up to 40% or even more of the total professional restoration costs.

Merely to hand the car over to a professional restoration company and glibly request a full restoration can cost a lot of money! For a start, no-one (not even the most experienced restorer) can state with 100% certainty exactly what work will need carrying out to the body until some of the welded panels have been stripped to reveal hidden metal (or a lack of it) underneath. Secondly, reputable restorers do not tend to employ low-paid, unskilled staff specifically to carry out tedious and time-consuming tasks, and so if the car has to be stripped to bare metal for a respray then the work will probably be undertaken by an over-qualified craftsman at a high hourly rate.

Quite frequently, cars come on to the market as unfinished restoration projects. Often, the vendors started work on the car in good faith but subsequently discovered that their welding skills were wanting, that their tools and facilities were not up to the job, or that they were simply out of their depth.

If you have doubts regarding your abilities, facilities or motivation to complete the job, it is best to think in terms of having the restoration work carried out professionally, and to assemble the car yourself.

DIY RESTORATION

The cheapest way to restore a Mini is to do it yourself provided that you already possess suitable premises and a full range of necessary tools and equipment. The outright purchase costs of a suitable garage, tools and equipment alone will represent a substantial percentage of (if not more than) professional restoration costs should you have to buy the lot from scratch.

As far as premises are concerned, it is essential only that they are dry and permit you sufficient light to see by and room to move around the car. However, there is a great gulf between what is possible and what is practical. It is possible, for instance, to carry out a restoration on the roadside but it certainly cannot be considered a practical method of doing so! Similarly, it is possible to work in cold and cramped conditions but to do so will have a terrible effect on morale and many people lose their motivation half-way through a restoration simply because they cannot face the prospect of returning to the work space again. It would be by no means impossible to work in a damp building, although any exposed metal would begin to rust overnight and tools would quickly become rusted and useless.

Ideally, the workshop should be wide enough to accommodate two cars (in order to restore one) and leave at least five feet clearance front and back. A garage eighteen to twenty feet long by twelve to fifteen feet wide (an ordinary double garage) would give a comfortable working area all around the car. Do check on local building and planning regulations before erecting a huge garage; it would be a shame to have to demolish it part-way through the restoration. Very large buildings like an old barn might seem ideal but will prove very costly to heat in the winter.

Illumination should not be confined to the ceiling but should also cover the sides of the car, something best achieved by fitting strip lights (with protective covering) around the walls at a height of 3' or so.

The place of work should have some form of heating, not only for the sake of the person working on the car but also to assist in drying paints and in drying off any panels or components which have to be washed. Heating systems which burn a fuel such as diesel or even solid fuel could prove dangerous when inflammable materials are being used.

The floor must be capable of supporting the weight of the car when concentrated into the four small footprints of axle stands. This calls for a concrete floor laid over proper foundations. The floor cannot be too strong; if it is too weak and cracks while your car supported on axle stands and perhaps partially stripped, then body distortion can result which may only be rectified using a jig. If a pit can be incorporated into the floor then so much the better, because its use can save hours.

Obviously, an electricity supply will be required,

and a water drainage system is useful. Another drainage system suitable for the collection and disposal of sometimes toxic or environmentally harmful materials should be provided, and a supply of running water will prove very useful. It is often a good idea to incorporate a pumping system to empty the pit if the water table is high or if there is much surface draining around the building. It is by no means unknown for a pit to continuously fill with water through its 'drain'. A drain must, in the UK, be built-in to a pit for the removal of fumes. Exhaust fumes will fall into the pit, fill it and possibly kill the person working therein. Petrol vapours will also fall into the pit and represent obvious dangers.

Security should not be overlooked. All classic cars are tempting targets for criminals as are classic car components and also good quality tools. Furthermore, the possibility of attack by vandals also points to a need for proper security measures. The workshop should therefore possess locking doors and locking or barred windows. An alarm system is a good idea.

Unlike the normal domestic garage building which houses cars but not people, a garage/workshop should have some measure of insulation in order to keep heat losses to a minimum. Garage workshops manufactured from pre-cast concrete sections, steel or other sheet materials obviously offer very little in this respect, and some can let in draughts. Such buildings may be both draught-proofed and properly insulated, but do not forget to leave some ventilation, especially at ground level where heavier fumes, whether explosive or toxic, might otherwise lie undisturbed. Far more satisfactory is brick and/or breeze block construction, preferably with a proper pitched roof and joists strong enough to support an engine hoist.

The workshop should be designed and built so that it is easily kept clean. Fillets at the edges of the floor will make sweeping up much easier, lots of wall-hanging cupboard space and tool racks will keep the paraphernalia of restoration off the floor. The concrete floor should be sealed to prevent it from soaking up oil, and gulleys should be incorporated to assist in periodic floor washing. Mice and insects should be discouraged by the absence of nooks and crannies for them to hide in during daylight hours. The typical workshop strewn with cardboard and old rags makes a comfortable habitat for a mouse family and within a couple of months the third generation descended from the original invaders could be setting up home in the upholstery of your car.

The ideal building, then, could cost almost as much as a full professional restoration! In some cases, existing buildings may be adapted, in others, less than satisfactory buildings will have to suffice. The ideal building is not essential, but like the proper tool for any task, it does make the job far easier.

Basic furnishings

A workbench is an absolute essential. The workbench should be solidly constructed from rot-treated 4″x4″ timber and bolted to both a wall and the floor for rigidity. It should be between two and three feet deep and stand waist high for comfortable working. On the wall behind the bench, shelving or cupboard storage should be built, and a large board on which tools may be hung is a great aid, especially if the tools are traced around so that if one goes missing you can tell at a glance which tool it is.

Also very useful are small drawers to hold specific sized nuts and bolts, washers, set screws and self-tappers, and to save hours of frustrating rumaging through mixed containers for these small items.

If strong joists are not used in the building then it pays to incorporate one central massive joist or preferably an RSJ on brick or block-built end pillars to hold an engine hoist. Portable hoists are quite expensive and take up quite an amount of room, whereas an old garage hoist can often be acquired at a low price and may be easily stowed to one side out of the way when not in use. The engine hoist should be situated at the far end of the building from the door, so that the engine can be lifted out and the car pushed backwards from underneath it.

For the sake of safety, a small door at the opposite end of the building from the main door will permit escape should the front door be cut off by a fire, something which is terrible to think about but ridiculous to ignore. Also, a fire extinguisher at each end of the building could save your car or your life.

THE TOOLS AND EQUIPMENT OF RESTORATION

Good quality tools are very expensive, yet offer the cheaper alternative in the long run. Cheap spanners, screwdrivers and other tools actually last only a very short time if given the kind of heavy usage encountered during a full car restoration, and some will have to be replaced many times.

Nowadays it is quite usual to find modern powered tools, which were previously only used by professional garages, in the workshops of restoration enthusiasts. Most of these tools make life very much easier for the restorer. Remember that there is nearly always an old-fashioned hand tool which can perform the function of the modern powered equivalent at lower cost, although the old-style tools will usually require a higher degree of skill and a lot of energy.

Probably the single most useful piece of equipment to the car restorer is the air compressor. This converts electrical energy into potential energy, stored in the form of compressed air which is contained within a cylinder. Unlike electrical power tools which each require a separate electric motor, air tools draw their power from the compressed air within the cylinder and are as a consequence not only often cheaper than electric tools of equal quality but far more able to withstand heavy usage and less likely to break down. Air tools are also far less likely to stall than their electric equivalents. Perhaps more importantly, air tools are far less likely to ignite fumes than electric tools.

Air compressors are graded according to the horsepower of their electric motors and the subsequent rate at which a volume of air can be generated, and the storage and pressure rating of their cylinders. Small compressors with low power motors and low capacity cylinders might be capable of operating a paint spray gun but will lack both the pressure and volume of air for a more power-hungry continuous use tool like an air chisel or random orbital sander. Such tools can be used with small compressors (provided that the air pressure is sufficient), although the user will have to frequently stop work while the compressor 'catches up' with the heavy air consumption tool. When air is compressed, heat is generated. A small compressor which might have to run almost continuously during spraying so that the motor gets hot and further pre-heats the air reaching the gun, causes dry spray. Use the largest compressor which you can afford.

The restorer should as a minimum requirement look for a compressor with a 1.5hp motor and a 25 litre tank, although this will prove wanting with some continuous use tools. Better, a compressor with

This SIP Airmate compressor has proven reliable and a very useful tool for general car maintenance, repair and restoration. A larger unit would be better for more air-hungry tools such as dual-action sanders, and spraying a large panel also left the 25 litre tank gasping for breath. However, its portability has on occasions been an extremely valuable asset, allowing the compressor to be taken to the work.

This gasless MIG, the SIP Handymig, is a very useful piece of equipment to have around even if you do not carry out a body restoration. It can be used to fabricate special tools and to repair broken ones, to build up worn metal surfaces or to fabricate special brackets. For the restorer, the gasless MIG has much to offer. The MIG is capable of welding 20g steel without burning through (subject to user skill) and yet it may be used to weld heavier section steel such as that found on the Mini's subframes.

a 100-plus litre air tank and a motor of 2hp or more will enable most tools to be used for comparatively long periods. Even this might prove inadequate for some tools, which effectively means stopping work for a minute or two while the compressor again builds up tank pressure.

Many people think of compressors merely as power sources for paint spray guns, yet a wide range of tools are available including air chisels and 'nibblers' which make light work of cutting out rusted panels, sanders and grinders which do not (unlike electric tools) become too hot to hold after extended use, wrenches, sand blasters, drills and so on. In addition to a paint spray gun the compressor can power a paraffin gun for cleaning off dirt and oil and the simple blow gun for putting out small

welding fires or blowing away the rubbish which you grind or sand off the metal.

The other important and relatively expensive tool for the restorer is welding equipment. Four different types of welding equipment may commonly be used. These are arc, MIG, gas and spot welders.

Arc welding equipment is comparatively cheap to buy but there are severe limitations on the thickness of metal it can be successfully used on. If the metal is less than ⅛″ thick (ie. all body panels) the fierce arc welder will quickly burn right through the metal which it is supposed to be joining! Arc welders are best suited to use on heavy section agricultural vehicle metal and are useless for most car restoration work. An accessory called the Kel Arc Body Welder is available, however, which is claimed to cut the hot amps from the arc welder and to have a stitching motion which lifts the rod on and off the metal, allowing it to cool and preventing the rod from either sticking to or burning through the metal. The author has not had the opportunity to test this equipment. The costs of the Kel Arc attachment and an arc welder will still be slightly under the purchase price of a MIG welder.

The MIG welder surrounds its electrode (in wire form) in an inert gas, so preventing the metal from burning through. It may therefore be used on the thin metal of car body panels. Two types are available. The more traditional MIG welder draws gas from either a small cylinder strapped to the unit or from a larger, remote cylinder, and different gasses are required for different metals. The newer type of MIG (the 'gasless' MIG) substitutes a substance contained in the wire for the gas. Because large gas cylinders are expensive and because small gas cylinders have to be replaced frequently at high cost this newer type of welder appears to offer advantages. The main advantage of the gasless MIG is that it possesses only one consumable (the cored wire) to run out of! The MIG welder is probably the best type for a newcomer to the art.

The majority of the welding covered within this book was carried out using an SIP 'Handymig' Gasless MIG welder; a unit which proved quite easy to use and which can produce first-class results. The cored wire needed for a gasless welder is more expensive than that for a gas MIG, although as no gas need be purchased for the former, the running costs of the two will not differ greatly.

Gas welding is arguably the most versatile of all methods, and can produce excellent results in the hands of a skilled person. Arc, MIG and spot welders all use electricity to heat a very small area, whereas in gas welding a gas torch is used to heat both metal and welding rod, and a larger area of metal tends to become very hot. The greatest drawback is that the heat which is necessary tends to warp body panels and can easily give a new panel a corrugated finish!

Spot welders are the easiest in use, although they are limited insofar as they can only be used (unless a range of quite expensive special arms are also available) for joining together the edges of two metal 'lips'. For such joins they provide an unbeatable combination of ease of use, strength and neatness. Few DIY restorers would go to the expense of buying a spot welder because of their limited applications, and most opt to hire them as and when necessary

from a DIY store or tool hire business.

Most welding equipment can only produce neat and strong results if the operator possesses the appropriate skill. The quickest way to acquire such skills is to enroll on a short welding course, perhaps an evening class at a college. Whilst it is true to say that you can teach yourself to weld, it is not recommended that you do so (especially using your own car as a guinea pig).

Using a MIG Welder

The MIG is (apart from the spot welder) arguably the easiest of welding devices for the beginner to use for general bodywork repairs. This does not, however, mean that it is an easy matter to produce clean and strong welds on typically thin body panels for, unless conditions and the user's skills are both excellent, there are many obstacles.

The worst problem to beset the novice is that of 'burning through', when the electric current melts straight through the metal which it is supposed to be joining. This can occur if the wire feed speed is too slow, if the gun is moved across the metal too slowly, if the current is set too high or if the shielding gas/core fails to do its job.

When the metal to be welded has become thin through rusting then the chances of burning through are greatly increased, and hence the advice to always cut back to not only clean but also to strong and thick metal before attempting to weld.

The correct preparation of the metal which is to be welded is important. All traces of rust, of paint, oil, grease and any other contaminant must be cleaned from the surface to avoid poor adhesion and spitting.

When a joint is being welded, both surfaces should be thoroughly cleaned and then clamped in some way so firmly that the heat of the welding process does not distort either. Small sections may be clamped, although longer runs are usually affixed using self-tapping screws or alternatively pop rivets.

When first attempting MIG welding, always practice on scrap metal and do not attempt any welding to the actual bodywork.

Safety is the most important consideration. Never weld in the vicinity of a petrol tank nor any other container which holds or has held combustible fluids especially if the container is now empty or near-empty (an empty petrol tank contains more explosive fumes than a full one).

In the top left photograph, two holes have been drilled in the top piece of steel for the plug welds, and the panel has been clamped firmly to the bottom one using pop rivets. After plug welding, the surplus weld is ground down using an angle grinder. (top right) The pop rivets are then drilled out and their holes filled with weld, which is finally ground down to give a smooth finish. (above).

Always use a proper welding mask. If you view the electric arc with the naked eye then you will later suffer an immensely painful phenomenon called arc eye. Arc eye is painful enough to drive most sufferers to seek hospital attention.

Always wear protective clothing, especially strong leather gloves and a hat (to prevent your hair from catching fire). It is as well to wear old, thick clothing, as you will inevitably burn holes in them.

Never take liberties with the electric current, which is quite powerful enough to kill you. Ensure that you weld only in dry conditions, and keep trailing leads off damp floors.

When firstly attempting to weld, try to run a bead onto a flat sheet of 16g-20g steel rather than attempting a joint between two pieces. Begin by cleaning the metal thoroughly of all rust, paint and grease. Trim the wire protruding from the MIG nozzle to around 10mm. Place the earth clamp on the steel, put on all protective clothing then switch on the machine. Place the wire against the steel, pull the face visor in front of your eyes then press the trigger and begin to push or drag the gun along the surface of the steel, keeping the gun at an angle of around 70 degrees from the horizontal.

When you first attempt to weld it will appear that everything happens at once, too quickly for you to establish gun movement before burning through begins. The solution is to keep on practising and adjusting the settings on the MIG to suit the steel you are welding until you master the art. The author is not possessed of particularly steady hands, and he has never found achieving good welds with the MIG an easy matter. The greatest problem is that of running the weld away from the intended join. He overcomes this problem to a great extent by resting the side of the MIG pistol grip against a solid object such as a length of scrap box section steel which is arranged so that it is in line with the intended join. Many people use proper head-mounted welding visors rather than the 'lollipop' type of mask typically supplied with cheaper welders, and this allows them to use their 'spare' (and heavily gloved) hand to help guide the MIG. Basically, the visor is tilted upwards so that the person can place the pistol grip onto the metal and support it using both hands (do not allow your hand too close to the 'business' end), then a flick of the head moves the visor downwards over the eyes, and welding can begin.

MIG 'plug' welding is an easy method of producing neat and strong joints. This simulates a spot weld, and is achieved by drilling holes in the uppermost of two panels which are to be joined, then clamping the panels together and filling the holes with weld. The weld fuses to the bottom panel and to the side of the hole in the top panel. After surplus weld has been ground down, the results can be very neat and strong.

The alternative to welding is to bring in a skilled welder as and when required. There are many self-employed and mobile MIG and gas welders who may be hired by the hour, and they are usually listed in the telephone directory.

When hiring a skilled welder it is as well to prepare as much work per visit as possible, otherwise the travelling expenses could eclipse the actual welding charges! For most DIY restorers, hiring a skilled welder is probably a better solution than learning to weld, because you will get better results and be able to drive your car safe in the knowledge that the sill welds will not spring open the first time you drive over a pothole!

Electric Tools

Those who already possess general purpose electric tools such as drills, jigsaws and angle grinders may not wish to duplicate those tools in air-powered form. The majority of these electric tools may be used satisfactorily, although drills and sanding devices especially should be in very good condition; an old drill with a chuck which vibrates will not be capable of producing neat holes. The electric cables should also be in very good condition, because when trailed across the workshop floor, a lead with poor insulation could easily short out against any metal or water lying on the floor.

The most useful electric power tool is the drill, because it can not only be used to drill holes but may also power a range of accessories. Second in usefulness is the palm sander or random orbital sander: avoid using disc sanding attachments in an electric drill for important sanding work, because it is very difficult to obtain a satisfactory finish using these.

The electric 4″ angle grinder is an immensely useful tool for cutting metal and for grinding away proud weld beads. It can also be fitted with flexible abrasive discs or with cup brushes for rapid paint and rust removal.

If you possess a small capacity compressor then many air tools will have too high an air volume requirement, and in this case, electric tools will be preferable. This is especially true for continuous use tools, such as sanding devices. A dual action air sander is undeniably the best tool for general bodywork/filler sanding, although if you can only work for a minute each time before the compressor runs out of 'puff' then an electric sander is the better choice. The small random orbital sanders which take a 1/3 glasspaper strip are cheap to buy and give excellent results, although the smaller palm sander which takes self-adhesive glasspaper discs allows you to work in smaller areas. Of the two, the author prefers the standard random orbital sander, because the consumables are cheaper than those of the palm sander. (One small point in favour of the electric random orbital sander over the air-driven equivalent is that you can also use it for general DIY household work).

Hand Tools

When a car is being restored it is important that nuts, bolt and screw heads are not distorted through the use of poor quality hand tools. Not only are the looks of the car spoiled by this, but also such fixings will prove difficult to remove in the future.

It is impossible to tell whether a tool is of high quality merely by looking at it, because the grade of

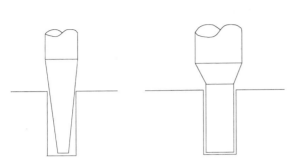

Tapered blade only touches shoulders of screw slot

Parallel blade gives greater contact area

Parallel bladed (right) and taper bladed (left) screwdrivers. Taper bladed screwdrivers can rapidly distort screw slots because the area of contact between the two is so small. They are popular because one size can be used with many different slot widths. Always try to buy parallel bladed screwdrivers, and build up a good set, because each has ideally to closely match the size of screw slot which it can turn.

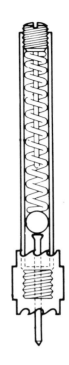

The Sykes Pickavant spot weld remover is a very simple device which cuts a hole around a spot weld so that two panels can be parted easily and without distorting either. These cost very little and can be used in any electric drill.

The joddler (also known variously as the joggler, jogger and jodder, and more properly as an edge stepper) is an immensely useful tool which places a step in the edge of a panel so that it can overlap yet remain flush with the panel to which it is to be joined. The joddler shown in the photograph incorporates a punch for making plug welding holes.

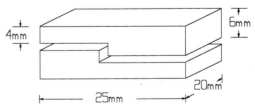

The author made his own joddler by firstly cutting and filing two small mild steel blocks as shown, then welding these into the jaws of an old pair of mole grips. Although this does not give such a neat result as the professionally made joddler, the improved leverage offered by the converted mole grips makes it easy to set an edge into heavier gauge steel.

metal used in its construction largely determines its quality, and this cannot readily be seen. The best guide to quality is the brand name attached to the tool. Within the motor trade, the very expensive (in the UK at least) 'Snap-on' tools are highly regarded, although their great cost is likely to prove too much for most amateur users. The tools marketed by Sykes Pickavant have a good reputation for quality; otherwise, it is best to buy from a motor trade dealer rather than a general motorist's store, where you will find many attractively priced but poor quality tools.

A selection of open-ended and ring spanners is essential, as is a high quality socket set with ratchet and cranked drives, plus extension bars. In both cases, the 'motorist's shops' seem to stock mainly poor quality products, and it is worth shopping around to find the quality which will be necessary for heavy use.

Screwdrivers must have parallel blades rather than the tapered blade which characterises carpenter's screwdrivers; a good selection will be necessary because the blade should exactly fit the screw head slot if it is not to distort it. Philips or Posidrive type cross-headed screws also demand high quality, properly fitting screwdrivers. Some of the cordless screwdrivers have excellent interchangeable blades.

Other hand tools are so useful so often that they will repay their purchase costs many times over; a pop-riveter can be used to hold panels in place during welding and to affix many items of trim. A mole wrench can be a small vice, can clamp metal for welding and can undo nuts or bolts with heads too distorted for spanners or sockets. An adjustable spanner saves wasting time looking for odd-sized spanners to fit non-original nuts and bolts. A spot weld remover enables panels to be removed with no distortion, and its use can thus save a lot of time, trouble and money.

The range of hand tools needed for each specific aspect of repair/restoration will be listed in full in the relevant section of the book.

ENGINE/GEARBOX REMOVAL

This is the real starting point for a full Mini restoration. Removing the engine and gearbox takes some 330 lbs of weight from the car, making it easier to manhandle around the workshop but more importantly reducing greatly unwanted stresses on the monocoque body while structural panel repair work is carried out.

There are two methods of removing the Mini's engine/gearbox unit from the car. The first is to unbolt the unit from the subframe and lift it out through the bonnet aperture in the normal manner. However, there is also the option of leaving the unit attached to the subframe and in effect 'dropping' this from the bodywork by lifting the bodyshell away. Four strong people can lift the bodyshell up and back from the entire engine, subframe and transmission.

Perhaps the greatest advantage of removing not only the engine unit but also the subframe is that no engine hoist or crane need be hired. The advantage in leaving the subframe in position is that the wheels, brakes and steering gear may still be attached and functioning, to make the vehicle mobile. Also, the subframe provides valuable reference points for the positioning of panels at the front of the car (provided that it is not itself distorted!).

Engine/Gearbox only removal

The Mini's engine and gearbox weigh considerably more than some larger capacity engines alone. The lifting gear employed should be capable of lifting much more than 330 lbs in order to give a margin of safety. If the lifting gear was to fail when the engine was at its maximum height above the engine bay, the results could be disastrous. The best option is probably to use a mobile engine crane, hiring one for the day if necessary. This will enable you to not only lift the engine from the body, but also to wheel the crane around the workshop and lift the engine onto the bench.

Not everyone will have access to a crane or a local hire shop which keeps cranes. Old garage ratchet winches can sometimes be acquired, and should be used only if your garage has a strong enough roof beam to take the engine's weight easily. The alternative to a proper winch is to opt for a 'block and tackle' of the type pictured, attached to a roof beam. These are obtainable separately (at low cost, the one pictured cost under £10) or at rather higher cost with specially constructed tripods. When static lifting gear is employed, the car must of course be rolled out from under the raised engine. It may sound too obvious, but do ensure that there is sufficient

This diminutive and very low cost block and tackle set allowed the author to lift the Mini engine and gearbox unit with no trouble. In recent years a number of cheap ratchet winch lifting and pulling devices have come on to the market. The author has no personal experience of these but a friend managed to break one without placing much force on it, so be careful to ensure that any lifting tackle you use is up to the job in question. The thought of the engine and gearbox crashing back down into the engine bay is frightening.

scribing around the nut washers to help alignment when re-fitting.

The carburettor(s) can then be removed. If fitted with the large air filter cover, undo the two wing nuts and ease the unit over the top of the piston damper cap of the carburettor. Remove the vacuum advance pipe, the breather hose, the fuel hose (taking care not to spill petrol), the choke and accelerator cables and their return springs. The carburettor is held with two nuts which run onto threaded studs set in the manifold. After removal of these, the carburettor may be lifted away. Take care not to invert the unit, as this allows sediments from the bottom of the fuel bowl to pass through the needle and jet, causing blockages.

Depending on the model, it may not be necessary to remove the grille, although access is improved by this and it is recommended. The grille is held by three self-tapping screws along its top front face, and by two smaller self-tapping screws around each headlight unit.

If the car has a heater air intake situated under the front wing, remove the front end of the pipe, and remove the plastic air scoop (where fitted) from within the engine compartment. Remove the heater control valve from the cylinder head and disconnect the heater hose from the radiator bottom hose adaptor.

It is not necessary to remove the manifolds. Remove the clamp from the manifold to exhaust down pipe junction. On cars fitted with a mechanical fuel pump, remove the inlet fuel hose then plug the hose, taking care not to spill fuel if possible.

Remove the clutch return spring from the operating lever, then unbolt the clutch slave cylinder and tie this out of the way.

Remove (if fitted) the ignition shield, then remove the leads from the sparking plugs, the coil high tension lead from the coil, the distributor cap and rotor arm from the distributor. The coil may also be

room for the car to be rolled clear of the suspended engine unit before starting work!

The first stage is to disconnect the battery, to drain the coolant and to drain the engine oil. Some Minis are fitted with radiators which have drain taps thoughtfully provided for this, others do not, in which case the bottom hose connection should be undone from the radiator.

Every wire, pipe and ancillary which connects the engine/gearbox unit to the rest of the car must be removed. If you are unsure of your ability to correctly replace wires and pipes, make tags out of folded masking tape, write on a description of where they go and apply these to each of the various wires and pipes as they are removed. Remove the bonnet, firstly

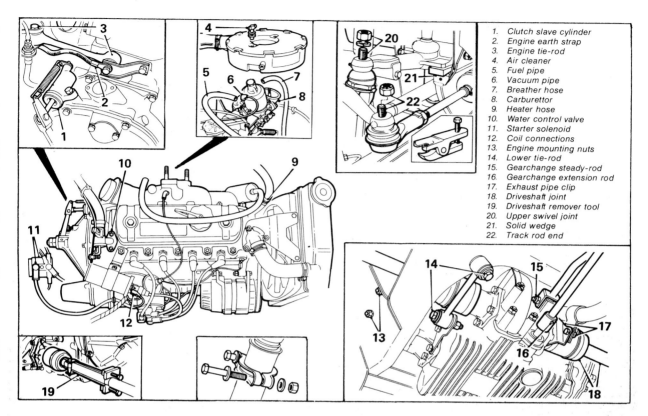

1. Clutch slave cylinder
2. Engine earth strap
3. Engine tie-rod
4. Air cleaner
5. Fuel pipe
6. Vacuum pipe
7. Breather hose
8. Carburettor
9. Heater hose
10. Water control valve
11. Starter solenoid
12. Coil connections
13. Engine mounting nuts
14. Lower tie-rod
15. Gearchange steady-rod
16. Gearchange extension rod
17. Exhaust pipe clip
18. Driveshaft joint
19. Driveshaft remover tool
20. Upper swivel joint
21. Solid wedge
22. Track rod end

This illustration summarises the components which have to be removed before the engine and gearbox unit can be lifted from the car. The inset shows the gearbox connections for the rod-type change, the direct gear select lever gearbox has fewer attachments. (courtesy Autodata)

removed from its bracket if wished. Disconnect the cable from the starter motor and remove the solenoid if it is fitted to the flywheel cover. Although not essential, it is as well to remove the starter solenoid where fitted to the flitch panel, to avoid damaging it.

Systematically work your way around the engine, checking that all wires (including the earth strap, which may be connected to the timing mark cover plate or to the engine tie rod) and pipes (including the oil pressure gauge pipe, where fitted) have been removed from the engine.

Remove the top engine tie rod. Slacken the road wheel nuts, chock the rear wheels, raise the front of the car and support it with axle stands placed at the rear of the subframe. Remove the lower engine tie rod.

The gear lever or remote control must be disconnected from the gearbox, and the method of

doing so depends on the type of lever or remote control mechanism fitted. On early cars with the direct (pudding stirrer) gear lever, remove the rubber boot surround and lift the boot slightly. From underneath the car, remove the gear lever retaining plate from the rear of the differential housing, then remove the gear lever, anti-rattle spring and plunger.

On early cars with a remote gear lever system, remove the four bolts holding the gear change extension to the differential casing, and allow the extension to hang down or preferably, support it on a block of wood.

On later remote gearchange cars, drift the roll pin from the collar which joins the extension to the selector shaft. These cars will also have a tie rod to the gearbox casing, and this should also be removed. Remove the exhaust pipe strap from the differential housing.

Remove the road wheels. Undo and part the track rod end ball joints, using a ball joint splitter if necessary. Raise the hub temporarily using a small bottle or scissors jack, remove the rubber packing piece and replace this with a thicker and solid wedge to keep the cone suspension compressed. Undo the nut from the swivel axle top ball joint, then part the

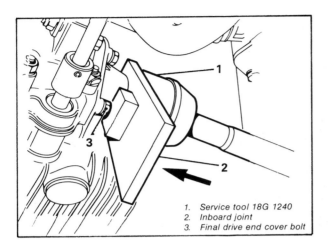

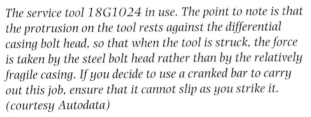

1. Service tool 18G 1240
2. Inboard joint
3. Final drive end cover bolt

The service tool 18G1024 in use. The point to note is that the protrusion on the tool rests against the differential casing bolt head, so that when the tool is struck, the force is taken by the steel bolt head rather than by the relatively fragile casing. If you decide to use a cranked bar to carry out this job, ensure that it cannot slip as you strike it. (courtesy Autodata)

The author made up this special tool to replace the much smarter service version. If you do not have access to a welder then simply run a nut and bolt through a hole in the bar. Offer the bar and nut up to the offset sphere joint and mark the correct position for the nut, ie, where it touches the bolt head.

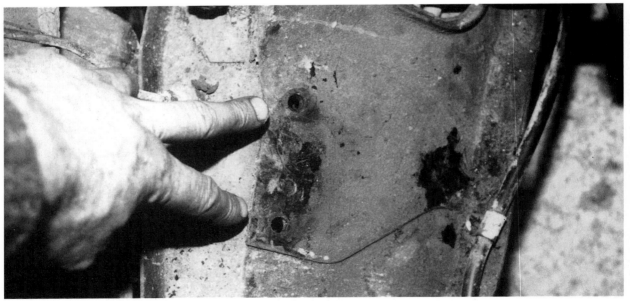

The engine mounting is bolted through two holes either side of the subframe, and removing them is not a pleasant nor an easy task due to very cramped access which prevents you from using a ratchet winch and relegates you to an open ended-spanner with a swing of about one flat at a time. Needless to say, this operation takes some time and makes your arms ache.

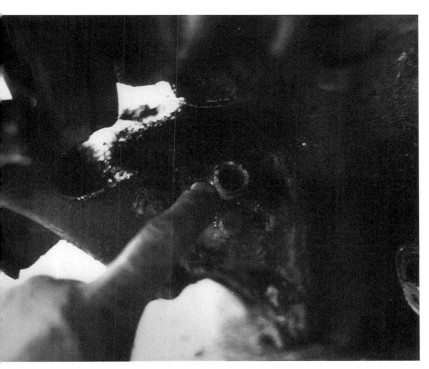

The speedometer cable is driven from the nearside of the differential unit. Access is only possible with the engine lifted part-way out from the bay.

With the engine removed, access to deal with all those niggling areas of rust becomes far better.

joint with a ball joint splitter. Lower the swivel axle until it comes free of the top lever then swivel it away from the car, avoiding placing stress on the brake hose.

Release the driveshaft inner ends. On early models, undo the nuts from the two rubber coupling 'U' bolts and pull the driveshafts away from the differential casing. On later models with offset sphere joints, a special tool (18G1240) is available to release the joints from the differential. In the likely event that this is unavailable, use a tyre lever or cranked bar, ensuring that pressure is applied to the bolt head (see illustration) rather than to the differential casing. The author manufactured his own version of the proper tool by welding a large nut onto a length of steel bar, (see photograph) and used this to free the offset sphere joints.

The offset sphere joint can then be pulled clear of the differential casing. The swivel axle will have to be pulled right down and also turned in order to give the necessary clearance. Reassemble the swivel axles and track rod ends.

With the car back on its wheels, attach the lifting gear. Special lifting brackets are available which locate under the rocker post nuts, and these automatically angle the engine so that the differential unit clears the subframe whilst lifting, although many people opt to wrap strong rope or chain around the entire unit or to attach ropes to the rocker shaft. In non-Clubman cars, there is not much clearance for the unit as it lifts, and it should be angled backwards initially so that the differential can clear the subframe. The Clubman engine bay is large enough to enable a straight lift. Take the weight of the engine using the lifting gear, then undo the engine mountings, situated fairly inaccessibly on the subframe. Two bolts pass through the mountings into nuts on the outside of the subframe. Remove the bolts before attempting to lift the engine. Begin lifting the unit out, stopping as soon as practical to remove the speedometer drive cable, which is hidden away at the rear nearside of the gearbox.

When the engine is lifted clear of the car, simply push the car rearwards, then lower the engine to the ground or preferably onto some form of support stand. It is a great help to have an assistant during this process, so that one person can steady the engine unit whilst the other pushes the car from underneath. The author, as usual, accomplished the job single-handed, just to prove to himself that the task could be undertaken safely by a single person. He will freely admit to a large dose of nerves as the engine rose out of its compartment, held by the flimsy-looking block and tackle already mentioned. Wishing to acquaint the engine unit with terra firma as quickly as possible before the lifting gear gave way, the author neglected to photograph the stressful but successful operation.

Engine and Subframe Removal

Before commencing, have Hydrolastic systems depressurised by an accredited dealer. If the system is then pressurised with a few psi of compressed air, it will still be drivable in relative comfort at slow speeds. If completely depressurised, it should not be driven at above 30mph (and, it must be added, this will be in some discomfort).

Proceed as before, omitting to disconnect the drive shafts. Remove the complete exhaust system (see Chapter 4 – exhaust) or, if a two-piece system has been fitted, remove the front half. Remove the speedometer drive cable.

Remove the brake master cylinder cap and place cling film or thin polythene over the neck before replacing the cap to reduce fluid loss. Disconnect the brake pipe unions or connectors where the system passes from attachment to the bodyshell to the subframe. These will vary according to the year of the car and whether a single line or dual circuit system is fitted. If the brake light activator switch is situated on the subframe, also remove the wires.

With the front of the car raised and the road wheels removed, remove the nut from and then split the track rod ends, using a ball joint splitter if available, then disconnect the lower ends of the dampers. On cars with remote gearchange, proceed as before and disconnect the gearchange rod from the selector input shaft, but also unbolt the remote assembly and remove this from the car. In the case of cars fitted with Hydrolastic suspension, remove the hoses from the displacer units. The road wheels may be re-fitted and the car lowered to the ground.

The number and positions of the subframe mounting nuts and bolts will differ according to the year of the car, although all years have two bolts per side situated in the toeboard (which can be reached by lifting the interior carpets) and two bolts at the front of the car. The subframe towers on early cars are secured by two nuts held by tab washers, on later cars the towers each have a single large bolt. This bolt takes a lot of starting; use a $1\frac{5}{16}''$ hexagonal impact socket and a long lever.

Check again that nothing is left which connects the subframe, engine or gearbox to the bodyshell. Support the subframe with wood blocks to prevent the unit from falling, then lift the bodyshell up and either push it back over the engine if you have three strong assistants, or pull the engine and subframe complete from under the shell if you have lifted the shell using lifting gear.

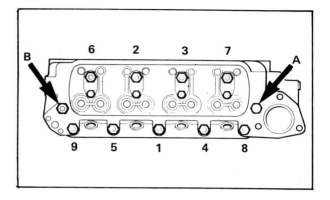

It is vital that you follow this sequence for both loosening and tightening the cylinder head nuts, as this gently and evenly releases the pressure from the cylinder head. Turn each nut by one flat in sequence, then by two flats, until all of the nuts turn easily. Failure to adhere to the recommended procedure can result in the cylinder head warping, in which case it would have to be skimmed. (courtesy Autodata)

THE CYLINDER HEAD

The cylinder head houses the inlet and exhaust ports, the valves and rocker gear, oilways and coolant galleries, heater take-off valve and thermostat. It is the 'busiest' part of the engine and therefore the part which most often requires some sort of attention.

Cylinder head problems are sometimes merely symptoms of real problems which lie with the carburation or ignition (although if you insist on putting unleaded fuel into a standard Mini, this will cause terminal cylinder head problems in next to no time). Running the car with too rich a mixture can cause the head to become fouled with heavy carbon deposits, running with badly set ignition timing can cause overheating, which can have long-term dire consequences. Always find and cure the cause of such cylinder head problems.

Cylinder head removal

Disconnect the battery and drain the coolant from the cylinder block plug (where fitted) or alternatively from the radiator bottom hose. Remove the rocker box cover and disconnect the throttle and choke cables, springs and vacuum advance pipe from the carburettor. Remove the air filter cover. Remove the ignition shield if fitted. If emission control equipment is fitted, remove this.

Slacken the clip holding the top hose to the thermostat housing, and pull the hose free. Remove the heater control valve. Disconnect the high tension leads. If you are not sure of your ability to replace the leads on their respective spark plugs, mark each using masking tape tags or by painting the corresponding number of bands with typist's correction fluid.

Disconnect the wire from the water temperature sender unit under the thermostat housing.

Remove the two nuts securing the carburettor to the inlet manifold, then remove the carburettor. Keep the carburettor upright at all times, as sediment in the fuel bowl will otherwise be disturbed and may foul the main jet on re-assembly. Disconnect the exhaust down pipe from the manifold.

Remove the radiator to thermostat bracket, then fully slacken one of the clips on the small bypass hose which runs from the underside of the cylinder head.

Slacken the cylinder head nuts in the order shown, turning each by no more than one or two flats at a time to avoid distorting the cylinder head. When all of the nuts are slack, remove them. The 1275 GT has two extra fixings which can become numbers 9 and 10 in the removal sequence. Remove the coil bracket where held under a cylinder head nut. The rocket shaft nuts may now be removed and the rocker assembly lifted away. Lift out the pushrods, placing them in a numbered rack (a piece of cardboard with holes punched in it and numbers 1-8 written on will suffice) in order that they can be replaced in the correct order.

Lift off the cylinder head. If it sticks, do not use any kind of lever in between the block and head, but tap the cylinder head using a rawhide mallet until it is free. Discard the old cylinder head gasket.

When using a valve spring compressor, it is best to place the cylinder head on a clean surface, as the collets are sometimes prone to dropping out as the valve spring is compressed. This compressor is actually far too large for the Mini, and had to be packed with an old socket which pressed against the valve head. Early valve spring collets have a groove, around which fits a cotter clip which should be eased off before the valve spring is compressed.

Gently stamping 1, 2, 3 or 4 dots on to the valves according to which cylinder they came from ensures that each is replaced in the correct position. Cylinder 1 is nearest the radiator, so that both the inlet and exhaust valves from the cylinder are given a single dot.

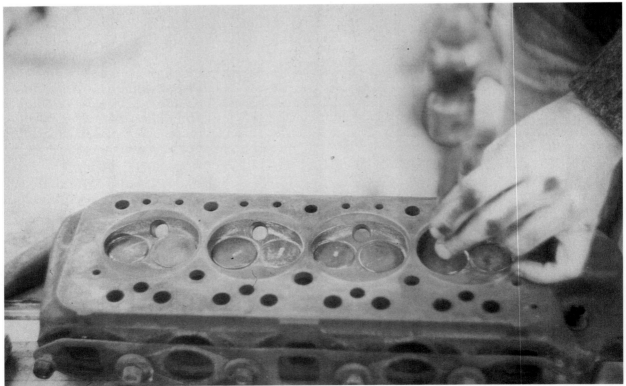

Stripping the cylinder head

Remove the spark plugs, the thermostat housing cover and the thermostat. Tap each valve cap sharply in case it is sticking to the valve stem. Using a proper spring compressor, compress each spring in turn, lift out the collets, pull off the oil seal then release the spring pressure slowly. The valve may now be withdrawn from the cylinder head. It is important that the valves are replaced in the correct sequence, so either place them in a numbered rack or stamp them with a number of dots according to whether they came from cylinder 1, 2, 3 or 4. Early cars may have small spring clips fitted over the collets, and these should be removed before the spring compressor is used.

Carefully clean all carbon deposits from the cylinder head. If very heavy dry carbon deposits are found then the engine could have been running far too rich. If oily black deposits are found then oil is leaking into the cylinders, most probably past the valve stems/guides. After cleaning the cylinder head, examine it for cracks, which usually run between two valve seats or between a valve seat and a coolant gallery. These can be repaired, although it may prove cheaper to obtain a replacement head from the breaker's yard.

Examine the valve seats and valves for deep pitting, and if this is found, the valves should preferably be replaced as a set along with the guides, and the valve seats will have to be re-cut (work best placed with a professional, although valve seat cutting equipment is available for the DIY enthusiast). Place each valve stem in its guide from the topside of the cylinder head, and feel for play between the valve stem and guide. There must be a reasonable amount of contact between these two, because the valve dissipates excess heat partially through its contact with the guide. If a valve begins to stick within its guide at some point of its travel, then the valve stem will be bent and the valve and its guide should be replaced; preferably, all valves and guides should be replaced together.

If the valves and guides are to be replaced, then it will pay to ask whoever re-cuts the valve seats to also fit the new guides. These can be drifted into position, but it is better to have them pressed in using a hydraulic press. At this point you have the option of fitting an exchange cylinder head, including those which have been altered so that they are suitable for use with unleaded fuel. The Cooper S valves are felt by some to be too large for the inserts necessary for use with unleaded fuel to be safely fitted. (See Chapter 6 Engine Modifications).

The valves may now be lapped in. You will need a very low cost tool (a stick with a rubber sucker on the end) and some grinding paste. Wet the rubber sucker, then attach the tool to the centre of the valve face, smear some of the coarser paste to the seating area, then place the valve into position. Rotate the tool between your hands, frequently lifting it and turning it through ninety degrees. Clean the paste from the valve and seat, then inspect both. You need to be able to see an unbroken circle with the matt finish produced by the paste, so repeat the process until this is achieved, then use the fine paste. When the valve and seat are properly lapped, the valve will bounce if dropped into its seat from a height of 1½″ or so.

ENGINE/GEARBOX STRIP

With the engine/gearbox unit removed from the car, the first job is to thoroughly clean it. This makes subsequent work on the unit much more pleasant and very much easier. More importantly, it lessens the chances of dirt entering the engine whilst it is being worked upon. If a tiny piece of grit finds it way into a main or big-end shell bearing, then the crankshaft will sooner or later have to be reground and the bearings in question replaced as a consequence, so clean the unit thoroughly and then work in the cleanest possible surroundings! Note the positions of any obvious oil leaks before starting work.

Begin by masking off the oilways in the cylinder block upper face and stuff clean oiled rags into the cylinders if the cylinder head has been removed (if not, then refit the rocker box cover to seal the engine). Mask the inlet manifold, speedometer take-off and differential drive shafts, then cover the alternator/dynamo (if still in place), the starter motor end and the distributor. Use small plastic bags to cover electrical components. Various cleaning fluids (such as Gunk) may be used with care during the subsequent washing-off process, although if the cylinder head has already been removed then it is best not to use any product which requires washing off with water. Alternatively, begin by scraping the

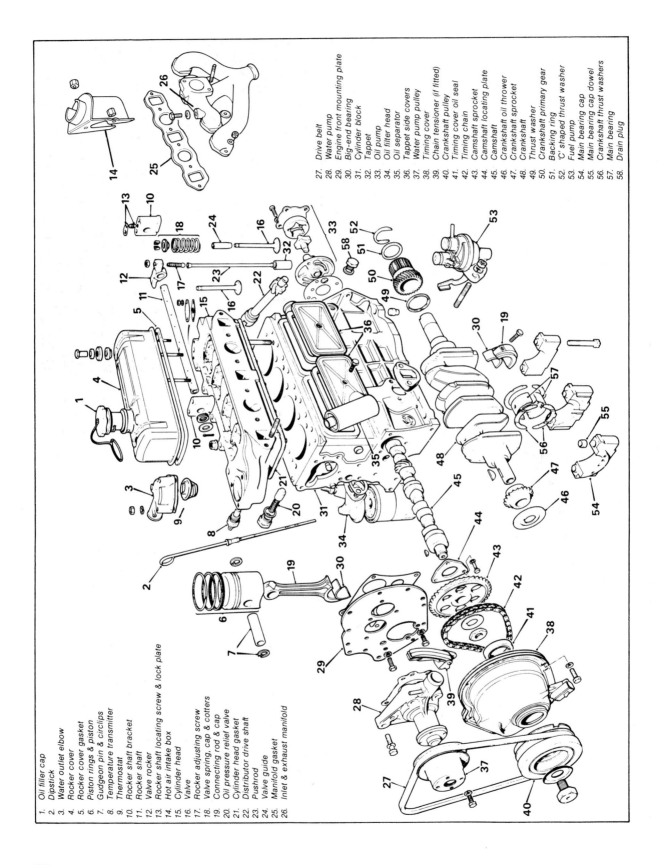

1. Oil filler cap
2. Dipstick
3. Water outlet elbow
4. Rocker cover
5. Rocker cover gasket
6. Piston rings & piston
7. Gudgeon pin & circlips
8. Temperature transmitter
9. Thermostat
10. Rocker shaft bracket
11. Rocker shaft
12. Valve rocker
13. Rocker shaft locating screw & lock plate
14. Hot air intake box
15. Cylinder head
16. Valve
17. Rocker adjusting screw
18. Valve spring, cap & cotters
19. Connecting rod & cap
20. Oil pressure relief valve
21. Cylinder head gasket
22. Distributor drive shaft
23. Pushrod
24. Valve guide
25. Manifold gasket
26. Inlet & exhaust manifold

27. Drive belt
28. Water pump
29. Engine front mounting plate
30. Big-end bearing
31. Cylinder block
32. Tappet
33. Oil pump
34. Oil filter head
35. Oil separator
36. Tappet side covers
37. Water pump pulley
38. Timing cover
39. Chain tensioner (if fitted)
40. Crankshaft pulley
41. Timing cover oil seal
42. Timing chain
43. Camshaft sprocket
44. Camshaft locating plate
45. Camshaft
46. Crankshaft oil thrower
47. Crankshaft sprocket
48. Crankshaft
49. Thrust washer
50. Crankshaft primary gear
51. Backing ring
52. 'C' shaped thrust washer
53. Fuel pump
54. Main bearing cap
55. Main bearing cap dowel
56. Crankshaft thrust washers
57. Main bearing
58. Drain plug

LEFT *The 998cc engine components. There are detail differences between this and other Mini engines. For instance, the 1275GT engine does not have tappet chest covers. However, all of the Mini engines are very similar to the one illustrated. If you encounter an engine component name which you do not know, refer to this illustration to see what it looks like and where it is to be found. (courtesy Autodata)*

ABOVE *Removing the distributor drive. This engages with the camshaft, and it will be necessary to rotate the drive shaft as it is pulled out from the casing, to disengage the drive to the camshaft.*

rich oil and mud mixture from the lower half of the unit and then clean off what remains with neat petrol and a brush (an old toothbrush is ideal), or paraffin. If you have a compressor and a paraffin gun then these can be used to very good effect.

If substantial remedial work is envisaged on the engine and especially the gearbox then it is strongly recommended that you opt for an exchange unit rather than attempting the work yourself. There are several reasons for this. Firstly, some major problem such as a cracked engine block could become apparent part-way through the reconditioning process; with an exchange unit, the company which carries out the reconditioning work will usually stand the loss involved. Secondly, there are a number of machining processes which could prove to be necessary on your engine, such as skimming the cylinder head and/or block, reboring the cylinders,

re-grinding the crankshaft, and so on. If you take these tasks individually to an engineer then the charges will reflect not only the time involved in doing the jobs but also the time needed to set up the machinery for each individual job, and will be far greater than the same costs in the case of a reconditioning company, which will work on a production-line basis and so keep costs down.

Thirdly, the costs of likely components for an engine rebuild plus the costs of commissioning machining operations on a one-off basis can easily outstrip the cost of a good quality exchange unit.

If you wish to carry out the engine overhaul yourself, you will need the use of a micrometer to check for oval mains and big ends, plus access to special equipment which allows the crankshaft to be checked for straightness. Alternatively, if there is an engine reconditioning business nearby then you can

The lower radiator mount must be removed to allow access to the crankshaft pulley.

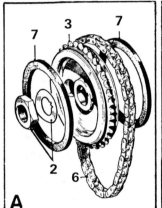
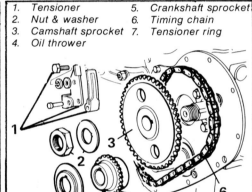

1. Tensioner
2. Nut & washer
3. Camshaft sprocket
4. Oil thrower
5. Crankshaft sprocket
6. Timing chain
7. Tensioner ring

Exploded view of timing chain and sprockets: (A) early type, (B) later type. (courtesy Autodata)

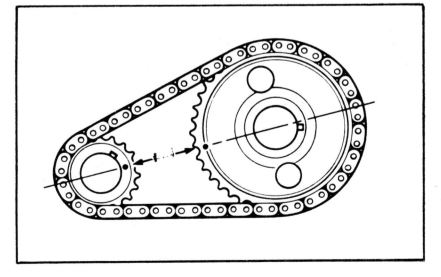

Timing sprocket marks aligned. (courtesy Autodata)

When lifting away the timing chain and its gears, try to keep and store them as an assembly unless the chain is to be replaced. Ensure that all of the crankshaft gear packing washers are retained and eventually replaced, because they are necessary to align the two gears.

take components along for checking as and when necessary. New gaskets and oil seals are available in sets, and should always be used on reassembly. The sets are for the cylinder head, the engine, gearbox and differential.

Begin by removing ancilliaries. These include the petrol pump, manifolds, dynamo/alternator, starter motor, spark plugs, radiator and hoses, water pump, fan and pulley, temperature gauge sender, dipstick, oil filter housing, pipe and banjo fitting, oil pressure gauge pipe or sender. Details of each will be found in the relevant following chapters. Remove the distributor then use a long 5⁄16″ bolt to lift out its drive, turning as you lift to disengage the drive from the camshaft gear.

Remove the cylinder head (see previous section), pushrods and tappets (cam followers). On the 1275cc engines which do not have external tappet covers, the tappets will have to be removed at a later stage by laying the cylinder block on its side after it has been split from the gearbox housing and the camshaft has been removed, then pushing the tappets out using a pushrod. Remember to re-fit the tappets before the camshaft goes back in when rebuilding the 1275GT! Ensure that all tappets, pushrods and valves (when you come to remove them) are identifiable and can be re-fitted in the correct position. Valves can be stamped with one, two, three or four dots using a centre punch; valves and pushrods can be placed in numbered racks, tappets may be tagged using masking tape.

Timing Gear

The timing gear consists of two gears which are connected by a chain. One gear is situated on the crankshaft end, the other on the camshaft end, so that the crankshaft drives the camshaft and hence the pushrods and valve gear. The timing gear is situated under a cover at the front of the engine.

Remove the lower radiator mount. Bend back the lock tab on the crankshaft pulley nut, prevent the engine from turning by placing a large screwdriver through the starter motor aperture in the transfer gear housing and against the flywheel ring gear, then remove the crankshaft nut using a 1 5⁄16″ socket (preferably a six-sided impact socket) and long lever. This nut can prove very difficult to start, and it may be necessary to use a 'T' bar and hammer.

Lever the pulley away using a puller or two large screwdrivers if necessary, then remove the woodruff key from the crankshaft end.

Remove the timing cover bolts and washers, then the cover and its gasket (which should be renewed). Align the marks on the two gears so that they are adjacent before dismantling, and keep them in this position. Remove the crankshaft oil thrower, bend back the tab washer on the camshaft end nut and remove the nut. This may prove reluctant to budge, and it may be necessary to lock the crankshaft as already described and use a socket, T-bar and hammer.

A large ring spanner may prove better

Lifting out the camshaft. On the 1275GT it is better to leave this until the engine and gearbox have been split when the cam followers can also be removed.

than a socket, if one is available, because this is a very shallow nut, and a socket will be inclined to jump off when it is hit, so rounding the nut. When removing difficult nuts which are very shallow and easily damaged by the socket slipping off, the best option is to take the unit to a garage and use their pneumatic impact driver.

The two gears and their chain may now be removed complete, after starting each gear with gentle leverage. Alternatively, (or if gentle leverage fails to start one or both gears) use a puller. The crankshaft gear will be packed with a number of

washers. This is to align it exactly with the camshaft gear, so note how many there are and place them somewhere safe until re-fitting.

The camshaft may be removed if desired at this stage, or it may be left until the engine front plate has been removed.

Clutch

The clutch disengages drive from the crankshaft to the gearbox when the pedal is pressed downwards.

The clutch bell housing removed.

Keep the marks at the top of the flywheel whilst it is removed.

The clutch pedal is connected to a master hydraulic cylinder, which pushes clutch fluid through piping to a slave cylinder, causing it to extend its arm and push the clutch operating lever.

The clutch mechanism consists of the flywheel, which is attached to and constantly driven by the crankshaft, a pressure plate, which is bolted through the flywheel to the clutch cover/diaphragm spring housing plate, and the friction plate which is sandwiched between the flywheel and pressure plate and which passes drive from the crankshaft to the gearbox via three gears collectively known as the transfer gears. The clutch friction plate is fixed to the uppermost transfer gear, the primary gear. The primary gear is concentric with the crankshaft, and drives the idler gear, which drives in turn the first motion (gearbox input) shaft gear.

When the clutch lever operates, it moves the clutch cover and hence the pressure plate towards the engine, so releasing the friction plate from its 'sandwich' and disengaging the drive from the crankshaft to the transfer gears and hence the gearbox.

The clutch may be removed with the engine in

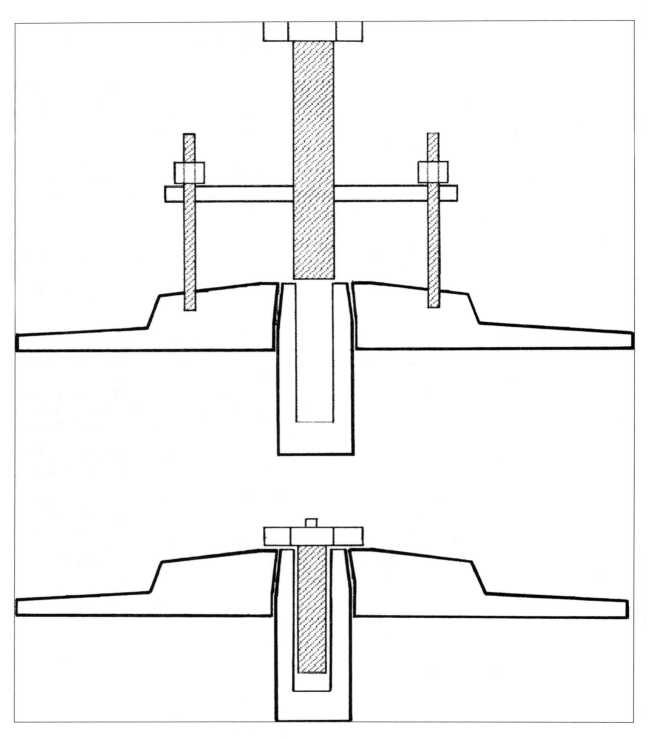

The flywheel retaining bolt shown in the lower drawing must be removed. The puller (top drawing) is then attached as shown. This illustrates the threaded type of puller, which gives lower pressure than a hydraulic type but which may be hit with a mallet if necessary to free the flywheel. Ensure that the puller boss (plate) is parallel to the flywheel before applying pressure, to ensure a straight pull.

the car by clearing everything from the adjacent inner flitch panel, removing the tie bars and (on many earlier cars) the radiator top bracket, undoing the offside engine mounting and jacking that side of the engine up to reveal the clutch bell housing. The Clubman gives rather better access than the standard Mini, although in either case this task could turn into a mini nightmare if the flywheel is reluctant to move (as most seem to be). If you wish to replace the clutch (or the bearings of the idler gear, which lives behind it) with the engine in the car then the author suggests that you follow the instructions within a workshop manual, because the job can hardly be considered a typical restoration task.

Clutch removal with the engine removed from the car can prove almost as frustrating as with the engine in situ, although the fact that you will not be working in an extremely constricted space does save skinned knuckles!

The clutch bell housing is held by a series of small bolts. Remove these, then tap the bell housing away using the shaft of a hammer or a rawhide mallet. Do not use any kind of lever in between the bell housing and transfer gear cover, nor, for that matter, to prise open any castings, because the mating faces are easily damaged (especially aluminium ones) and will usually fail to seal properly afterwards. Note whether one of the bolts also holds the earth strap, and do remember to reconnect this afterwards, so that the engine has a good earth, rather than having to earth itself through the throttle and choke cables, the covers of which can catch fire due to the immense power drawn by the starter motor!

Three types of clutch have been fitted to the Mini. Very early cars had a coil spring arrangement. The majority of Minis were fitted with the Borg and Beck type which is dealt with here. Some models were fitted with a Verto clutch.

Turn the engine over until the timing marks are at the top of the flywheel. The crankshaft must be prevented from turning so that the timing marks remain in this position until the clutch has been removed. Remove the diaphragm spring plate, which is held by three bolts. Bend back the locking tab on the flywheel nut, prevent the engine from turning by holding a screwdriver in the flywheel teeth through the starter aperture, and remove the flywheel nut. Now for the part which could ruin your whole day . . .

The flywheel is located on a taper on the crankshaft end. It is normally held so tightly that extreme force is necessary to remove it. Using a flywheel puller, place the three studs into the holes provided, feed the puller boss onto these, then tighten the nuts behind the boss so that it is parallel to the crankshaft and so that the central pushing component of the puller rests against either the end of the crankshaft or preferably a sacrificial piece of steel. The author used a small piece of ⅜″ mild steel, cut from the bar, for this purpose. Begin tightening the puller.

There are two types of puller. The most common possesses a threaded central pusher component, and if this is struck smartly with a two pound hammer whilst the flywheel is under pressure then the flywheel may come free, sometimes with a quite startling 'crack' like a rifle shot! The other type of puller (shown in the photographs) is a more splendid hydraulic type, which may not be struck with a hammer. In this case, the flywheel itself should be struck periodically with a steel bar and heavy hammer.

The author's 1275GT (in the photographs) refused point-blank to cooperate and would not move, even under the huge pressure of the hydraulic puller and a severe hammering to boot.

At this stage, there is a great temptation to reach for a sledgehammer, but the author opted instead to try heating the flywheel centre hub with a small blow torch.

After ten to fifteen minutes heating, the hub had expanded sufficiently to be pulled from the crankshaft end with relative ease.

The flywheel, friction plate and pressure plate may now be removed from the crankshaft/primary gear. You may notice that the clutch components (friction plate excepted) are all stamped with the letter 'A', and when the clutch is reassembled these marks will all have to align with the timing marks, and the crankshaft will have to be turned so that these marks are all at the top.

The components are all balanced, and hence the necessity for correct alignment. The friction plate and pressure plate may now be removed from the primary gear.

Examine the pressure plate and flywheel for marks caused by a badly worn friction plate, and replace as necessary. Examine the friction plate and renew if the material is wearing low. Remember that there is no point in skimping at this stage.

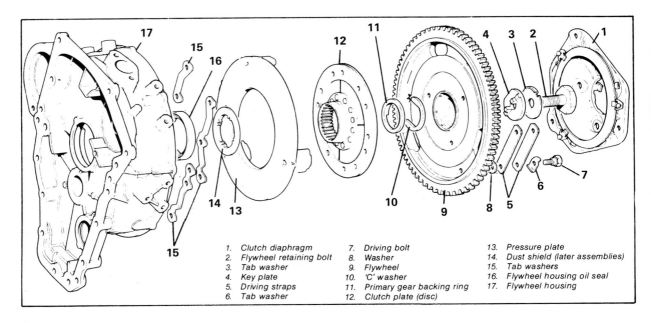

1. Clutch diaphragm	7. Driving bolt	13. Pressure plate
2. Flywheel retaining bolt	8. Washer	14. Dust shield (later assemblies)
3. Tab washer	9. Flywheel	15. Tab washers
4. Key plate	10. 'C' washer	16. Flywheel housing oil seal
5. Driving straps	11. Primary gear backing ring	17. Flywheel housing
6. Tab washer	12. Clutch plate (disc)	

The Borg & Beck diaphragm clutch. (Courtesy Autodata)

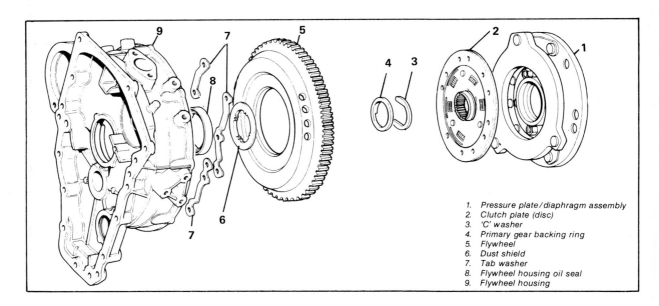

1. Pressure plate/diaphragm assembly
2. Clutch plate (disc)
3. 'C' washer
4. Primary gear backing ring
5. Flywheel
6. Dust shield
7. Tab washer
8. Flywheel housing oil seal
9. Flywheel housing

The Verto clutch. (Courtesy Autodata)

Removing the clutch from the flywheel – often the lull before the storm of trying to remove a reluctant flywheel! (Courtesy Autodata)

The alternative to an expensive hydraulic flywheel puller is the type shown, which has the advantage that it may be struck to assist (sometimes!) in freeing the flywheel. (Courtesy Autodata)

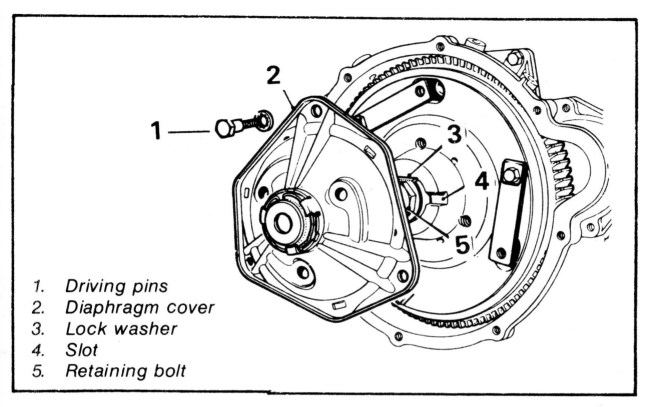

1. Driving pins
2. Diaphragm cover
3. Lock washer
4. Slot
5. Retaining bolt

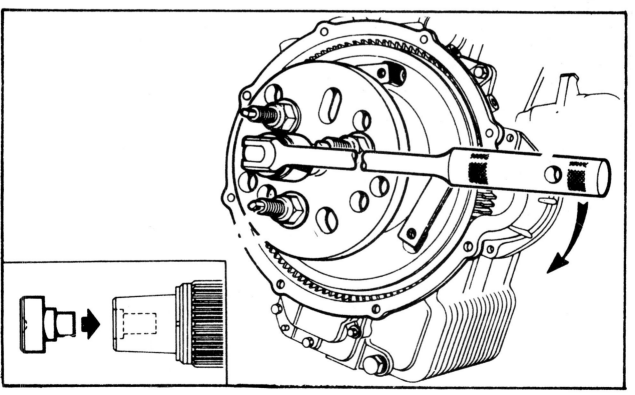

This hydraulic puller was kindly loaned by Alan Gosling from Central Garage, Martley. It exerts a huge force on the flywheel but even this failed to break the grip of the flywheel on the crankshaft taper. Eventually, the author resorted to the application of heat to cause the flywheel hub to expand slightly and release its grip on the flywheel taper. (See text).

The clutch friction plate meshes with and drives the primary gear. The friction plate and pressure plate may now be removed.

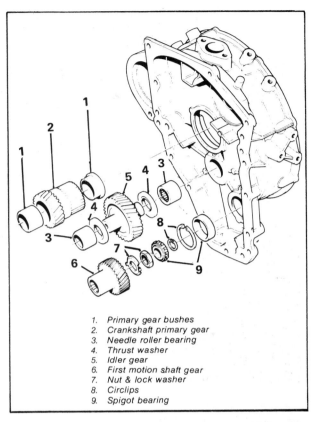

1. Primary gear bushes
2. Crankshaft primary gear
3. Needle roller bearing
4. Thrust washer
5. Idler gear
6. First motion shaft gear
7. Nut & lock washer
8. Circlips
9. Spigot bearing

ABOVE *The primary gear and its bushes (top) and the idler gear (centre) may now be removed. It is imperative that the thrust washers are retained and refitted in the correct positions. Take the opportunity to replace the idler gear bearings at this stage. (courtesy Autodata)*

LEFT *This is the 'C' shaped washer which can cause such problems if you try to remove the flywheel without correctly aligning it first (see text).*

Transfer gears

The primary gear is retained on the crankshaft by a thrust washer which is secured into a groove on the crankshaft by a 'C' washer. If you had attempted to dissemble the clutch without keeping the timing marks and 'A' marks at the top, this washer could have dropped and fouled a flywheel groove, preventing the removal of the flywheel.

The transfer gear housing sits between the clutch mechanism and the crankcase. It is secured by a number of nuts and bolts, some of which are held by tab washers. Removal of these permits the housing to be tapped from the crankcase. The primary and idler gears may be removed, along with their thrust washers.

Note the positions of the washers to aid correct assembly, and if any of the components appear unduly worn, replace them.

The idler gear bearings should only be removed using a special tool number 18G581. If you try to use force to remove the bearing situated in the flywheel housing then you will risk damaging the aluminium housing. Immersing the housing in hot water may expand it and allow the bearing to be extracted with less force. A small internal puller may be used in place of the special tool. Alternatively, fill the blind hole with grease and then sharply tap the idler gear journal back into this; the hydraulic pressure may push the bearing out.

The oil pump retaining bolts and then the pump may be removed, inspected and replaced at this stage.

Removing the oil pump. The oil pump should be inspected and the rotor removed and examined. If it appears to be in good condition, replace the rotor and place a straight edge across the mating face of the pump. Measure the endfloat and if it is .005" or more, replace the unit.

Push one arm of the inner rotor fully into a matching female part of the outer rotor. If the gap between the opposite inner rotor arm and the raised portion of the outer rotor adjacent to it is more than .006" replace the unit.

Measure the outer rotor to body clearance and if this is greater than .01" replace the unit. In fact, having gone to all the trouble of removing the engine and stripping it, it is probably best to renew the oil pump as a matter of course. It would be a shame to have to repeat the whole exercise in 10,000 to 20,000 miles time, just to replace a worn oil pump!

*Removing the crankshaft bearing
cap bolts.*

*If the engine front mounting plate
has not previously been removed, do
so now.*

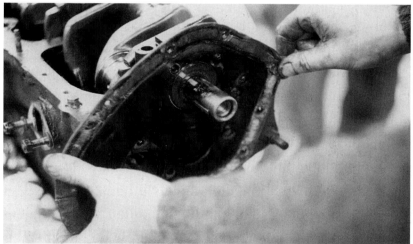

Engine/gearbox split

The engine and gearbox are held together by a
number of nuts and bolts. Remove these. The engine
may now be lifted from the gearbox although,
because the engine is very heavy and the gearbox
relatively light, it makes sense to invert the two and
lift the gearbox from the engine. It may stick a little,
in which case a few gentle taps with a rawhide mallet
should cause it to become free. Take care not to
get dirt into either the engine or the gearbox as they
are split.

Engine bottom end strip

Lay the engine on its side then undo, in turn, the
bolts holding each big end cap (these will be held by
tab washers) or the multi-sided nuts in the case of the
1275GT, then remove the cap. Refit the big end cap
immediately back onto its connecting rod once it has
been removed from its cylinder, or mark each in some
way for identification before moving on to the next,
because it is important not to mix these up.

The crankshaft bearing caps are held with six
bolts. Remove these, then lift off the lower bearing
caps. The crankshaft may now be removed, along
with its bearings and thrust washers. The pistons and
connecting rods may now be pushed upwards and
out of the cylinders. Mark everything with the

The crankshaft may now be lifted from the crankcase.

With the 1275GT engine, you can now remove the cam followers by pushing a pushrod downwards to force the followers out into the crankcase. Do not forget to replace them when you come to rebuild!

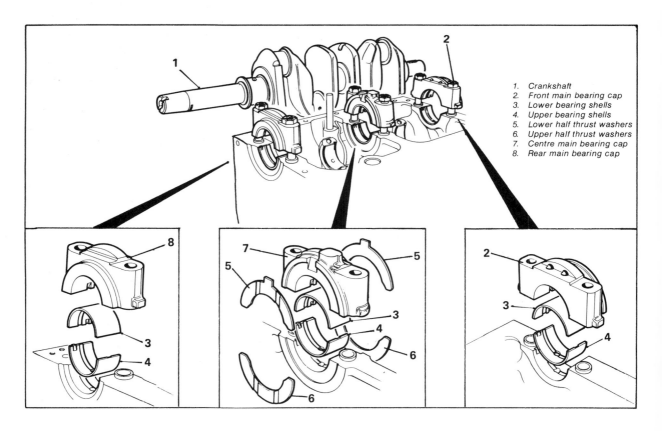

1. Crankshaft
2. Front main bearing cap
3. Lower bearing shells
4. Upper bearing shells
5. Lower half thrust washers
6. Upper half thrust washers
7. Centre main bearing cap
8. Rear main bearing cap

appropriate cylinder number to ensure correct replacement.

The pistons are held to the connecting rods by a variety of methods. In 850cc engines a small clamp arrangement is used. Slacken this, and the piston pin may be eased out. On 998cc and 1098 the piston pins are floating and retained by circlips at either end. Remove the circlips, and then press out the piston pin. If the pin is tight, try immersing the piston in hot water to expand it slightly. On 1275GT engines, the piston pin is an interference fit on the small end and should preferably be removed at an authorised workshop.

Clean all traces of old gasket material from the engine block.

Engine wear and faults

Specialised measuring equipment, some of which is described here, is needed for a thorough examination of the engine internals. It is a good idea to take the major components (block, pistons, crankshaft etc.) along to an engineering works or an engine rebuilders' premises and ask the staff to check everything for you.

Examine the crankshaft bearing surfaces visually for signs of scoring. If any damage is apparent, then the crankshaft will have to be reground. Many companies will undertake such work, but not all will give equally good results. To locate a good business for the work, take advice from your nearest performance car preparation company. You should ideally use a micrometer to check that none of the journals or crankpins are oval. You should also have access to a flat machined metal plate and two machined steel blocks with large 'V' cuts machined from the tops. The outer main journals sit in these, and a dial gauge assembly is used against the centre main journal as the crankshaft is rotated slowly by hand. This is necessary to check that the crankshaft is not bent. If you cannot obtain such equipment, then have the crankshaft checked at a machine shop.

If the crankshaft is bent or if it has already been

The centre crankshaft bearing thrust washers must be replaced with the oilways facing outwards as shown in the illustration. Measure the crankshaft endfloat (see text) and replace the thrust washers with thicker ones if necessary. (courtesy Autodata)

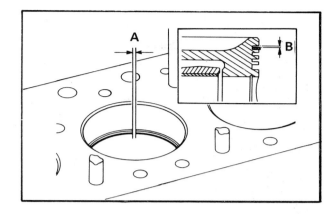

Measuring the piston ring gap (A) and the groove clearance (B). (courtesy Autodata)

ground to the extent that you are advised by the company you have chosen to carry out the re-grinding not to remove any more metal, they may be able to supply you (at slightly higher cost) with a reground crankshaft from a competition car. These will often be deemed unfit for competition work by their owners even though they still have plenty of 'meat' on the mains journals. The author took this option, and the cost was 30% higher than for a straight re-grind of his old crankshaft. A new crankshaft would have cost 3 to 4 times as much.

Examine the cylinder bores for scoring and other marks, tapering and ovality. You require a bore gauge for this, and if you cannot gain access to one, it is best to have the bores professionally checked. If the taper in the bore exceeds .006″ top to bottom then the cylinders must be rebored and oversized pistons fitted. Also check your pistons for ovalness. The piston rings should be replaced as a matter of course. If the bores are satisfactory, use a glaze-buster tool or alternatively fine emery cloth (clean the bores thoroughly afterwards) to remove the glaze.

Insert a piston ring squarely into each cylinder (use an inverted piston for this) and measure the gap in the ring. If this is above that listed in the specifications for your particular engine, use another set of piston rings. Also, check the clearance of the grooves with the rings fitted (see illustration).

Examine the transfer gear teeth for chipping or un-even wear. Remember that two meshing gears should be replaced together if one is faulty, because the apparently sound one will have worn out of true from continual contact with the other.

This piston ring compressor is easily fabricated from 20g steel. The distance between the inner sides of the two holes should be three times the diameter of the piston. It is important that the sides of the compressor are parallel.

The upper thrust washers are fed into position after the crankshaft has been placed in its shells. The lower thrust washers (those with tabs) can be fitted along with the centre cap as indicated.

If the crankshaft, cylinder bores and pistons are all suspect, then you may be better advised (and it may well be far cheaper) to opt to reassemble the unit and acquire an exchange 'short' engine.

Engine Rebuild

It is essential that the engine is rebuilt in very clean surroundings and it is advised that all components are thoroughly cleaned then lightly oiled immediately prior to re-fitting. All oilways in the cylinder block should be cleared, either by compressed air or by poking a piece of wire through them.

Refit the crankshaft bearings, ensuring if the original bearings are re-used that they go back into the positions from which they came. Ensure that the locating tags are properly engaged. If you find that half of the bearings do not have oil holes, then fit these into the bearing caps and fit the bearings with the oil holes into the top (crankcase). It is not unknown for some people to fit the blank bearings into the crank case side and so block off their oilways!

Apply oil generously to the bearings before fitting the crankshaft, then oil the crankshaft journals before fitting the caps. Fit the upper and lower thrust washers each side of the main bearing cap so that the oilways face away from the bearing. Tighten the main bearing bolts down to 63 ft lbs. The crankshaft should rotate easily and smoothly. If there is any roughness or drag then dissemble the crankshaft and bearings, clean everything thoroughly and

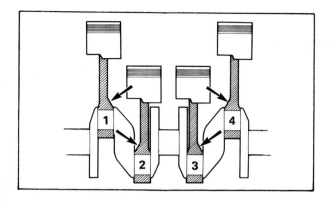

The connecting rods simply will not fit their journals if you get the offset the wrong way around! (courtesy Autodata)

reassemble. Check the crankshaft endfloat using a feeler gauge inserted between a thrust washer and the crankshaft face with the crankshaft pushed firmly in one direction, if this exceeds .005″, obtain and fit thicker thrust washers.

The piston rings should be replaced using the proper compression tool. Naturally, the author did not possess one and so quickly fabricated an alternative from 20g steel strip. Some rings may have 'Top' marked on one face and, if so, this face should be uppermost in the engine. If the top ring is stepped (for use in worn bores) then ensure that the step is at the top of the piston when the ring is fitted. The step is there to avoid the wear ring in the bore, and if these rings are fitted upside down then they will probably break up when the engine is started up. Before fitting the pistons, move the piston rings so that their gaps are evenly spaced on the non-thrust side of the piston.

Ensure that each connecting rod will have the correct offset when fitted (see illustration). Oil the bores and piston rings with clean engine oil, then re-fit the pistons and connecting rods, ensuring that the arrows on the pistons point towards the front of the engine. The connecting rod and piston can be fed into the cylinder and gently tapped home. Ensure that the connecting rod does not lodge against the crankshaft by turning the latter before you tap the piston down.

Fit the bearings in the connecting rods and caps, then apply oil to the crankpins before pulling each connecting rod down fully into position and attaching the cap. Tighten the nuts (33 ft lbs) or bolts (37 ft lbs) and, in the case of the bolts, knock down the locking tabs.

On 1275GT models, refit the cam followers, then the camshaft. On other models, fit the camshaft alone, because the cam followers can be added later through their inspection panels. Fit the engine front plate using a new gasket, then the camshaft locking plate so that its white metal face is towards the camshaft journal. Fit the dynamo/alternator adjuster bracket on to the cylinder block. Turn the crankshaft so that its keyway is at the 12 o'clock position and turn the camshaft so that its keyway is at the 2 o'clock position. Reassemble and fit the timing gears and chain as a single entity, then check the timing gears for correct alignment by placing a straight edge across them. Ensure that the dimples in the gears are opposite each other. Secure the camshaft with the nut and lock washer, then refit the chain tensioner (where applicable) and the timing gear cover.

Refit the crankshaft end primary gear assembly. If not already done, refit the gearbox assembly. Replace the idler gear, then the flywheel housing.

GEARBOX STRIP

This describes the later gearbox on cars fitted with the remote gearchange. Details on stripping early gearboxes with direct gearchange levers will follow. You will require large and small circlip pliers, two large sockets (preferably hexagonal rather than twelve-pointers) in 1⁵⁄₁₆″ and 1½″ sizes, and (probably) access to a large compressor and pneumatic impact wrench.

Remove the differential assembly. On cars fitted with rubber coupling inner drive shaft joints, remove the split pins and castellated nuts. Remove the nuts which secure the two side casings, and remove these, along with their shims. On later cars with remote gear levers, remove the selector shaft detent assembly, consisting of a sleeve, spring and ball bearing. Remove the main differential casing bolts, then lift off the casing and the differential unit.

Remove the speedometer drive pinion cover and the pinion. Remove the engine mounting and the speedometer drive housing (front cover assembly). Remove the oil pipe blanking plate from the outside of the gearbox casing, then the bolts securing the strainer assembly and suction pipe. Pull the pipe from the strainer, which may not itself be removed yet.

Remove the internal circlip from the first motion shaft roller bearing. The circlip is too small for many

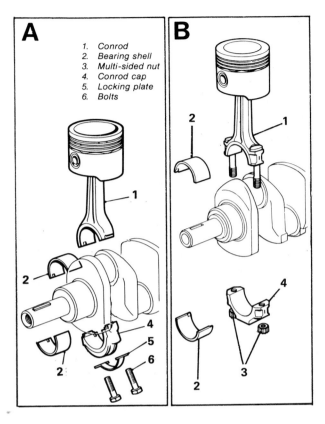

A
1. Conrod
2. Bearing shell
3. Multi-sided nut
4. Conrod cap
5. Locking plate
6. Bolts

B

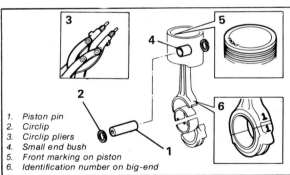

1. Piston pin
2. Circlip
3. Circlip pliers
4. Small end bush
5. Front marking on piston
6. Identification number on big-end

pneumatic impact wrench for this purpose, and then had to seek out a larger compressor to power it. The gearbox assembly is so light that the best option may be to take it to a garage premises and have this and the 1½″ nut on the other end of the mainshaft removed with a pneumatic impact wrench.

Before the mainshaft and first motion shaft nuts can be turned, the transmission has to be locked to prevent it from turning. This is achieved by firstly removing the selector shaft from the bellcrank levers by aligning the three levers and turning the shaft anti-clockwise, then engaging first and fourth gears similtaneously. To do this, simply push the two synchromesh hubs away from each other. Bend back the lock tabs on the mainshaft and first motion shaft nuts, then remove them.

Remove the mainshaft bearing bracket from the centre web, along with its shim and the layshaft/reverse gear shaft locking plate. Measure the laygear endfloat, and if it is greater than 0.006″, make a note to obtain the appropriate thrust washers. Using a soft faced drift, tap the layshaft out of the casing, then remove the laygear and thrust washers.

The first motion shaft bearing is retained by a large circlip. Remove this, then carefully tap the bearing and first motion shaft out from the casing, using a thin soft faced drift. Using the same drift, tap

1	Transmission case	58	Second speed gear	114	Shaft lever
2	Control shaft bush	59	Bush or needle roller bearing	115	Lever screw
3	Flywheel housing dowel	60	Interlocking ring	116	Washer
4	Idler gear bearing	61	Third speed gear	117	Reverse check plunger
5	Bearing circlip	62	Bush or roller bearing	118	Plunger spring
6	Operating lever pin	63	Third motion shaft thrust washer	119	Spring plug
7	Remote gearchange mating face	64	Thrust washer peg	120	Plug washer
8	Drain plug	65	Spring	121	Front cover
9	Plug washer	66	Third/top synchroniser	122	Cover joint
10	Oil strainer	67	Ball	123	Cover screw
11	Sealing ring	68	Spring	124	Washer
12	Strainer bracket	69	Baulk ring	125	Mounting adaptor stud
13	Screw to strainer	70	Bearing retainer	126	Washer
14	Washer	71	Lock washer	127	Nut
15	Screw to casing	72	Screw	128	Crankcase joint washer – RH
16	Washer	73	Bearing shim	129	Crankcase joint washer – LH
17	Oil suction pipe	74	Final drive pinion	130	Bearing cap oil seal
18	Joint washer	75	Nut	131	Grease nipple
19	Pipe flange	76	Washer	132	Needle roller bearing journal
20	Joint washer	77	Spedometer pinion	133	First/second synchro hub
21	Pipe screw	78	Bush	134	Reverse gear & first/second s coupling
22	Washer	79	Bush assembly	135	Baulk ring
23	Sealing ring	80	Joint washer	136	Split needle roller bearing
24	Primary gear	81	Bush screw	137	Locking plunger & spring
25	Gear bush (front)	82	Washer	138	Synchro balls & spring
26	Gear bush (rear)	83	Washer	139	First motion shaft spigot bear
27	Idler gear	84	Speedometer spindle & gear	140	Circlip
28	Idler gear thrust washer	85	End plate	141	Seal
29	First motion shaft gear	86	Plate joint	142	Thrust washer
30	Nut	87	Screw	143	Differential pinion
31	Lock washer	88	Washer	144	Roll pin
32	Reverse gear	89	Reverse fork	145	Bush
33	Bush	90	Reverse fork rod	146	Spring ring
34	Reverse shaft	91	Fork rod selector	147	Washer
35	Reverse operating lever	92	First & second speed fork	148	Thrust washer
36	Pivot pin circlip	93	First & second speed fork rod	149	Differential thrust block
37	Layshaft	94	Third & fourth speed fork	150	Differential gear
38	Laygear	95	Third & fourth speed fork rod	151	Differential pinion
39	Locating plate	96	Selector screw	152	Thrust washer
40	Bearing	97	Washer	153	Roll pin
41	Distance piece	98	Locknut	154	Differential cage
42	Retaining ring	99	Plunger fork end	155	Bush
43	Thrust washer (rear)	100	Plunger spring	156	Bearing
44	Thrust washer (front)	101	Plug	157	Differential pinion pin
45	First motion shaft	102	Plug washer	158	Gasket
46	First motion shaft roller bearing	103	Gearchange gate (interlock)	159	Differential end cover
47	First motion ball bearing	104	Gearchange shaft	160	Bush
48	Circlip	105	Oil seal	161	Oil seal
49	Third motion shaft	106	Operating lever	162	Inboard joint
50	Third motion shaft bearing	107	Key	163	Oil seal
51	Circlip	108	Lever screw	164	Bush
52	First speed gear	109	Washer	165	Differential end cover
53	Synchroniser ball	110	Change shaft lever	166	Gasket
54	Spring	111	Lever screw	167	Shim
55	Second gear synchro plunger	112	Washer	168	Bearing
56	Baulk ring	113	Remote-control shaft	169	Final drive gear
57	Second speed gear thrust washer				

circlip pliers to cope with, and the author welded two small panel pins to an old pair of pliers to make a crude circlip plier for this purpose. Using two screwdrivers or a very small puller (if available), pull the roller bearing from the first motion shaft end.

The mainshaft/first motion shaft assembly is retained at each end by large nuts which are very difficult to remove. At the first motion shaft end, the nut is 1⁵⁄₁₆″ and very shallow, so that there is a tendency for a socket to jump off the nut when the 'T' drive bar is struck. The author 'borrowed' a

Text continues on page 116

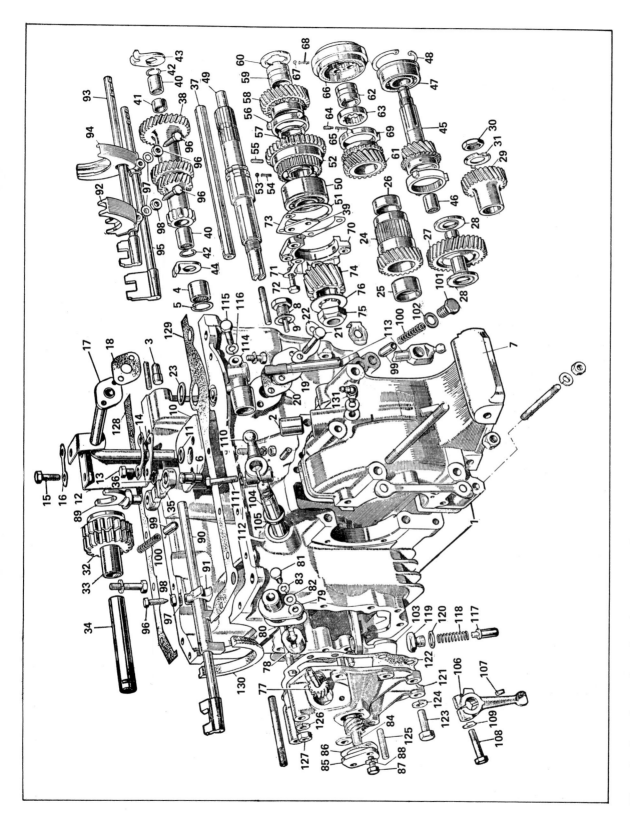

The earlier 3 synchromesh gearbox. (courtesy Autodata)

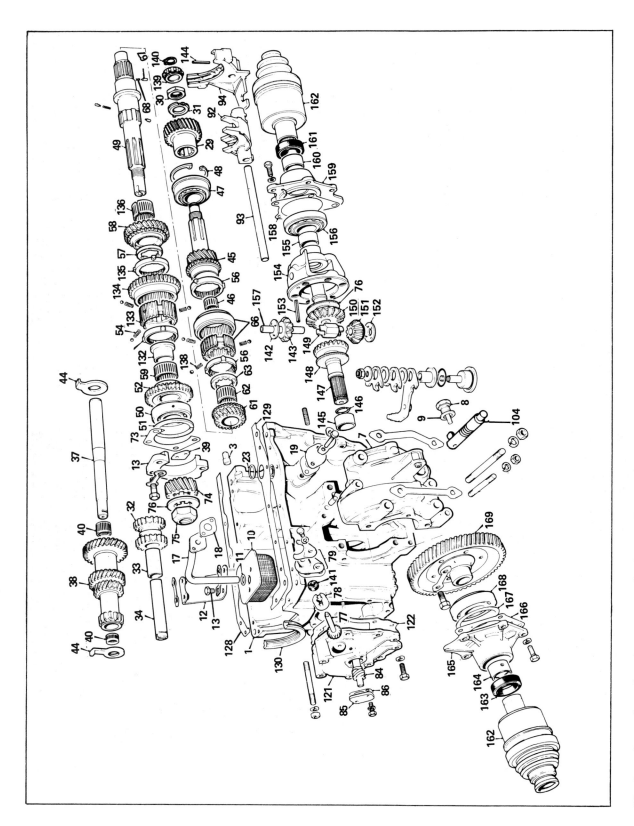

The 4 synchromesh gearbox. (courtesy Autodata)

Lifting off the differential side cover.

The selector shaft detent mechanism.

Lifting off the differential housing.

The differential.

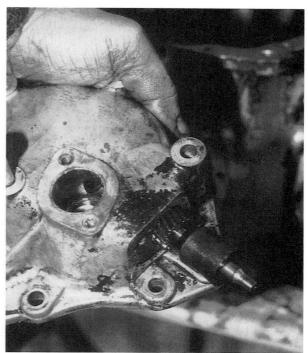

The speedometer housing and pinion.

Remove the oil blanking pipe.

Unbolt the strainer assembly.

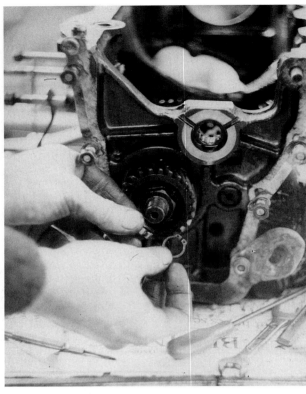

ABOVE, LEFT AND RIGHT *The first motion shaft roller bearing circlip is tiny, and the author was unable to find circlip pliers small enough to fit. Two panel pins welded to a pair of pliers eventually did the job. The roller bearing was in a terrible state and needed replacing.*

LEFT *The first motion shaft nut is so shallow that even a well-fitting hexagonal impact drive socket tended to jump off when a 'T' bar was used. This quickly rounds a nut and thereafter its removal may prove impossible. An impact driver was tried to no avail and finally a pneumatic impact wrench moved it.*

To remove the mainshaft nut, you ideally require a 1½" hexagonal impact socket, a 10" extension bar with ½" square drive and a pneumatic wrench of some substance coupled to a largish compressor.

Move the two synchromesh hubs away from each other to similtaneously engage 1st and 4th gear. This locks the transmission whilst the mainshaft/first motion shaft nuts are removed.

Removing the mainshaft bearing bracket. Incidentally, the Mini Spares Centre (see appendix for address) is now offering a 5-speed conversion for the Mini gearbox.

Measuring the layshaft endfloat (see text).

Drift the layshaft out from the gearbox casing, then remove the layshaft and its thrust washers.

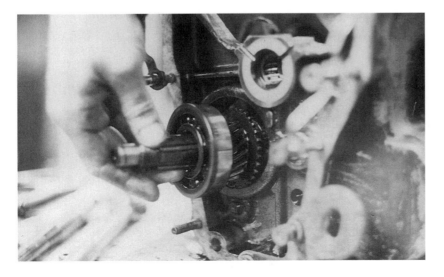

Removing the first motion shaft.

Exercise extreme caution when tapping the bearing out from the centre web, because the web is easily damaged and may not be repaired if broken. As soon as possible, use two screwdrivers against the circlip to ease the bearing the rest of the way.

The synchromesh hub and baulk rings. There are several opportunities during the stripping and reassembly of the mainshaft and the gearbox for the three captive ball bearings contained within the synchro hubs to be powered into free flight (they travel up to six feet through the air) by their springs. Proceed with caution when dealing with the mainshaft.

When reassembling a synchromesh hub, fit the springs into the inner section, then assemble it as shown in the photograph. In turn, push each spring inwards using a ball point pen or similar and press that edge of the outer part of the hub downwards to keep the ball in position. When all three ball bearings are properly held, snap downwards to push the inner fully into the outer.

Using two screwdrivers simultaneously will enable you to initially move the first gear bearing journal. It may come free enough to be removed by hand, although if it sticks, use a three-leg puller to move it the rest of the way.

the far end of the mainshaft until there is a 1″ gap between the first gear and the mainshaft bearing, then tap the bearing gently out from the centre web. Tap both sides of the bearing alternately to prevent the bearing from jamming sideways. As the bearing starts to emerge, screwdrivers can be used carefully against the circlip to lever it the rest of the way. It is as well to lay cloth over the top of the gearbox casing during the first part of this operation, because the collar of the third/fourth gear synchromesh hub is liable to move and allow three ball bearings and their springs to fly out. In a crowded and dirty workshop, these ball bearings can take some finding; the author once wasted a day and a half looking for one!

The mainshaft can now be lifted from the gearbox casing, and the oil strainer may be removed. Tap out the reverse gear shaft and lift out the gear.

Drift out the roll pin securing the third/fourth gear selector yoke, then slide out the shaft and withdraw the two yokes. The bellcrank levers may be removed after their retaining bolt has been undone. Finally, the interlock spool and the selector shaft may be withdrawn from inside the casing.

Examine all gear teeth for signs of uneven wear and chipping, and replace if necessary, remembering to order not just the faulty gear but also that which meshes with it. Remove the three roller bearings from the laygear and examine both these and the corresponding areas of the layshaft for wear, and renew as appropriate.

Refer to the photographs which appear in the description of the mainshaft rebuild. To strip the mainshaft, firstly remove the third/fourth gear synchromesh hub assembly and baulk rings. Carefully pull the outer from the inner sections and be sure to catch the three ball bearings which can otherwise be propelled a considerable distance! Third gear is retained by a splined thrust washer, held in turn by a spring-loaded plunger. Using a very small screwdriver or similar implement, push the plunger inwards towards the centre of the shaft, then turn the thrust washer so that it locks the plunger down. The third gear, its roller bearing and thrust washer can now be removed, along with the plunger and spring.

At the other end of the mainshaft, slide off first gear and its needle roller bearing. Use two large screwdrivers to slide the first gear roller bearing journal off the mainshaft. The first/second synchromesh hub assembly and its baulk rings may now be removed and stripped in the same way as the third/fourth synchromesh hub.

The second gear is retained by a thrust washer which is held by two spring loaded plungers. Push in the plungers using two small screwdrivers, then turn the thrust washer to lock them into the mainshaft. The thrust washer should now be free to come easily off the mainshaft (according to some manuals!), but in reality it is anything but easy to remove it. The author found that precise alignment of the washer and the mainshaft splines could be followed by a gentle tap on the mainshaft end with a soft faced mallet whilst the second gear was firmly held.

He then employed the shanks of two pop rivets to compress the plungers whilst the second gear was removed from the mainshaft. The second gear sits on a split roller bearing, which is the final removal of the gearbox strip!

Clean all bearings and gears (the author used neat petrol – DO NOT use paraffin) to remove all traces of grease which can hold tiny pieces of grit. Apply a thin coating of oil to all components unless they are immediately going to be re-fitted, to prevent surface rust from forming. The oil should be removed prior to reassembly, because it may have picked up and will of course hold dirt. Examine the journals and bearings for damage, renewing while you have the chance if necessary.

The second gear split roller bearing. The rollers are quite prone to becoming detached from the shell if the bearing halves are dropped, so take care when handling these. Ensure that the rollers are all spotlessly clean and, if not, clean them in a petrol bath before oiling and fitting them.

Place second gear on to the mainshaft before fitting the plungers. Minimal pressure may be required to the plungers in order that the gear can slide over them.

It is best to hold the mainshaft using wooden 'V' blocks in a vice whilst reassembling the gears. Here, a small screwdriver and the round tang of a swiss file are being pressed into service compressing the two plungers whilst the locking ring is fitted.

After sliding the first/second gear synchromesh hub and baulk rings into position, the first gear roller bearing journal can be tapped into position.

With the first gear roller bearing and the gear itself fitted, fit the third gear roller bearing, spring and plunger, then the third gear. It is now necessary to depress the plunger whilst the thrust washer is fitted.

Gearbox rebuild

Reassemble the synchromesh hubs by replacing the three springs and ball bearings in the inner section and then resting this in position part way onto the outer section. Apply pressure to the inner section, and push each ball bearing inwards in turn, allowing the inner section to angle slightly as it drops slightly to retain the ball. Then push the two sections together. It is best to hold the assembly in an open-topped box, so that the ball bearings cannot fly too far if you allow them to slip out of position!

Oil then replace the two halves of the second gear bearing and the spring and plungers. Replace the second gear to retain the bearing, depressing the plungers slightly if necessary. Slide the thrust washer over the plungers, then compress the plungers using two lengths of stiff wire, pop rivet stems etc., so that the washer can pass over them. Rotate the washer to allow it to lock home.

Refit the first/second synchromesh hub and the inner baulk ring, then tap the first gear roller bearing journal into position. Replace the second baulk ring, then refit the needle roller bearing and first gear.

At the flywheel end, refit the third gear needle roller bearing, the spring and plunger, third gear, and finally the thrust washer. Depress the plunger, slide the thrust washer over it, the rotate the washer to lock it. The third/fourth synchromesh hub assembly and its baulk rings can now be replaced.

Clean the gearbox casing, both inside and out. Replace the selector shaft and interlock spool, then

The small plunger has to be pushed right in before the thrust washer can be turned to lock into position. It pays to try and arrange to have some assistance during this and other operations concerning stripping and reassembling the mainshaft.

Replace the third/fourth synchromesh hub and its baulk rings. When the mainshaft is refitted into the gearbox, pay constant attention to this synchromesh hub, because it is easy accidentally to move the outer sufficiently to allow the three ball bearings to escape!

the bellcrank assembly. Do not fit the selector mechanism to the bell crank at this stage.

Place the third/fourth selector yoke in the casing and push the shaft into the casing, then place the first/second selector yoke next to it and push the shaft fully home. A new roll pin should be used to secure the third/fourth yoke.

Hold the reverse idler gear in place, and insert its shaft. Replace the oil strainer.

Offer the mainshaft assembly into position, then push on the centre web bearing and drift this home. Fit the first motion shaft bearing in position, then feed the assembly into position, drift it back into the casing and refit its circlip. Assemble the three roller bearings into the laygear, position the thrust washers and laygear within the casing, then feed the layshaft through the laygear. Refit the mainshaft bearing retainer and measure the gap between it and the casing. Shims are available from .005″ to .015″ in .002″ increments. If the gap is large enough for the next size of shim, then this must be fitted. Remove the bearing retainer, refit the layshaft/reverse idler shaft lock plate and the aforementioned shim, then fit the bearing retainer and fold over the locking tabs on the four bolts.

The final drive pinion and its lock washer may now be fitted. To tighten the 1½″ nut, lock the gears as already described, then torque the nut to 150 ft lbs. At the other end, so to speak, refit the first motion shaft gear and lockwasher, and torque this to 150 ft lbs. Move the two synchromesh hubs to their centre positions, align the three notches of the bellcrank assembly, then feed the selector shaft and interlock spool into the bellcrank assembly.

Drift the first motion shaft roller bearing onto the shaft and refit the small circlip. Further reassembly is the opposite of stripping.

Stripping the early Gearbox

Stripping the earlier gearbox is not so very different from stripping the later versions, although in order to save the reader from constantly having to refer back and forth between two sections, the stripping process for the early gearbox is described in full.

Remove the differential assembly. Undo the hexagonal plug (or the reversing light switch) from the front of the casing, then the reverse detent and its spring. Remove the idler gear and thrust washers.

The gear shaft is held to the selector lever by a

clamp, remove the bolt from this then withdraw the shaft, taking care not to allow the woodruff key to drop out. The selector lever may now be lifted out. Remove the speedometer drive pinion cover and the pinion. Remove the engine mounting bracket and the speedometer drive housing (front cover assembly). Remove the interlocking change speed gate.

Remove the bolts securing the oil strainer assembly and suction pipe. Pull the pipe from the strainer, which may not itself be removed at this stage.

Remove the internal circlip from the first motion shaft roller bearing. The circlip is too small for many circlip pliers to cope with, and the author welded two small panel pins to an old pair of pliers to make a crude circlip plier for this purpose. Using two screwdrivers or a very small puller (if available), pull the roller bearing from the first motion shaft end.

The mainshaft is retained at each end by large nuts which are very difficult to remove. At the first motion shaft end, the nut is 1⁵⁄₁₆″ and very shallow, so that there is a tendency for a socket to jump off the nut when the 'T' drive bar is struck. The author 'borrowed' a pneumatic impact wrench for this purpose, and then had to seek out a larger compressor to power it. The gearbox assembly is so light that the best option may be to take it to a garage premises and have this and the 1½″ nut on the other end of the mainshaft removed with a pneumatic impact wrench.

Before the mainshaft and first motion shaft nuts can be turned, the mainshaft has to be locked to prevent it from turning. This is achieved by engaging first and fourth gears simultaneously. To do this, simply push two of the selector rods in or out. Bend back the lock tabs on the mainshaft and first motion shaft nuts, then remove them.

Remove the mainshaft bearing bracket from the centre web, along with its shim and the layshaft/reverse gear shaft locking plate. Measure the laygear endfloat, and if it is greater than 0.006″, make a note to obtain the appropriate thrust washers. Unlock the mainshaft. Using a soft faced drift, tap the layshaft out of the casing, then remove the laygear and thrust washers. Remove the two interlocking plunger plugs and the plungers from the lower rear face of the gearbox casing.

The first motion shaft bearing is retained by a large circlip. Remove this, then carefully tap the bearing and first motion shaft out from the casing, using a thin soft faced drift. Using the same drift, tap the far end of the mainshaft until there is a 1″ gap between the first gear and the mainshaft bearing, then tap the bearing gently out from the centre web. Tap both sides of the bearing alternately to prevent the bearing from jamming sideways. As the bearing starts to emerge, screwdrivers can be used carefully against the circlip to lever it the rest of the way.

Lift the mainshaft assembly from the casing. The oil strainer may now be removed. Tap out the reverse gear shaft and remove the gear and its selector fork. Slacken the locknuts and remove the selector fork screws, then slide the selector rods from the casing and remove the forks. Remove the circlip from the reverse shift lever and lift out the lever.

THE FUEL SYSTEM

Petrol is drawn from the fuel tank by a pump, which can be either mechanical, integral with and driven by the engine, or electrically powered and mounted on the rear subframe. The fuel reaches the carburettor, where a partial vacuum created in the carburettor throat by the air being sucked in by the engine draws the fuel upwards through the main jet so that it mixes thoroughly with the air before being drawn into the combustion chambers, forming the fine mist which is burnt to power the engine.

The fuel tank

The fuel tank (there are two on the Cooper S) is situated on the nearside of the boot space, secured by a metal band. Before carrying out any operations to or in the vicinity of the fuel tank, disconnect and remove the battery. Remember that petrol vapour is easily ignited, and a spanner accidentally dropped across the battery terminals could easily spark off an explosion if petrol vapour (which is heavier than air and which will therefore tend to fall down towards the battery compartment) is present in the boot. Remove the spare wheel.

To remove the tank, it is advisable to firstly remove the boot lid in order to improve access. Undo the six nuts which secure the boot lid to the hinges, then, with a helper holding the lid to prevent it from falling, remove the screws which fasten the ends of the support wires and lift the boot lid away. Then

remove any material coverings from within the boot which could absorb petrol (if you spill any). Syphon the fuel from the tank. The fuel pipe is situated just above the bottom of the tank and will have to be disconnected before the tank can be removed from the boot. It is necessary to drain the fuel to a level below that of the fuel pipe outlet if spillage is to be avoided. If you are syphoning fuel into a metal container then it is wise to run a length of wire which will earth both the container and the car, to prevent static electricity from jumping from the car to the container, which could ignite the fuel.

Instead of syphoning the tank, you could alternatively undo the connection between the rubber pipe leading from the tank and the metal pipe underneath the car and drain the fuel into a container. Alternatively, on cars fitted with the electric fuel pump, you could pump it out by disconnecting the carburettor fuel line and joining this to a pipe leading to a petrol container. Switch on the ignition, and the pump will empty the tank for you. When the fuel has been drained, the outlet pipe may be disconnected and plugged or sealed with plastic tape.

On some Mini saloons the tank retaining band runs over the top of the tank, and is easily disconnected by removing the lower fixing bolt.

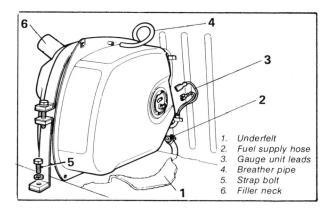

1. Underfelt
2. Fuel supply hose
3. Gauge unit leads
4. Breather pipe
5. Strap bolt
6. Filler neck

The standard Mini saloon fuel tank. Access to the retaining band bolt is good. This is not true of models fitted with the diagonal retaining band. When replacing fuel tanks fitted with the diagonal band, it is worth remembering that a knocking noise from the tank (which results from it moving when the car is mobile) can be cured by inserting two lengths of steel around ⅛″ thick under the tank lower rim before tightening the retaining band. (courtesy Autodata)

On other models (including the 1275GT) the band runs diagonally from the top front to the bottom rear of the tank. Remove the nut and bolt which secure the lower end of the metal retaining band. The bolt head should be captive, in which case a deep socket may be used to remove the nut.

Do not be surprised to discover that on your car the bolt head is not held securely, in which case it will be necessary to try and jam it in some way to prevent it from turning whilst the nut is undone. Remove the filler cap and the wires from the fuel gauge sender unit. If you have not already done so, slacken the screw clamp on the fuel line connection, then pull the line from the tank outlet. The tank may now be eased out from the boot.

Examine the tank for rot and, if any is discovered, replace it. It is possible to repair fuel tanks, although this is a job which is strictly the province of the experienced professional, because trying to weld any sort of container which has held fuel could prove a highly explosive and terminal experience! Various types of repair kit are available for fuel tanks (but are not recommended), as are chemical solutions which are placed in the tank and swilled around, and which are supposed to seal pin holes. However, if a tank has rust holes then it will have tiny flakes of rust inside which, sooner or later, will cause a blockage somewhere within the fuel system. Even though Mini fuel tanks are not particularly cheap, replacement is advised rather than repair.

If you are tempted to opt for a tank repair, bear in mind that, unlike many cars which have their fuel tanks slung underneath in the open, the fuel tank of the Mini is contained within an enclosed area where explosive fumes could build up. To make matters worse, the battery is right next door . . . Beware of this potentially disastrous combination, and act with due caution.

The fuel gauge sender unit may be removed from the tank by gently tapping the retaining ring until its lugs are free and the unit may be lifted out. When refitting the unit, use a new seal. If the tank is to be scrapped then it is a good idea to immediately fill it with water until it can be safely disposed of. If it is to be re-used then stuff rags in the filler and gauge sender unit holes, and preferably store the tank in a separate building for safety's sake.

Examine the metal and rubber sections of the fuel line, and replace any sections which show signs of corrosion or, in the case of the rubber sections, perishing or cracking.

Carburettor

The SU HS2 and HS4 carburettors fitted across the Mini range are simple, robust and extremely reliable units. They differ mainly in their size, the HS4 being a rather larger unit than the HS2.

Refer to the illustration opposite to identify the components mentioned in the following description. Fuel is fed under pressure by the pump into the separate float chamber half of the carburettor (18). When the fuel rises to a set level, the float arm pushes a needle (22) into a jet to cut off the supply until the level again drops. This prevents the carburettor from flooding.

From just above the bottom of the float chamber (where sediment can settle out safely), the fuel is piped off to the carburettor main jet (39). A needle (11) slides up and down in this jet to vary the size of the hole through which fuel is able to pass, so richening and weakening the mixture. The needle is attached to a piston (9) situated within the top bell chamber (7), and the piston rises as the speed of the air passing through the carburettor throat rises, and vice versa, to allow the fuel mixture to remain stable irrespective of the amount of air being sucked in by the engine.

At the top of the carburettor is a damper piston rod (15), which passes into a small cylinder at the top of the main piston. This cylinder is filled with oil to dampen the action of the piston and prevent 'flutter'. The piston itself also has a return spring (10), to ensure that it drops back promptly to reduce the fuel supply when the amount of air passing through the throat drops.

Two cables control the actions of the carburettor. The throttle cable is attached to the throttle disc (32), which rotates to vary the effective internal size of the throat and hence the volume of air/fuel mixture which the engine can draw. As the accelerator pedal is depressed, the valve rotates to increase this size and the amount of mixture reaching the engine to increase its revolutions, and vice versa. The choke is a device for richening the fuel content of the air/fuel mixture, to assist starting the engine in cold conditions. The choke cable is connected by a lever to the main jet (39), and because the choke is engaged the jet is pulled downwards to allow more fuel to be drawn into the air mixture.

A rubber pipe connects to the upper face of the carburettor on the cylinder head side of the bell housing. This is the vacuum advance pipe. As the throttle is depressed and the engine revolutions begin to pick up, air passes more rapidly through the carburettor throat, causing a slight vacuum. The vacuum extends up into the vacuum advance pipe, which leads to the distributor and causes it to advance the ignition slightly to enhance performance. This pipe must be in good condition and its end connections must be airtight. If the vacuum advance pipe leaks at either end or if it is perished then the timing will not be advanced, and neat air will be drawn back into the carburettor throat,

The HS4 carburettor. The HS2 is essentially a similar, though smaller unit. Refer to this illustration when following the text. (courtesy Autodata)

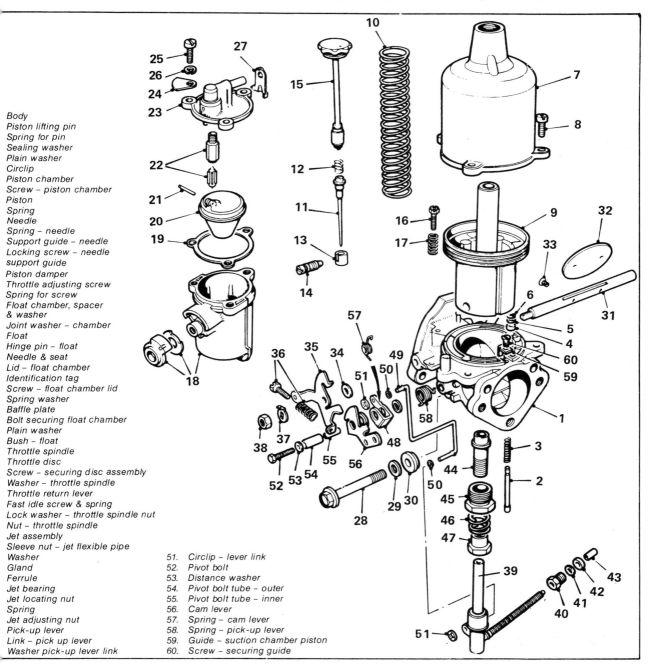

Body
Piston lifting pin
Spring for pin
Sealing washer
Plain washer
Circlip
Piston chamber
Screw – piston chamber
Piston
Spring
Needle
Spring – needle
Support guide – needle
Locking screw – needle
support guide
Piston damper
Throttle adjusting screw
Spring for screw
Float chamber, spacer
& washer
Joint washer – chamber
Float
Hinge pin – float
Needle & seat
Lid – float chamber
Identification tag
Screw – float chamber lid
Spring washer
Baffle plate
Bolt securing float chamber
Plain washer
Bush – float
Throttle spindle
Throttle disc
Screw – securing disc assembly
Washer – throttle spindle
Throttle return lever
Fast idle screw & spring
Lock washer – throttle spindle nut
Nut – throttle spindle
Jet assembly
Sleeve nut – jet flexible pipe
Washer
Gland
Ferrule
Jet bearing
Jet locating nut
Spring
Jet adjusting nut
Pick-up lever
Link – pick up lever
Washer pick-up lever link

51. Circlip – lever link
52. Pivot bolt
53. Distance washer
54. Pivot bolt tube – outer
55. Pivot bolt tube – inner
56. Cam lever
57. Spring – cam lever
58. Spring – pick-up lever
59. Guide – suction chamber piston
60. Screw – securing guide

123

slightly weakening the mixture. The combination of retarded ignition timing and a weak mixture will have a serious effect on performance.

Carburettor removal

Disconnect the battery. Remove the air filter. Disconnect the throttle and choke cables, the return springs and the vacuum advance pipe. Slacken the clip which fastens the fuel pipe to the top of the float chamber, and pull the pipe away, taking care not to spill fuel.

The carburettor is held by two nuts on threaded studs which are screwed into the inlet manifold. Remove the nuts, then withdraw the carburettor. Take care not to hold the carburettor at an angle, but keep it upright at all times to prevent sediments in the fuel bowl from getting into the jet pipe. On models fitted with emission control equipment, there will be a varying number of extra pipes to remove. Make a note of where each pipe resides before removal!

Carburettor overhaul

It is not too difficult to overhaul an SU HS series carburettor whilst it is attached to the cylinder head, although it is made much easier by improved access if the work is carried out whilst the unit is removed from the car during the restoration.

Clean the outside of the unit. This makes it far easier to work with but also reduces the chances of dirt being allowed to enter the carburettor, where it could clog up the main jet. The author prefers to use an old toothbrush and neat petrol for this. Allowing the petrol to soak well into the mixture of dirt and oil typically found on a carburettor quickly loosens it, so that it may be easily washed and brushed away.

Lift the piston manually and allow it to fall, noting whether there is any roughness (caused by the piston fouling the bell housing or dirt thereon). The piston should drop to the jet bridge with a soft 'click'; if it does not then the jet will have to be centred.

Remove the three screws from the top of the float chamber, then lift off the top and the float/needle and jet assembly. Empty the float chamber. Disconnect the fuel outlet pipe and clean the sediment from the bottom of the float chamber. Remove the fuel inlet needle (22) and examine it for a ridge which indicates that it is worn and should be replaced, along with its

An amazing amount of muck can collect in the bottom of the float chamber. If you remove the carburettor for any reason such as when servicing the cylinder head and allow the carburettor to lie at a angle, some of this sediment can find its way into the main jet and lodge there. To clean out the bottom of the fuel bowl, use neat petrol and a small paintbrush to loosen the sediment, then swill it out.

jet. Examine the float for damage.

Remove the three screws (8) from the bell housing, then lift the bell housing and the piston return spring (10) from the carburettor. Carefully lift the piston (9) from the main body, taking care not to place any stresses on the needle. Examine the needle for ridges and, if the slightest ridge is found, replace both the needle and the jet. Undo the screw which retains the jet and withdraw this from the carburettor body. Examine the jet for ovalness, and, if it is the slightest out of true, replace both it and the needle.

There are a range of needles, jets and piston return springs available for all SU carburettors to suit varying conditions. In order to fully assess which combination is required for your engine really demands that the car is properly set up on a rolling road, with exhaust emission equipment. However, for most purposes, you could select the standard option and tune the engine yourself.

If roughness could be felt when the piston was lifted, clean it and the inside of the bell housing and

Lifting away the bell housing reveals the spring and piston. If the spring is suspect, do not attempt to stretch it (which will merely weaken it) but replace it with a new one. Examine the inside of the bell housing for wear marks which are usually caused by the piston picking up grit. These may be very carefully polished out if necessary.

Be very careful not to bend the needle when lifting the piston from the carburettor main body. The needle is fairly fragile and easily damaged, so store the piston in such a way that no strain is placed upon it. If the needle is already bent or if there are any ridges on its side then you should replace both it and the main jet together because the needle will have worn one side of the jet away.

Refit the jet bearing nut.

Refit the jet adjusting nut without the spring which is shown being fitted in this photograph.

then examine both for signs of contact wear. This may be very gently removed using metal polish. If this fails to prevent the piston from sticking then both the piston and the bell housing should be renewed as a set. Both are manufactured to very close tolerances and should only ever be used in the set.

Examine the throttle spindle (31) for looseness within its bushes. If wear is apparent (this will allow air into the system and weaken the mixture) then the spindle and throttle disc may be exchanged, although wear in the bushes can be treated successfully only by replacement of the carburettor body. The best option may be to obtain a replacement carburettor from a breakers' yard. The SU HS2 and HS4 were used on such a wide range of cars that obtaining one should be easy.

Finally, examine the float body for damage. Holes will already have been made apparent because the carburettor will have regularly flooded, although small cracks should be dealt with by replacement. Lubricate all external moving parts using a light oil (engine oil will suffice).

Carburettor reassembly

If removed, re-fit the jet bearing (44), jet bearing nut (45) and the jet adjusting nut (47) to finger tightness, but do not fit the spring (46). Fit the main jet assembly (39) into the base of the unit. Fit the needle into the piston.

The jet has to be centered so that the needle is positioned concentric with it, otherwise, the needle and jet will rapidly wear. Refit the piston and dashpot, then tighten the jet bearing nut whilst holding the piston down (this can be achieved by pushing a length of rod down through the dashpot bell housing). Lift the piston then allow it to fall onto the jet bridge. It should land with a soft 'click'. Lower the jet adjusting nut, then let the piston fall again. If it does not still land with a click then repeat the whole procedure.

Slide out the jet assembly, then refit the spring (46), adjusting nut and choke lever. Connect the fuel pipe to the float chamber. Fit the float chamber needle and float, then refit the unit to the float chamber body with the three securing screws.

Screw the main jet upwards until it is level with the bridge, then turn it back by two complete turns (twelve flats). The carburettor may now be refitted.

Setting the carburation

Ideally, the air/fuel mixture should be set with the assistance of emission measuring equipment or, in the case of fast road or competition cars, with a rolling road. It is possible, however, for the amateur working alone at home to achieve reasonably accurate results with care.

Before attempting to set the mixture, all elements of the ignition system should be checked and the timing set. The engine should firstly be warmed to normal operating temperature, and the air filter cover then the elbow which connects the filter and carburettor should be removed.

Some SU carburettors (sealed type) have covers over the throttle adjusting screw and mixture adjusting nut, and these should be removed. Set the idle revolutions using the throttle adjusting screw. If the carburettor has a lifting pin, use it to lift the piston and listen to the engine revolutions as you do so. If they rise noticeably and remain higher, then weaken the mixture by screwing the jet adjusting nut upwards. If the revolutions die away when the piston is lifted then richen the mixture by screwing the jet adjusting nut downwards. When the mixture is correctly set and the piston lifted, the engine revolutions should rise momentarily, then settle back to where they were. On carburettors without lifting pins, raise the piston by hand through about $\frac{1}{16}''$. Setting the mixture will probably have an effect upon the idle revolutions, so re-adjust using the throttle adjusting screw.

The fast idle speed may be set by rotating the choke operating lever to the point at which it is about to lower the jet, then adjusting the fast idle screw until the correct revolutions are obtained.

After setting the carburation, take the car out on to the road, and accelerate hard from about 30mph in fourth gear. If the engine pinks, richen the mixture slightly by unscrewing the jet adjusting nut by just one flat.

Twin carburettor installations

The Cooper S models have two linked SU carburettors which are more difficult to set up correctly because they must be in balance. Slacken the pinch bolts on the throttle and choke linkage spindles to allow the carburettors to operate independently. With the engine at idle speed, use a length of rubber hose held against the ear and in the throat of each carburettor in turn to gauge the volume of air being taken by each carburettor. Adjust each throttle stop screw in turn using the throttle adjusting screw until an even rush of air through each carburettor is detected. Tighten the pinch bolts on the throttle linkage, making sure that the two lost motion levers are pressed downwards against their respective pins so that the carburettors operate similtaneously. Then adjust each throttle stop screw by an equal amount until the correct idle speed is obtained. Low cost vacuum gauge carburettor setting kits are available, and are very worthwhile.

Re-tighten the choke clamp bolts, ensuring that the pegs are similarly positioned relative to their respective forks.

To set the mixture, proceed as for a single carburettor, but working firstly on one carburettor, then the other and back again to the first, until the desired results are achieved. The setting up of multi-carburettor installations is best carried out on a rolling road.

Some cars are fitted with emission control equipment, consisting basically of an air pump which supplies air to the exhaust manifold to help burn off gasses and to the inlet manifold via a gulp valve to weaken the mixture during deceleration and on the overrun. The same cars have an evaporative loss system, consisting of a charcoal cannister which essentially absorbs fuel vapours and feeds them into the engine via the rocker cover. This equipment requires special tools and knowledge for testing and repair, and so work should only be carried out by an accredited dealer.

Fuel pump

Two different types of fuel pump may be fitted. The electric pump is situated on the rear subframe, whilst the alternative mechanical pump is attached to the side of the engine unit, underneath the carburettor.

To remove the electrical type pump, raise the rear of the car and support it on axle stands (the battery MUST be disconnected and preferably removed). Remove the electricity feed and earth wires from their terminals. Using a brake hose clamp or a small pair of mole grips with heavily padded jaws, clamp the rubber pipe which runs from the fuel tank to the pump to prevent fuel loss, then remove the pump inlet and outlet pipes. It is as well to have a

large, shallow container under the pump to catch any fuel which does escape. Undo the fuel tank pipe immediately. Remove the nut from the pump bracket, and the pump may then be removed from the car.

Remove the end cover and inspect the contact points. Following any period of inactivity (ie. a restoration) the points are liable to surface corrosion which may be gently cleaned off. If the points are burned or have pitting then they and the rocker assembly and spring blade should be replaced. Check that the gap between the outer rocker and the main coil housing is 0.07", and adjust the spring blade until this is achieved.

To gain access to the diaphragm, mark the relative positions of the main pump body and the coil housing, (also noting on which fixing screw the earth wire is attached), the undo the screws and separate the two halves of the pump unit. If the diaphragm requires replacement then it should be replaced along with its spindle.

Two types of mechanical fuel pump were fitted to the Mini. The earlier type 700 may be user serviced, whilst the later type 800 is a sealed unit which must be exchanged. Access to the mechanical fuel pump is very awkward with the engine in the car, and a number of other components including the carburettor and manifolds should be removed firstly in order to gain access. During an engine-out restoration the opportunity to replace the pump should therefore not be missed. It is possible to perform a rough check on the operation of the pump by covering in turn the inlet and outlet whilst operating the unit. If the inlet is covered (sealed with your finger) and the pump operated through three strokes, an audible hiss of air should accompany the removal of your finger. If the outlet is similarly blocked and the pump operated, the lever should not return for around fifteen seconds.

Access to the mechanical fuel pump is so awkward that, even though the earlier type 700 can be user-serviced, it is recommended that the unit is exchanged rather than repaired.

127

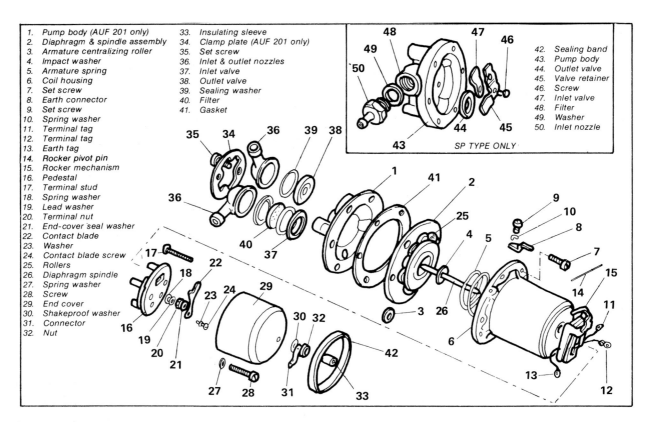

1. Pump body (AUF 201 only)
2. Diaphragm & spindle assembly
3. Armature centralizing roller
4. Impact washer
5. Armature spring
6. Coil housing
7. Set screw
8. Earth connector
9. Set screw
10. Spring washer
11. Terminal tag
12. Terminal tag
13. Earth tag
14. Rocker pivot pin
15. Rocker mechanism
16. Pedestal
17. Terminal stud
18. Spring washer
19. Lead washer
20. Terminal nut
21. End-cover seal washer
22. Contact blade
23. Washer
24. Contact blade screw
25. Rollers
26. Diaphragm spindle
27. Spring washer
28. Screw
29. End cover
30. Shakeproof washer
31. Connector
32. Nut
33. Insulating sleeve
34. Clamp plate (AUF 201 only)
35. Set screw
36. Inlet & outlet nozzles
37. Inlet valve
38. Outlet valve
39. Sealing washer
40. Filter
41. Gasket
42. Sealing band
43. Pump body
44. Outlet valve
45. Valve retainer
46. Screw
47. Inlet valve
48. Filter
49. Washer
50. Inlet nozzle

SP TYPE ONLY

ABOVE *The most common problem with fuel pumps on cars which have been restored appears to be light corrosion of the points, which is easily rectified. If the diaphragm requires replacement then be sure to replace all seals and gaskets, along with the filter. Many people elect to obtain a replacement reconditioned unit rather than service the fuel pump themselves. This does ensure that this vital component is fully serviceable. (courtesy Autodata)*

LEFT *The mechanical type fuel pump is rather awkward to get at with the engine in the car, as can be seen from this photograph. Note the position of the exhaust manifold and imagine that the inlet manifold, carburettor etcetera were in position, and you will see just how awkward work on the pump can be! Always take the opportunity to deal with these fuel pumps whenever the engine is removed from the car.*

THE EXHAUST SYSTEM

The exhaust system serves two basic functions. The more obvious is to suppress the very loud noise generated when the exhaust valve opens and suddenly unleashes hot exhaust gasses which expand rapidly under their high pressure. The second purpose is to draw those exhaust gases away from the exhaust manifold quickly and efficiently. Were this not to happen then the resultant back pressure would compromise the clean exiting of the next cylinder full of exhaust gases and so adversely affect performance.

The internal volume and the basic design of the silencer should match the requirements of the engine to which it is attached if the two are to operate efficiently together. Fitting larger bore exhaust systems has long been regarded by many as a quick and easy way in which to make their tired old Minis go faster, when in fact most achieve only an increase in exhaust system noise! When used in conjunction with the right carburation, however, a larger bore exhaust of the correct size can give a further power increase. Some systems from performance specialists are claimed to give an absolutely guaranteed power increase.

The standard exhaust is a one-piece steel system with a single silencer (early cars) or a rear and intermediate silencer on later cars. The Mini Cooper has a three branch manifold attached to a front pipe and separate rear section incorporating the silencer, although some Coopers have an additional intermediate silencer.

There should be four attachment points for the standard Mini exhaust system. The down pipe is attached at the combined inlet/exhaust cast iron manifold by a simple clamp. At the bend under the car there is a bracket which attaches to a bracket on the gearbox differential casing, and the silencer at the rear is supported by two rubber-mounted brackets attached to the subframe. This is a flexible mounting system, made necessary by the forwards and rearwards movement of the transversely mounted engine.

The most common problems with an exhaust system are rusting and blowing. Some mild steel exhaust systems can last a very short time before rust weakens a joint between the pipe and a silencer box. When this happens, flexing of the two can soon cause a hole to appear. An exhaust blows because a hole allows gasses to escape, which could be caused by rusting as already outlined, or by impact damage or even poor welding when the system was fabricated.

Exhaust repairs are possible but they do not usually last very long. The most obvious solution is to weld a patch over the offending area, and this can give a reasonable repair as long as the exhaust is holed due to impact damage and not to rust, because the weakened rusty exhaust system will soon develop other holes or even flex sufficiently to buckle the new plate. Various non-ferrous repair materials are available, including pastes and bandages. Again, such repairs might be quite long lasting on a sound but damaged system, but they will last a very short time on a rusted exhaust. Exhaust systems for Minis are not too expensive, so that replacement is usually a better option than repair.

Exhaust removal

Let the engine cool first! Remove the air filter cover and disconnect the throttle return spring from the

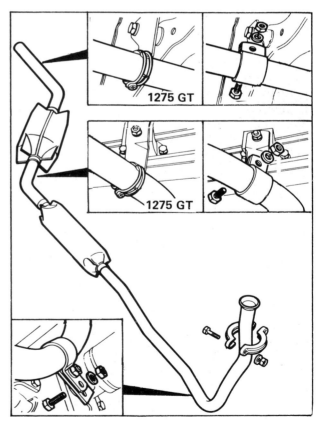

Exhaust system installation. (courtesy Autodata)

exhaust clamp. Undo the nut and bolt from the clamp and remove the clamp.

Raise the offside of the car and support it on axle stands. Working from underneath the car, undo the nut and bolt from the gearbox/exhaust bracket, then temporarily chock the front of the system so that it does not place strain on the rear mountings.

Remove the nuts from the intermediate and rear mounting brackets, then lower the system to the ground, turn it through ninety degrees so that the down pipe clears the bulkhead, and withdraw the system from under the car.

Which Exhaust?

When exhaust replacement time comes around you are faced with three fundamental choices. You could opt for a plain mild steel system, a stainless steel system or a performance system. The mild steel exhaust can last a relatively short time if used in adverse conditions, ie, on salted roads in winter. The engine pushes quite an amount of water through the exhaust, and with water, mud and salt splashing on to the outside of the system, it is little wonder that mild steel systems succumb with such regularity. The stainless steel system will last many times as long as mild steel alternatives, but has a higher cost and can have a tinny exhaust note which is not to everyone's taste. On economic grounds, the stainless system wins in the long run.

Not all stainless exhaust systems are created equal; there are many grades of 'stainless' steel, and the lifespan of a stainless system will depend both on the quality of steel used and the thickness used. The more flimsy systems also have the problem that they can be badly damaged by 'grounding' – especially on a low-slung car like the Mini – so that it always pays to buy the best you can afford.

Performance exhausts abound for the Mini, and come from some well respected companies. One long centre branch (LCB) manifold, coupled to the matching system, was advertised as capable of achieving a 16% increase in the power of the Mini engine. If this is correct, then the exhaust would be well worthy of consideration for higher power versions of the Mini. Be sure to obtain written confirmation of the performance increase which can be anticipated from an exhaust (or retain the advertising literature in which the claim is made) before parting with too much money, though.

Exhaust re-fitting

The author prefers to offer a one-piece system up and to support it at approximately the correct height before attaching it to save stressing the brackets. It would be quite acceptable, however, firstly to attach the bracket at the lower end of the down pipe, followed by the rear brackets (keep them all loose until all are connected) then finally the manifold clamp. The brackets may now be tightened.

With two or three piece systems, it pays to trial assemble the system and to compare it with the one which you have just removed, so that the angles of the separate pieces to each other can be established (and marked for ease of assembly under the car) and to ensure that the system is actually the correct one for your car. It can prove awkward to try twisting a tight joint whilst you are lying on your back underneath the car! Begin at the front and work your way backwards. Attach the down pipe first at the manifold and differential bracket then offer up the centre (or rear, in the case of two piece systems) section, followed by the rear section, using plenty of sealant around the joints.

Check that the exhaust does not foul any part of the bodywork, and that ground clearance is adequate, before the sealant hardens and adjustment becomes much more difficult. Start the engine, and check that the exhaust cannot rattle against any part of the body or ancillaries and that it is well clear of the main battery feed. A hot exhaust can burn through battery feed insulation very quickly and provides an excellent earth guaranteed to start an electrical fire where you need it least – in the boot next to the fuel tank.

THE ELECTRICAL SYSTEM

Safety

It is imperative that all aspects of the car's electrical system are maintained in perfect working order for safety's sake, because something as seemingly insignificant as an area of poor insulation on a wire or a loose spade connector can start an electrical fire which will reduce your car to a burnt-out wreck in a few harrowing minutes.

When a live wire shorts to earth, the battery discharges at its maximum amperage (current) rate through the wire. The resultant wattage (energy) passing through the wire is far higher than it is able to tolerate, so it quickly becomes red-hot. This firstly melts and then ignites the insulation, causing a fire. A wire's ability to pass current depends basically upon its cross sectional area, so that thin wires become hot and burn off their insulation with far lower currents than thick wires are able to tolerate. This is why it is vital that any wires which are replaced are replaced with wire of the same thickness and colour.

Even the huge main battery feed wire has a limit to how much power it can transmit. If it shorts directly to earth (it is not unknown for a loose exhaust pipe to burn through the insulation) then the battery will discharge to earth at its maximum amperage. The amount of power in question is more than enough to physically move the car (as can be proved by using the starter motor with the car in gear), so that even this high capacity wire can start an electrical fire.

An electrical fire can start just about anywhere on the car. If it starts near a fuel line or the petrol tank then the results can be explosive. If an electrical fire begins behind the instrument shroud or anywhere else within the car then it will be full of choking fumes within perhaps ten to twenty seconds.

No matter how collectable and original a car, there is a strong case for fitting a battery isolation switch, which may be reached from the driver's seat and which immediately disconnects the battery should there be any sign of an electrical fire starting. Such switches are widely available and cannot be accidentally operated because they must be both lifted and twisted in order to disconnect the battery.

Electrical component repair and replacement

The Lucas components used across the entire Mini range and including the dynamo/alternator, switches and relays, in the ignition system, may all still be obtained either brand new or, in the case of larger items such as the starter motor and generator, on an exchange basis as fully reconditioned units. There cannot, therefore, be any legitimate reason for attempting DIY repairs to any of these components, bearing in mind that a poor DIY repair to an electrical component which leads to the failure of the

component can at best leave car and driver stranded and at worst cause an electrical fire which could be terminal for both car and driver.

Many of the car's electrical circuits are fused. A fuse is a thin strand of wire which has no insulation and which is of a specific thickness and consistency to melt if the electrical energy which passes through it exceeds a pre-determined level. Fuses are rated according to the current which they can carry, and their job is to protect wiring and electrical components from damage due to too-high electrical energy. If a fuse 'blows' then there will be a reason, and on no account should the blown fuse be replaced until the fault has been found and rectified. A blown fuse should never be replaced with one of higher rating, with strips of metal foil, etc, because this will not cure the fault which lead to the fuse blowing and it will allow more electricity to pass down the wire than it is intended to handle. The insulation can melt down and an electrical fire can soon start.

Electrical power is generated by either a dynamo or an alternator, and stored in the battery for use in starting the car and in making up any shortfall when demand outstrips supply (if all electrical devices are simultaneously switched on). The dynamo wires run to the control box and the alternator wires run directly to the starter solenoid (the solenoid is a kind of electro-magnetically operated switch which uses a small current from the ignition switch to complete a circuit with a much more powerful current which is sufficient to turn the starter motor).

Minis up to 1969 were fitted with a positive earthed circuit, whilst later cars had a negative earth. To determine which polarity your own car is, simply check the battery terminals – the terminal which is connected by a short length of thick wire to the bodyshell is the earth, and will be marked with a '+' or '−' sign.

Battery

The battery must be firmly clamped into position within its compartment, any potential for movement is an MOT (UK Ministry Of Transport car test) failure point. Also, spilled battery acid will quickly destroy paintwork and corrode metal.

The battery is a 12 volt lead/acid type which is situated in the boot (saloons) under the rear seat (estate) or behind the driver's seat (van and pickup) and which usually requires little in the way of maintenance. The level of the electrolyte (fluid) should be periodically checked and maintained (using only distiled water) at a height of ¼″ above the lead plates. Every three to six months the battery may be removed, disconnecting firstly the earthed then the live side, and the specific gravity (SG) of the electrolyte checked using a hydrometer. This should range between 1.268 and 1.296 for a fully charged battery and 1.098 and 1.126 for a fully discharged one.

If the SG of different cells shows variation then either a plate will have buckled and the battery will soon fail or the electrolyte in the low reading cells contains too high a concentration of distiled water. In this case, some may be siphoned off and replaced with fresh electrolyte, which is readily obtainable from garages.

If the car is used only for short trips or under conditions of high current drain (at night with the lights on) then the battery may need recharging from time to time. It is recommended that the battery is charged at the lowest possible rate of amperage (current) and that 'boost' chargers are not used on a regular basis, because too rapid a charge rate can cause damage to the battery.

When the battery is removed from the car, clean the terminals and cover them with a thin layer of petroleum jelly; also, inspect the battery for cracks or leakage, which should be washed away at once, and check the battery compartment for corrosion.

One terminal of the battery is earthed (connected to the car's bodyshell) and the other is connected by a thick wire to the starter solenoid.

The Loom

The wires which carry electrical energy via fuses and switches to the majority of electrical components are contained tightly-bound within the loom. The wires are colour-coded so that they may be traced easily and compared to wiring diagrams, and some colours are used widely to denote certain functions. Brown, for instance, is usually used to signify that a wire is permanently live and may well be independent of any fuse. Black wires all run to earth and red wires are usually found in circuits which operate independently of the ignition switch, such as parking light circuits.

In many examples of the Mini it may be discovered that previous owners have run wires of inappropriate colour, sometimes to bypass a length of damaged wire and sometimes when fitting an electrical accessory. Such wires should be replaced with others of the correct colour and amperage rating, so that future problems can be traced more easily.

If a car has too many lengths of inappropriate wire or if the loom itself shows signs of damage, then it will be worth replacing the loom completely. These are widely available for all years and models of the Mini.

Before replacing the loom, lay the new one out alongside the car so that the terminals lie in their approximate respective positions. Using a circuit diagram and comparing the new loom to the old (still fitted in the car), make a tag from folded masking tape for every terminal on the new loom and write on it the correct terminal for the wire. Do not start to fit the loom until every terminal has been identified in this way. If you have 'spare' terminals or if the new loom lacks terminals, then you have the incorrect loom for the car.

When all terminals on the new loom have been tagged, cut out the old loom, leaving a short length of wire on every terminal for identification purposes.

The electric units at the rear of the car are powered through a section of the loom which passes up the nearside roof pillar, along the semi-enclosed section at the side of the roof, then down the rear roof pillar. If the loom has to be replaced or removed (for welding to the roof sides, guttering or top edge of the car's side), attach a length of strong string to the end terminals before pulling the loom out. This can later be used when refitting the loom, which could otherwise prove very difficult, especially as far as the front roof pillar is concerned.

Dealing with electrical faults

Electrical faults never 'cure' themselves, and intermittent faults which can appear to correct themselves are bound to re-emerge. An apparently inconsequential intermittent fault can in fact be a symptom of a far more serious fault, such as a loose spade connector on a permanent-live and non-fused brown wire which, if allowed to fall away and come into contact with the bodywork (earth) can cause a fire within seconds.

Always trace and rectify electrical faults as soon as they become apparent. If for any reason you are unable immediately to tend to a fault then at the very least you should note down the exact nature of the fault and the exact circumstances in which it occurred (ie, which devices were in use at the time, whether it was raining etc). This will make it far easier to later trace the fault.

Think Safety. Always begin by disconnecting the battery. Check the relevant fuse to see whether it is either blown or heat-discoloured, in which case too high a current has passed through it. Remember at this stage that a blown fuse is not a fault but a symptom of one; do not merely replace a blown fuse without locating the real fault. Many people replace blown fuses, switch on the appropriate circuit and watch to see what happens. This is often dangerously misleading if the fault fails to re-occur, because it then appears to be cured. The fault might, however, occur only during cornering or going over a bump due to a wire moving and shorting, or after the car has been out in the rain due to water entering the car and short-circuiting a wire.

To trace electrical faults, you will require a circuit testing device, which could range from a Multi-meter down to a small battery, bulb and crocodile clip tester.

The first step is to disconnect the battery earth lead, then to identify the components associated with the fault, which in addition to the component in which the fault is apparent (ie, wiper motor, light bulb etc.) might include a switch or switches, fuse, relay and wires, and which may be traced via the circuit diagram. Locate each component in turn and ensure that it is the correct one for your particular car, because a previous owner may well have substituted an almost identical alternative which may have different terminals. Test switches by connecting a multi meter or small battery/bulb tester across the earth and feed terminals, then operating the switch.

On the wiring diagram, back-trace the wires which lead from the faulty unit through any switches or relays to the power source. It is often helpful at this stage to make a small simplified sketch of the circuit, clearly marked with relevant details, such as wire colours, terminal numbers and so on. This will be far easier to work with than a full wiring diagram. Check that the correct colour wires are actually fitted to the power source, switch, earth, etc.

Remember that one side of the battery is earthed, that is, it is connected to the bodyshell of the car. One side of any electrical unit can also be earthed, so that the bodyshell acts as a length of wire between the two. Many electrical faults can be traced quickly to a poor earth connection, so check this before wasting too much time elsewhere. The use of the bodyshell in this way reduces the amount of cabling in comparison with that needed in GRP-bodied cars, but it also increases the chances of a short-to-earth fault occurring, because any live wire or connector which comes into contact with any part of the bodywork will cause a short-circuit which allows the battery to discharge at its maximum rate (until the wire actually melts).

Think logically. If a unit fails to operate and a fuse is not blown somewhere within its operating circuit, then either there is a disconnection in the power feed or the earth connection is suspect. Check the earth first, and if this proves sound then use the circuit tester to check continuity between the various elements in the circuit back to the main power feed. Check also that the relevant switch is operating properly, using the circuit tester. If no faults in the circuit are apparent then the unit is faulty.

If a unit fails to operate and an in-line fuse is found to have blown, then there will probably be a short to earth somewhere in the wiring between the fuse and the unit or in the unit itself. Isolate each section of wiring and each electrical component in turn and use the circuit tester, with one terminal earthed, to check for a short circuit. If none is found then the fault could lie with the component itself, or there could be an intermittent earth problem somewhere within the circuit. A blown fuse could also be due to one of too low a rating having been previous fitted.

TRANSMISSION, SUSPENSION AND STEERING

The transverse engine/gearbox front wheel drive transmission configuration which is today taken for granted and used by all major motor manufacturers was quite revolutionary when it first appeared in the Mini. Power from the engine is fed through the clutch then 'downstairs' to the gearbox by the transfer gears. The gearbox drives the differential, which in turn feeds power through one of several types of universal joint (rubber coupling, Hardy-Spicer or offset sphere) into the drive shafts, then through the constant velocity joints to the wheels.

If the car is driven in a 30′ diameter circle (or a part thereof ie. cornering) then the outer wheel will have to rotate around 13% faster than the inner (because the outer wheel travels further than the inner one) if the two wheels are not to 'fight' each other for road traction and therefore lose adhesion. The differential allows one wheel to rotate more quickly than the other when necessary. It also, incidentally, allows one wheel to spin whilst the other is stationary, and those who drive in off road conditions where such a situation is commonplace (one wheel in a muddy rut, the other on firm dry ground) usually fit a limited slip differential to ensure that the wheel which has traction will turn.

The drive shafts are driven by the differential, although because the outer end of each shaft is connected to a roadwheel and to all intents and purposes at a fairly constant height relative to the road, and the inner end is connected to the differential and therefore to the engine and bodywork with a variable height relative to the road, a joint is needed at either end of the drive shaft to allow it to swivel to cater for suspension movement and steering.

The inner joints need allow only for vertical movement; the outer (constant velocity) joints must also allow the wheels to be turned in the horizontal plane in order that the car can be steered. Work involving the transmission, suspension, steering or the front brakes can involve the same routines for stripping and rebuilding these components; rather than separate the functions of the components and duplicate instructions too many times or make constant referrals to other chapters there follows a description of a complete strip and rebuild.

Swivel Hub Removal

The special tools required for this are a universal ball joint splitter, 1⁵⁄₁₆″ AF or ¾″ Whitworth socket (preferably hexagonal impact sockets) and an extremely long lever!

Disconnect the battery. Put the car in gear, apply the handbrake and chock the front wheels. Remove the split pins from the driveshaft retaining nut castellations and 'start' the nuts. The nuts are torqued to either 150 ft lbs (Cooper S and 1275GT) or 60 ft lbs; in both cases, the nuts can prove very difficult to start without considerable leverage.

Loosen the roadwheel nuts, then transfer the wheel chocks to the rear wheels, raise the front of the car and support it on axle stands, placed well out of the way under the subframe.

Remove the roadwheels. Using the ball joint splitter, remove the track rod ends from the steering arms. It is sometimes possible to get by without a ball joint splitter by hitting both sides of the steering arm end similtaneously, so distorting the hole and allowing the track rod end to break free. However, the ball joint splitter will usually prove necessary. There are two types of ball joint splitter; the cheaper is a simple split wedge which is hammered into the joint until it parts, and the other is the more expensive scissors-type splitter. Do not be tempted to buy very cheap scissors ball joint splitters, because they can break, as the author has discovered to his cost. If a ball joint splitter is unavailable, you can alternatively unbolt the steering arms.

Unbolt the brake calipers (disc brakes) and support them so that no weight falls on the length of flexible brake hose, then remove the disc dust cover. If drum brakes are fitted, it is necessary to clamp the flexible brake hose before removing the union at the wheel cylinder when the hub is removed. See the relevent section of this chapter for more details of dealing with the front brakes.

Raise the suspension one side at a time with the jack, then remove the rebound buffers and replace them with non-crushable packing pieces. These keep the suspension compressed and the top support arm raised so that the hub can be removed.

Remove the nuts from the top and bottom swivel hub ball joints and separate these using the ball joint splitter. The swivel hub may now be removed (disc brakes) or removed and then separated from the brake hose (drum brakes). Keep a receptacle under the union to catch any escaping fluid. When separating the flexible brake hose from the wheel cylinder, do not twist the hose; grip the metal end fitting and rotate the hub assembly. It will be necessary to support the hub assembly whilst tapping the driveshaft end using a soft-faced mallet to free it.

Constant Velocity Joint Removal

It is not necessary to remove the driveshaft from the car if only the CV joints are to be replaced. Remove the soft wire binding or alternative CV boot fixing and push the boot back out of the way, turning it

ABOVE *If you forget to start the hub nuts before removing the wheel (or after the entire subframe assembly has been removed from the car, as in this photograph), you can lock the hub by passing a large bar through the hub studs. Place short lengths of steel tube over the studs to prevent damaging them.*

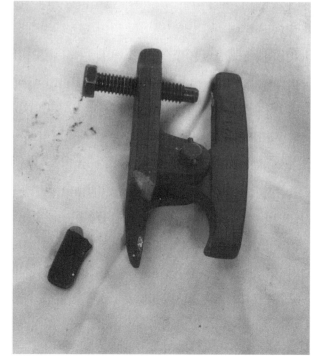

RIGHT *If you buy cheap tools then this is what you can expect. The ball joint splitter seemed a bargain, and survived around one dozen 'outings' before suddenly snapping. When this happens, always try to find another way around the problem, such as removing the steering arm from the front hub assembly.*

135

partly inside-out. Grip the driveshaft then gently tap the CV joint with a wood or rawhide mallet until it moves forwards slightly. It may now be pulled from the driveshaft end.

Driveshaft Removal

Undo the four locknuts from the 'U' bolts (rubber couplings) or from the flange (Hardy Spicer joint). The driveshaft may now be removed. If the car has offset sphere joints, a special tool (18G1243) can be used, although few DIY restorers will have access to

these. Alternatively, pull the driveshaft an inch out of the joint, then sharply tap the end of the shaft to release it.

To remove the offset sphere joint, use special tool 18G1240 or alternatively a cranked bar placed against the joint and a differential housing bolt head – NOT the housing, which can crack – then strike the other end of the bar or tool to lever off the joint. Not having access to the special service tool (as usual!), the author manufactured his own by simply welding

Front suspension components – rubber cone. (courtesy Autodata)

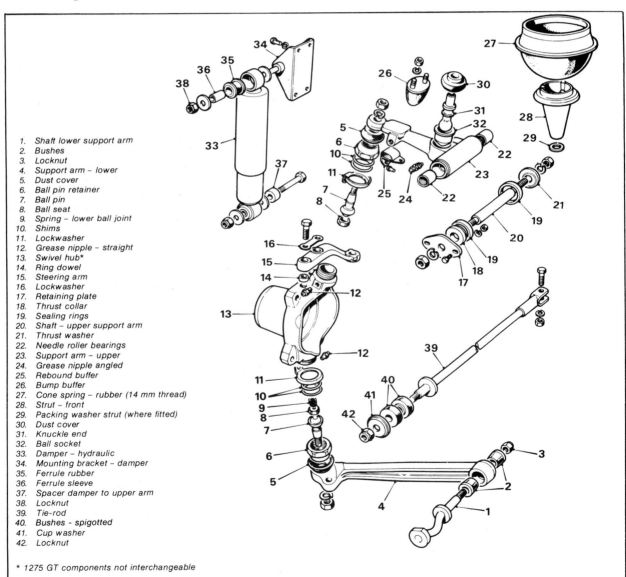

1. Shaft lower support arm
2. Bushes
3. Locknut
4. Support arm – lower
5. Dust cover
6. Ball pin retainer
7. Ball pin
8. Ball seat
9. Spring – lower ball joint
10. Shims
11. Lockwasher
12. Grease nipple – straight
13. Swivel hub*
14. Ring dowel
15. Steering arm
16. Lockwasher
17. Retaining plate
18. Thrust collar
19. Sealing rings
20. Shaft – upper support arm
21. Thrust washer
22. Needle roller bearings
23. Support arm – upper
24. Grease nipple angled
25. Rebound buffer
26. Bump buffer
27. Cone spring – rubber (14 mm thread)
28. Strut – front
29. Packing washer strut (where fitted)
30. Dust cover
31. Knuckle end
32. Ball socket
33. Damper – hydraulic
34. Mounting bracket – damper
35. Ferrule rubber
36. Ferrule sleeve
37. Spacer damper to upper arm
38. Locknut
39. Tie-rod
40. Bushes - spigotted
41. Cup washer
42. Locknut

* 1275 GT components not interchangeable

a large nut onto a length of steel bar. Offer the steel bar into position so that it lodges behind the offset sphere joint, then position the nut so that it sits on top of the differential housing bolt head. Mark this position on the bar and then weld on the nut. If you do not have access to a welder then simply drill and hole through the bar and fit a nut and bolt. The photograph of the special tool is in the section of this chapter dealing with engine/subframe removal. Another special tool 18G1243 is used to remove the offset sphere joint from the driveshaft.

If the constant velocity joints or the offset sphere joints have been removed following the discovery of a split in the boot, dismantle and clean them, before reassembling with plenty of grease. The constant velocity joints require Duckhams Q5795, and the offset sphere joints must be lubricated with a special grease available from BL/Rover Group dealers.

Rear Suspension

The rear suspension components of the Mini are carried on a detachable subframe. Although the subframe is made from heavy steel, it will often be found to have rotted to such an extent that replacement becomes essential. When this happens, many of the associated components will either be similarly rotten and require replacement, or be damaged during removal. Changing the subframe is thus the ideal opportunity to rebuild the entire rear assembly; brakes, suspension and bodywork.

The wheel hubs are located on pivoting radius arms which are attached to the front end of the subframe. The bushes of the radius arms can wear (especially if they are not properly lubricated), along with the pivot shaft, allowing the arm to move from side to side, which causes rear wheel steering – an undesirable effect. Another problem is a partial seizure of the arm, which can occur after a car has been off the road for a long period.

A rear-end rebuild is thus mainly concerned with the subframe and the radius arms. Whilst the car is stripped, the opportunity should be taken to assess the condition of the brakes, their cables and pipes, and the dampers, in addition to the actual bodywork which is revealed when the subframe is removed.

For rear subframe removal In the case of vehicles fitted with Hydrolastic suspension, it will be necessary to have the system de-pressurised at a Rover Group garage. Do not attempt to do this yourself, because

the fluid is at a very high pressure. The car may then be driven slowly (and uncomfortably) up to 30mph or so afterwards. Alternatively, the garage may be persuaded to partially pressurise the system with a few psi of compressed air to provide 'air springs' which will make the drive home more comfortable; unlike the fluid of the Hydrolastic system, the air could be safely released after the car had been driven home. This would certainly make the drive home safer and more pleasant.

Disconnect and remove the battery; remove the earthed terminal firstly, then remove the non-earthed terminal from its lead and pull the lead out of the boot area from underneath the car. Drain then remove the petrol tank(s), taking care not to spill petrol into the boot area if any welding is envisaged. On some later cars, the tank is held by a metal band, retained in turn by a bolt and nut which pass through a bracket at the lower end. The bolt should be held by a tab to prevent it from turning as the nut is undone, if not, then this is a rather awkward job. Earlier cars have fuel tanks held by a metal band which runs over the top of the tank, the fittings of which are far easier to undo. With the retaining band released, remove the tank gauge sender wires from the side of the tank and the fuel outlet pipe from the underside. The filler spout may be eased from the rubber surround and the tank withdrawn from the boot. For more details on this operation, see the section of this chapter dealing with the fuel system.

Chock the front wheels, slacken the rear wheel nuts then jack up the rear end of the car and support this on axle stands. If you envisage carrying out any

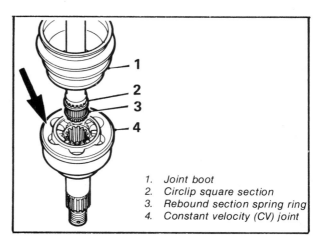

1. Joint boot
2. Circlip square section
3. Rebound section spring ring
4. Constant velocity (CV) joint

Separating drive shaft from constant velocity joint. (courtesy Autodata)

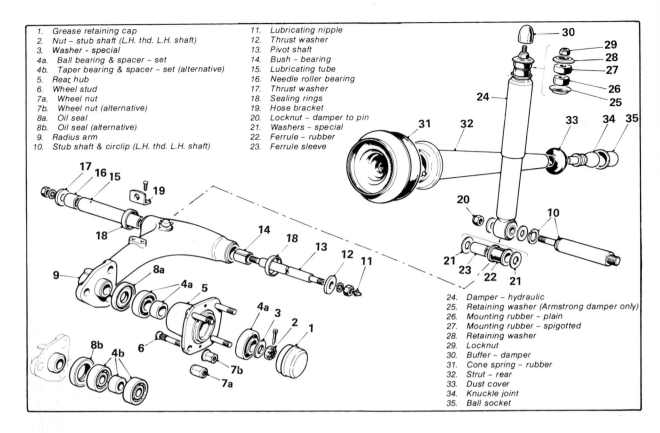

1. Grease retaining cap	11. Lubricating nipple
2. Nut – stub shaft (L.H. thd. L.H. shaft)	12. Thrust washer
3. Washer - special	13. Pivot shaft
4a. Ball bearing & spacer – set	14. Bush – bearing
4b. Taper bearing & spacer – set (alternative)	15. Lubricating tube
5. Rear hub	16. Needle roller bearing
6. Wheel stud	17. Thrust washer
7a. Wheel nut	18. Sealing rings
7b. Wheel nut (alternative)	19. Hose bracket
8a. Oil seal	20. Locknut – damper to pin
8b. Oil seal (alternative)	21. Washers – special
9. Radius arm	22. Ferrule – rubber
10. Stub shaft & circlip (L.H. thd. L.H. shaft)	23. Ferrule sleeve

24. Damper – hydraulic	
25. Retaining washer (Armstrong damper only)	
26. Mounting rubber – plain	
27. Mounting rubber – spigotted	
28. Retaining washer	
29. Locknut	
30. Buffer – damper	
31. Cone spring – rubber	
32. Strut – rear	
33. Dust cover	
34. Knuckle joint	
35. Ball socket	

Rear suspension and hub bearing. (courtesy Autodata)

bodywork at the rear of the car then it is advisable to support the entire width of the car on sturdy wooden or steel beams, located away from the area to be repaired.

Remove the roadwheels, and check the condition of the radius arm bushes by attempting to swing the end of each arm in and out. If any movement is apparent, the arms will have to be reamed out, new bushes and possibly a new pivot shaft fitted, work best undertaken (and relatively inexpensive) professionally.

Slacken off the brake adjusters and remove the brake drums and shoes. If the adjusters are seized solid then use releasing fluid and/or heat. From behind the backplate, remove the wheel cylinder retaining circlip. To minimise brake fluid loss during subsequent operations, remove the cap of the master cylinder and place a thin sheet of polythene over the filler hole before replacing the cap.

Undo the brake pipes from the wheel cylinders. It pays to place newspaper underneath the area to soak up any escaping brake fluid, or to use a large, shallow

container. Work backwards through the pipe and hose connectors to the regulating valve (early cars) or the twin connectors on dual-circuit models. It is wise to block off the exposed ends of brake pipes to prevent dirt from entering, and masking tape may be used for this purpose. For further details of working on the rear brakes, see the relevent section of this chapter.

Remove the entire exhaust system or, if a two piece system is fitted, the rear portion.

From inside the car, remove the handbrake cable adjusting nuts and their tensioning springs and washers (early cars), or the single nut of later cars. This may be removed from the car after the cable guide plate has been removed, or, alternatively, it may be left in the car and the cables freed from the radius arm pivot and subframe mounted guide.

The subframe will be easier to manhandle if the radius arms are removed. Firstly remove the dampers or the rear helper springs if Hydrolastic suspension is fitted. Lower each radius arm as far as it will go. In some cases, it will be partially seized and some force may be needed. The strut should then be removed from the rubber cone – again, this may be seized and require force. The strut may then be pulled backwards to disengage the knuckle joint. The rubber cone may then be removed. If Hydrolastic suspension is fitted, pull the strut backwards to disengage the knuckle joint and then forwards from the displacer unit.

Remove the handbrake cable moving sectors, or gently prise them open and remove the cable. Remove the split pin from the cable end to operating lever, and then pull the cables clear of the subframe.

From underneath the car, remove the radius arm inner retaining nut. The radius arm outer end is held by a bracket, secured by four bolts (which are often rusted solid). Remove these if possible, or drill them out otherwise. The radius arm may now be removed.

Support the subframe using a trolley jack and a length of wood across the width of the frame. The subframe is held by eight bolts (two at each corner) which are often very reluctant to move. Use releasing fluid first; if that fails, try heat. If one or more of the bolts will not move, then they have to be drilled/chiselled off (the studs may prove easier to deal with after the subframe has been removed).

With all nuts and bolts removed, gently lower the subframe to the ground and withdraw it from under the car. The opportunity to examine and repair as necessary any newly revealed bodywork should not be missed.

Examine the subframe. Although these are immensely strong fabrications, advanced corrosion

An old radius arm can be very reluctant to pivot far enough downwards to allow the suspension cone and trumpet to be parted. Use foot power if necessary. Even with the radius arm as far down as it can travel, there is still little clearance between the cone and trumpet to allow them to be removed. You may have to use force to part the two, as the alloy trumpet oxidises and 'glues' itself firmly into the cone.

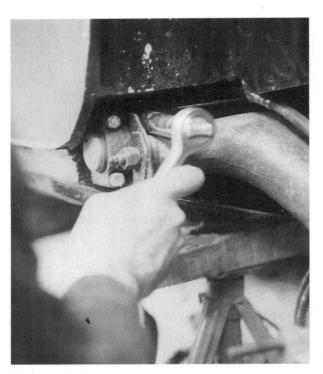

Two of the radius arm outer bracket bolts are on the underside of the bracket out in the open, and easy to get to. The other two are situated top and bottom of the arm within the bracket. The lower one can only be removed using a thin walled ½" socket, there being no room for anything larger.

If you do not possess a trolley jack, then go out and buy one today, for these are amongst the most useful of tools. Here, the author is placing a length of 4" by 3" timber over the trolley jack, then raising the two to support the subframe whilst its retaining nuts and bolts are removed.

If you are removing an old subframe, anticipate the front bracket bolts being complete seized. Worse, they may have corroded and the heads snap off as pressure is applied (as happened to the author).

This subframe eventually came off the author's car after almost every nut and bolt along the way had proved highly reluctant to start. Even this disgraceful example of a subframe was still strong enough to do the job.

can severely weaken them and if any doubt exists regarding their strength then replace them. Repair sections for the subframe are available and may be used to keep an ailing car 'alive' for an extra year or so, although rear subframes are not too expensive, and restorers will invariably opt for a straight replacement rather than a patched repair. If you do decide to weld on repair sections, remove the fuel tank, the fuel line and, where fitted to the subframe, the fuel pump. There is probably the same amount of work involved in replacing the subframe as there is in patching it.

Refitting the subframe

Although this is essentially the opposite of removal, there are a few points which may prove helpful. Firstly, the bodywork in the vicinity of the subframe mountings should be examined and any weakness or rust rectified. This is explained in depth within Chapter 5. The subframe should either be replaced or cleaned and painted if it is in good condition. If a new subframe is fitted, it pays to give this as much paint protection as possible. Also, run a tap through the captive nuts for the radius arm mounting bracket. These are normally covered internally with paint, which makes fitting the bolts very hard work unless the threads are firstly cleaned up.

Before offering the subframe into position, fit the front mounting brackets. You may find that it is easier to raise the frame into position before fitting the rear mountings if the adjacent rear valance end closing panels have been replaced as space can be quite tight.

Front Suspension

The front suspension is either of the rubber cone variety, found on very early and recent cars, or the Hydrolastic type found on cars manufactured between 1969 and 1974 (excluding the vans and the estates).
Prior to any work being carried out on a Hydrolastic equipped car, the system must be depressurised by an acknowledged dealer who has the special equipment necessary for the job.

The suspension comprises upper and lower pivoting arms, which are held top and bottom of the swivel axle via ball joints. Forward and aft movement

With the subframe removed. The length of ½" threaded rod was firstly screwed into the captive nut at the bottom of the rubber cone. As the cone thread was damaged, the threaded rod cut its own thread as it was screwed in. Quite a lot of pressure was needed for this, but two locknuts on the rod proved adequate for the job. With the nuts separated, the lower one was then used to bear against the washer and compress the cone spring. A huge pressure is needed to compress this. If the threads inside the cone give way then you are in serious trouble.

is prevented by a tie rod, which is fixed to a bracket at the front of the subframe and to the lower suspension arm.

To strip the front suspension, firstly remove the damper then the track rod end, using the proper ball joint separator, then remove the brake caliper (disc brake cars), and support this out of the way so that no weight falls on the length of brake hose, remove the brake drum, shoes and wheel cylinder (drum brake cars).

The rubber cone springs must then be compressed to take pressure from the suspension. Above the subframe towers on top of the bulkhead crossmember are two bolts (early cars) or a 1⅟₁₆" hexagonal headed bolt (rubber mounted subframe cars), which hold the towers to the crossmember. Remove per side either the two small bolts (easy) or the single large bolt (not so easy – 200 foot pounds or thereabouts seemed necessary to start those on the

Then the nut on the end of the top suspension lever pivot shaft was removed.

Remove the bolts from the thrust collar retaining plate. Be very careful during the whole of this operation not to place your fingers anywhere near the suspension cone or the top lever, just in case the threads inside the cone give way and cause serious injury.

The top lever pivot shaft could then be withdrawn.

Then the top lever could just be coaxed out. Take great care when releasing the pressure from the cone spring. It may not have much travel but it packs a lot of force, and you should not to screw the threaded rod out of the cone spring whilst the latter was still compressed.

authors car). The cone spring is underneath. The cone spring bears against an aluminium cone strut, in the lower end of which is a knuckle which locates into a socket on the upper suspension arm. The rubber cone spring is under some compression even with the suspension arm in its lowest position, and so it must be compressed before the suspension arm can safely be removed.

The cone spring may be compressed using the special tool 18G754B. This consists of a threaded rod which can be screwed into a nut which is welded on to the underside of each rubber cone, and a ratchet arrangement which then pulls the rod and hence the spring to compress the latter. The author, as usual, did not have access to the special tool, and attempted to lever the cone out without it, which proved impossible. Shining a torch down through the rubber cone showed that the threads of both nuts were in poor condition because someone had attempted to compress them using some sort of apparatus which had the wrong thread. There was thus nothing to be lost by making up a tool with another 'wrong' thread to do the job. The author and publishers cannot be held responsible for the consequences of anyone trying to compress the cone suspension using a makeshift tool.

A length of threaded ½" rod was found and fitted with two nuts and a large washer. Locking the two nuts allowed the rod to be threaded into the nuts of the rubber cones, using a spanner to turn the threaded rod. By then separating the two nuts and turning the lower one against the washer (which was bearing against the top of the turret), the cone slowly compressed. The small rebound rubber buffer was then removed. Still, there was insufficient clearance for the cone strut ball end to clear the upper suspension arm, but at this stage, the upper arm should be free of spring pressure, and the pivot shaft may be removed by firstly undoing the nut from the one end and the retaining plate from the other. With the pivot shaft removed, there should be sufficient clearance for the suspension arm and then the cone strut to be removed.

Pressure on the spring may now be released. Ensure that you do not screw the threaded rod out of the cone whilst the latter is still under pressure, and if the rod turns with the nut, then lock the upper end of the rod using two nuts, or grip it with mole grips. Replace the turret mounting bolts or nuts.

With the pressure removed from the suspension, remove the tie rod. The outer fixing nut is easy to

remove but the inner end can be almost impossible at this stage, when the application of heat (which proved necessary in the case of the car in the photographs) will set the rubber cover of the swivel axle lower ball joint on fire! If the bolt at the end of the tie rod will not come out easily, wait until the unit is removed from the car, then use heat to expand the surround, after which the bolt should come out easily. If the bolt still resists all attempts to remove it then it will have to be drilled out and a replacement fitted.

With both ball joints separated, the swivel hub can be removed. Take care to keep the bearings inside clean and free from air-bourne dust. The lower suspension arm may now be removed.

Front subframe removal

For instructions on removing the subframe and engine together, see the relevant earlier section of this chapter. The front subframe can not by itself be removed unless the engine has already been removed.

If the two large turret fixing bolts (or the nuts of

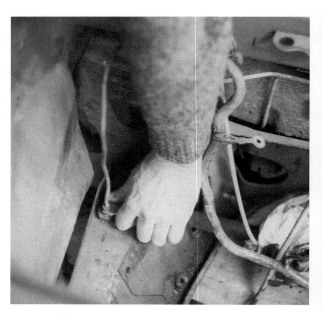

The brake pipes pass through the front subframe and so have to be removed before the subframe can be removed from the car. Be absolutely certain to drain the system thoroughly unless you wish to splash corrosive fluid all over the subframe.

Again, the little trolley jack comes into its own. Position the length of wood aft of the centre of the subframe, so that the latter balances better and is easier to handle.

Who left that exhaust pipe threaded through the subframe? That's right, the author. It is easy to overlook one of the cables, wires, pipes etcetera which thread through the front subframe.

Just hope that you have raised the front of the car high enough to give clearance for the subframe, atop the trolley jack, to be wheeled out. The author left the front suspension in place during this operation. The extra weight does not seem to make the job any more difficult, and it is easier to deal with the suspension when the subframe has been removed from the car.

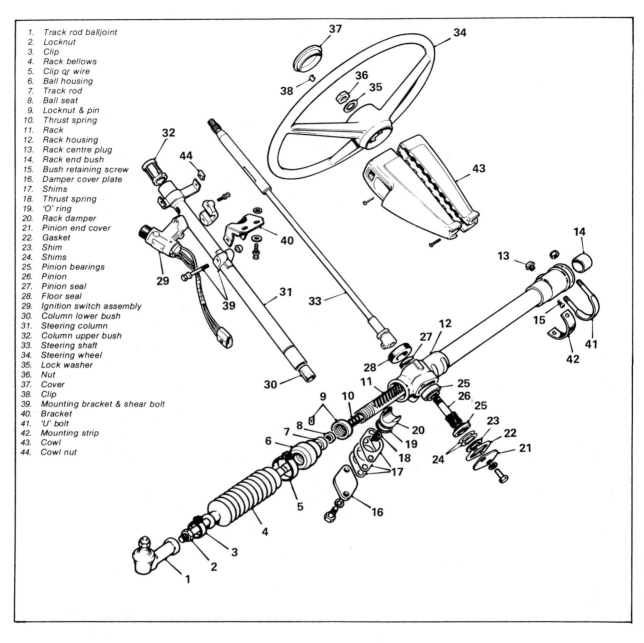

1. Track rod balljoint
2. Locknut
3. Clip
4. Rack bellows
5. Clip or wire
6. Ball housing
7. Track rod
8. Ball seat
9. Locknut & pin
10. Thrust spring
11. Rack
12. Rack housing
13. Rack centre plug
14. Rack end bush
15. Bush retaining screw
16. Damper cover plate
17. Shims
18. Thrust spring
19. 'O' ring
20. Rack damper
21. Pinion end cover
22. Gasket
23. Shim
24. Shims
25. Pinion bearings
26. Pinion
27. Pinion seal
28. Floor seal
29. Ignition switch assembly
30. Column lower bush
31. Steering column
32. Column upper bush
33. Steering shaft
34. Steering wheel
35. Lock washer
36. Nut
37. Cover
38. Clip
39. Mounting bracket & shear bolt
40. Bracket
41. 'U' bolt
42. Mounting strip
43. Cowl
44. Cowl nut

The steering rack assembly exploded view. Although it is possible to service and repair the rack at home, it is not recommended, especially in view of the extent of work necessary to remove and refit it should anything go wrong! (courtesy Autodata)

ABOVE RIGHT *The steering column mountings. (Courtesy Autodata)*

RIGHT *The steering column bushes. (Courtesy Autodata)*

146

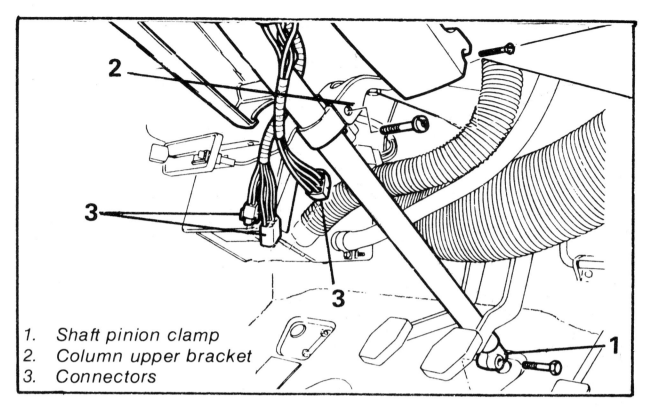

1. Shaft pinion clamp
2. Column upper bracket
3. Connectors

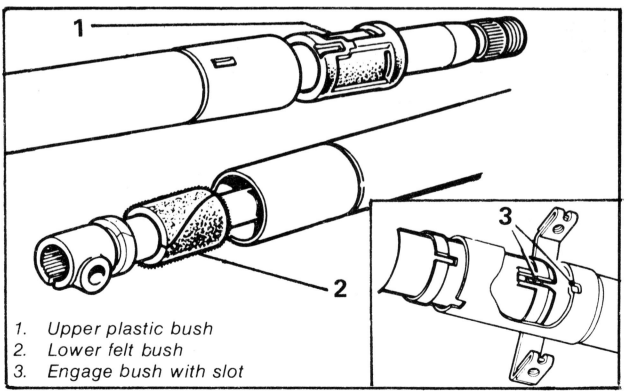

1. Upper plastic bush
2. Lower felt bush
3. Engage bush with slot

earlier cars) were removed previously to permit removal of the suspension, they must be refitted. Remove the brake pipes from the top of the subframe (bleed the system first), and check that no wires or pipes remain attached to the subframe. The main battery feed wire is held to the subframe with a number of brackets which are secured with self-tapping screws, be sure to remove this. Also, if the exhaust system is still in place, remove it, because the down pipe threads through the subframe.

Support the subframe on a trolley jack with a piece of wood long enough to support both sides of the subframe on top, then undo the nuts and bolts which secure the front and rear mountings. The author prefers to leave the turret mountings until last, although if the later type (the large bolt which can take a terrific amount of force to start it) is fitted, be sure to loosen this before removing the other mountings. The subframe may now be lowered, easing it past the front panel on the Clubman cars, and 'wheeled' out from under the car on the trolley jack.

Steering

A ball joint splitter will usually prove necessary to remove the track rod ends, although if you are in a hurry to strip the steering and are unable to split the ball joint, the steering arm may alternatively be removed from the swivel hub assembly.

The steering wheel is held by a single $1\frac{5}{16}$" nut which can be accessed after the steering wheel central cover (which will vary with the type of steering wheel fitted) has been removed. Remove all fitments from the steering column outer sleeve, which will vary according to the year of the car in question. In the case of later cars, there will be two plastic mouldings which cover the steering lock/ignition key and the switches for lights, wipers and horn. Removal of these fitments is straightforward, each being held by a single self-tapping screw. The direction indicator cancellation stud and locknut on early cars must be removed. The steering lock/ignition switch should have been fitted using shear bolts. These are bolts which have a thin cross sectional area immediately underneath the hexagonal head, and this shears as the bolts are tightened as an anti-theft precaution. Many people appear to replace the shear bolts with ordinary ones, but if shear bolts are fitted (and have sheared) then

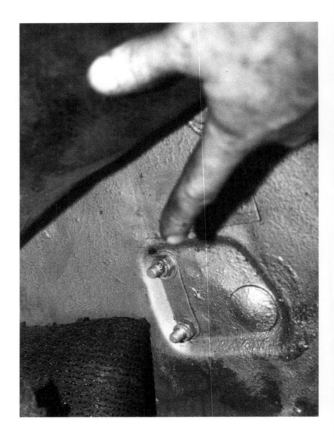

The steering rack 'U' bolt ends are situated on the toe board, above the front subframe mounting points.

they will have to be drilled out or drilled and the studs removed using a stud extractor. The fact that shear bolts are fitted does not necessarily mean that they will automatically shear when you attempt to remove them; on the author's car, they came out without a murmur.

Remove the pinch bolt from the lower end of the steering column, then the nut and bolt which hold the main steering column bracket. The column may now be removed.

The steering column has a plastic bush at the top and a felt 'bush' at the lower end. Check both the inner rod and the outer tube for straightness, then fit a new plastic bush in the tube and lubricate it with graphite grease, wrap new felt (soaked in engine oil) around the bottom of the rod, and feed the rod back into the tube.

The steering rack is held by two 'U' bolts which pass through the main bulkhead and are held by nuts which may easily be reached from inside the car.

Undo these, then simply lift the steering rack from the bulkhead.

If the steering rack has to be removed with the front subframe (or worse, the subframe and engine) in situ, it will be necessary to lower the subframe (plus engine and ancilliaries, which means that just about everything must be disconnected) by around 3″ in order to gain the necessary clearance. Having gone this far, it may be deemed preferable to remove the engine/subframe assembly complete! The prospect of that alone should encourage the restorer to fit a reconditioned steering rack when the opportunity arises during the restoration.

It is possible to recondition the steering rack at home, although this is a complicated and difficult task, and it is recommended that you opt instead for an exchange reconditioned and guaranteed unit. If you were to recondition the rack yourself, refit it and then discover some fault of your own making, you would be faced with the daunting prospect of removing the rack again, but with the engine, subframe and ancilliaries in situ; a task best avoided.

When re-fitting the steering gear, do not tighten the steering rack 'U' bolt nuts until the steering column is in place, then remove the grommet from the bulkhead adjacent to the nearside 'U' bolt mounting, remove the plastic plug from the steering rack, and use a 6mm twist bit shank to centralise the rack. The 'U' bolt nuts and the column pinch bolt may now be tightened.

Irrespective of whether the engine and subframe were removed as a unit or separately, it is better to refit the two as a single unit. If the car has been stripped to a shell for a complete body restoration, then the subframe will have to be fitted in order to correctly align the front end panels. The author would personally favour then removing the subframe, building up the suspension into it, mounting the engine unit on to it, then lifting the lightweight front end of the body into position over the assembly.

A drum brake consists of a drum which is attached to the hub flange and which rotates with it and hence the wheel, and two frictional shoes attached to the non-rotating backplate which expand to contact the inner face of the drum and so slow the rotation of it and the wheel.

Disc brakes consist of a large steel disc which is attached to the hub flange and so rotates with the wheel, and a caliper unit (which is attached to the non-rotating swivel hub) containing two frictional pads which are pushed against the sides of the disc to slow it and the wheel.

The shoes are caused to expand against the drum and the pads to press against the disc by a hydraulic system which is actuated by the brake pedal. Pressure on the brake pedal causes a piston to move within the master cylinder and force non-compressible brake fluid down the brake piping system. The fluid in turn moves two small pistons contained within the wheel cylinder (drum brakes) or calipers (disc brakes), to move the shoes and/or pads respectively.

The handbrake is operated independent of the hydraulic system by a cable. This passes to the rear brakes and causes a simple lever system to spread the two shoes in each brake so that they press firmly against the inside of the drum and prevent the wheel from rotating.

Disc brakes are self-adjusting, although drum brakes require periodic adjustment to compensate for wear in the frictional shoe linings. Adjustment of the rear brakes also adjusts the handbrake. An inefficient handbrake is not corrected by tightening up the operating cable, but by adjusting the rear brakes then adjusting the cable so that it has the correct amount of travel to engagement.

The brake pads and shoes must be replaced before the frictional material wears away. Failure to replace either will result in metal from the pad backing or from the shoe rivets scoring the drums and discs, so that they also have to be replaced.

It is vital that the brake hoses and pipes are not contaminated internally with dust. When any are removed, either plug or seal off the open ends.

BRAKES

All versions of the Mini were fitted with rear drum brakes. The 1275GT and Cooper S versions had disc brakes at the front, whilst all other versions had front drum brakes.

Bleeding the brakes

If the brake pedal feels soft and spongy, then there is air within the system. Unlike brake fluid, air can be compressed, and the soft feel of the pedal is due to the fact that pushing it is compressing air rather than pushing non-compressible fluid to operate the brakes. In this case, the brakes have to be bled. The brakes also have to be bled after any part of the hydraulic system has been temporarily disconnected.

Bleeding the brakes entails pumping fluid through the pipes until the fluid which contains air bubbles is removed from the system via one of the bleed valve nipples. The nipple is turned to allow fluid to escape as the pedal is pumped, then tightened before the pedal returns. To prevent air from entering the system via the bleed nipple, a short length of transparent plastic pipe is attached to it and the other end is immersed in a container of clean brake fluid.

To bleed a brake (or the clutch slave cylinder) you will require an assistant to push the brake (clutch) pedal for you. Attach the pipe to the brake nipple and immerse the other end of this in a small container of brake fluid. Open the nipple by turning it and call for the brake pedal to be depressed and held down. When your assistant has done this, tighten the nipple. Repeat the exercise until clear fluid with no air bubbles can be seen coming from the nipple. Ensure throughout this operation that the level of the fluid in the master cylinder is correctly maintained.

One-man brake bleeding kits, which are fitted with a small non-return valve to prevent air from being sucked back into the system, are available. The author has tried various of these and found that, while some work satisfactorily, some of the cheaper kits gave problems with the non-return valve. As ever, you are advised to buy the very best tools which you can afford.

Rear Brakes

To strip the rear brakes, firstly disconnect the battery, place the car in gear (do not engage the handbrake) and chock the front wheels, slacken the rear wheel nuts, raise the rear of the car and support it on axle stands situated under the subframe. Remove the roadwheels.

Each brake drum is held by two Philips-headed set screws. Remove these, then back off the brake adjuster. The brake adjuster has a square stud which protrudes from the top of the backplate, and this must always be adjusted with the appropriate tool, because damage to the stud could result from using ordinary spanners.

If the adjuster refuses to turn, do not use excessive force for fear of breaking the stud. Soak the

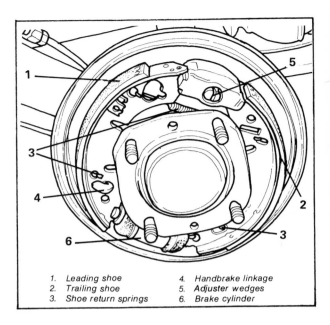

1. Leading shoe	4. Handbrake linkage
2. Trailing shoe	5. Adjuster wedges
3. Shoe return springs	6. Brake cylinder

Rear brake. (courtesy Autodata)

thread (which can just be seen under a cover strap) in penetrating oil and try again after a few minutes. If the stud still refuses to move, then heating it can usually help, although the studs are uncomfortably close to the fuel tank, and a totally seized stud will have to be dealt with by removal of the backplate, after which as much heat as is necessary may safely be brought to bear. In order to remove the backplate, remove the brake drum and strip the assembly as detailed below (shoes and springs, handbrake lever and master cylinder). Remove the hub nut and the hub, then remove the three nuts and bolts which clamp the assembly to the radius arm. The backplate may now be removed. The brake drum, however, may prove impossible to move. This will be due to the fact that the adjuster is holding the brake shoes in the expanded position. If this proves to be the case, then the radius arm assembly complete will have to be removed from the car. The moral is to frequently adjust the brakes to prevent the adjuster from seizing!

Back off the brake adjuster fully, then attempt to pull the brake drum off. If the brake drum will not move or if it sticks part-way off, then tap the outside of the drum using a soft-faced mallet until it comes away free.

Lift the brake shoe ends free of the adjuster mechanism, then from the wheel cylinder. Disengage the handbrake operating lever, and remove the brake shoes and springs, noting the positions of the latter. An elastic band or small clamp may now be placed so as to keep the wheel cylinder pistons in position.

The drum will contain asbestos dust which presents a health risk and which should not be breathed in. Use a dust mask, then gently clear the dust from the inside of the drum using a soft brush and methylated spirit. It is preferable to clean the drums out of doors to keep the dust out of the workshop air. Examine the shoes and drum for contamination from oil, grease or brake fluid. Examine the shoes for wear and replace if necessary. Small traces of oil and grease may be cleaned using petrol or paraffin, and traces of brake fluid should be cleaned with methylated spirit and the source of the contamination established and dealt with. Usually, the wheel cylinder will be found to have leaked the fluid, in which case the piston boots should be replaced.

Apply a little very high melting point grease to the brake adjuster thread, to the adjuster wedges, to the tips of the brake shoes (where they contact the wheel cylinder and adjuster) and a tiny smear to the raised portions of the backplate where the shoe sides contact. Take care not to get any of the grease on to the drum or the shoes!

Check the handbrake operating lever. The pivot point on this must be quite free to move, and if it is not, then it should be removed (remove the boot from the backplate, then disconnect the cable end), cleaned and re-lubricated.

The wheel cylinder may be stripped in situ, although it is preferable to remove it if wear in the cylinder or pistons is suspected. Clamp the length of flexible brake hose using the appropriate tool or alternatively mole grips with heavily padded jaws (this reduces brake fluid loss, but it will still be necessary to bleed the brake after reassembly). Unscrew the nut which holds the brake line to the wheel cylinder, taking care not to twist the brake pipe in the process. Remove the bleed valve. The wheel cylinder is held by a circlip. Remove this, then draw the wheel cylinder from the backplate.

The wheel cylinder should only be stripped in clean conditions. Remove the rubber boots then the pistons, noting the positions of each. Clean the cylinder and pistons in clean brake fluid, and examine both for signs of scoring. Replace as necessary. Use a new gasket between the cylinder and the brake backplate, use new piston seals and rubber boots.

Front Drum Brakes

These differ significantly from the rear drum brakes in having two adjusters and two wheel cylinders. To strip the brakes, firstly disconnect the battery, engage the handbrake, slacken the front wheel nuts, then raise the front of the car and support it on axle stands.

Remove the road wheels. Slacken off the brake adjusters then remove the drum fixing set screws and pull the drum away, tapping the sides with a soft-faced mallet if necessary.

The wheel cylinder pistons may be fitted with shoe steady springs (this does not apply to all models), and these should be removed. Lift the leading edges of the shoes from the wheel cylinders, then the trailing edges from the adjusters, and lift the shoes and return springs away together. Use an elastic band or small clamp to hold the wheel cylinder pistons in position.

Inspect the drums and shoes for contamination, which should be dealt with as per the rear brakes. Wearing a dust mask, clean the asbestos dust (see health warning – rear brakes) from the inside of the brake drum, preferably out of doors. Inspect the drum for scoring and replace if necessary, and inspect the shoes for wear, replacing again if necessary.

When rebuilding, remember to place the shoe toes (the trailing edge with the greater length of exposed steel platform) in the wheel cylinders. Lightly grease the adjusters and apply a small quantity to the

Front drum brake. (courtesy Autodata)

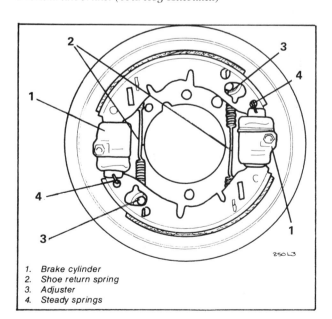

1. Brake cylinder
2. Shoe return spring
3. Adjuster
4. Steady springs

raised shoe support portions of the backplate.

To remove the wheel cylinders, clamp the flexible brake hose, then slacken its end fitting which is screwed into the front wheel cylinder and remove the bleed nipple from the rear cylinder. Remove the bridging pipe unions and the bolts which retain the cylinders. The rear cylinder may be withdrawn; the front cylinder may be pulled forwards and then disconnected from the flexible brake hose. Keep the hose end still and turn the cylinder. The wheel cylinders should be stripped, inspected and rebuilt largely as per the rear wheel cylinders.

Front Disc Brakes

Before working on the disc brakes, the disc should be checked for run-out. This requires specialised equipment consisting of a dial gauge and bracket, and should be carried out at a garage. If run-out is found to exceed .002″ then the disc should be renewed. If the disc is to be removed, slacken the hub nut before raising the front of the car.

To remove the brake pads, squeeze together the two legs of the split pins using pliers, and pull the pins from the calipers. The two spring steel retainers will come free. The pads may now be removed. They may prove to be quite tightly held between the caliper

Front disc brake. (courtesy Autodata)

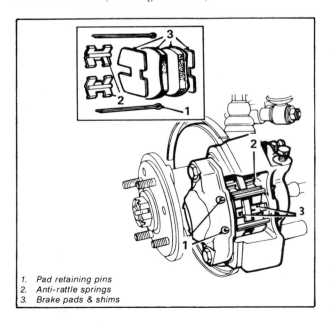

1. Pad retaining pins
2. Anti-rattle springs
3. Brake pads & shims

pistons and the disc. If new pads are to be fitted, the caliper pistons will have to be pushed back into their cylinders in order to make room. This may be achieved using a variety of levers. Take care not to force the pistons into their cylinders at an angle.

To strip the disc brake assembly, firstly clamp the length of flexible hose which runs to the caliper and slacken the hose connector at the caliper. Remove the pads as already detailed. The caliper is held by two large bolts which are prevented from shaking loose by lock tabs. Bend back the tabs then remove the bolts and lift the caliper free. Hold the flexible brake hose still and unscrew the caliper from it. It pays to have a shallow tray situated underneath the assembly during this operation to catch the small amount of brake fluid which will escape.

If the disc is to be removed, undo the hub nut and slide the disc off the stub axle, taking care not to allow the wheel bearings to fall out. The disc may now be separated from the hub. If the disc is scored, it may be repaired or replaced; replacement is the better option.

The caliper pistons may be removed by hand, although normally some assistance will be required from a low-pressure compressed air source. A foot pump will suffice, and if a compressor is to be used then turn down the pressure if possible or alternatively, take most of the air from the cylinder until the pressure is no more than 20 psi. If you try to use higher pressure air, the pistons will fly out at great speed! Fit a clamp (a small G-clamp is ideal) to retain one of the pistons, then use the air to move the other piston forwards but not out of the caliper. Open up the G-clamp to accommodate the freed piston, then use the air to drive the other out of the caliper. The first piston should now be removable by hand.

Examine the pistons and their bores for scoring and replace if necessary. Inspect the dust sealing ring and piston sealing ring for cuts or undue wear, and replace these if necessary. Before reassembly, lubricate the cylinder bores and pistons with clean brake fluid. Fit the piston sealing ring, then the piston. Push the piston in until approximately ⅛″ remains proud, then finally fit the dust sealing ring and its retaining ring.

Master Cylinder Removal

The master cylinder is connected to the brake pedal top by a cleavis pin, the removal of which is a nightmare owning to the very restricted access within the footwell and to the variety of sharp objects in the vicinity on which to cut your hands!

To bleed the cylinder, bleed the nearest front brake continuously until no fluid remains in the master cylinder, then re-tighten the bleed nipple. Disconnect the hydraulic pipe union from the master cylinder. The cylinder is secured to the bulkhead by two nuts. Take care not to spill brake fluid when removing the master cylinder.

To remove a tandem master cylinder, it is necessary to empty both cylinders by bleeding two brakes, one on each circuit. On some systems it will be necessary to bleed both front brakes, on others, to bleed one front and one rear brake. Follow the brake lines to establish which. It is not necessary to remove the brake pedal cleavis pin because the cylinder may be lifted away independent of the push rod. On replacement, both brake circuits have, of course, to be bled independently.

Handbrake

Early cars were fitted with twin independent handbrake cables; later cars had a single cable running from the lever to the compensator assembly, with a single cable connecting this to both brake backplate handbrake operating levers. In both instances, removal of the cables and lever from the interior of the car is a simple process requiring no special instructions here.

To remove earlier cables (which may be removed independently for repair), disconnect the end within the car, disconnect the battery, chock the front wheels and slacken the wheels nuts on one or both wheels then raise the rear of the car and support it on axle stands.

Remove the appropriate wheel(s), then remove the split pin and cleavis pin from the handbrake operating lever and disconnect the cable end from the abutment bracket. Prise open the radius arm moving sectors, and remove the cable. From underneath the car, pull the cable from the floor pan hole and from the subframe guide channel. The cable may now be withdrawn through the hole in the subframe.

To remove the later cable, proceed as before, but thread the secondary cable ends through the subframe from the outside in. Pull the single first cable back through the compensating assembly, then gently prise open the lugs so that the secondary cable may be removed.

(COURTESY AUTODATA)

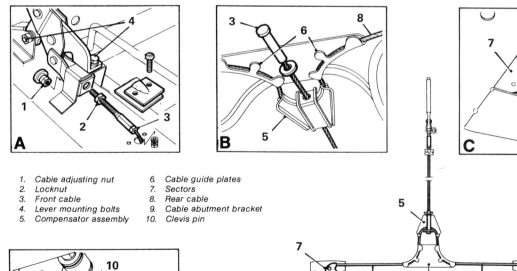

1. Cable adjusting nut
2. Locknut
3. Front cable
4. Lever mounting bolts
5. Compensator assembly
6. Cable guide plates
7. Sectors
8. Rear cable
9. Cable abutment bracket
10. Clevis pin

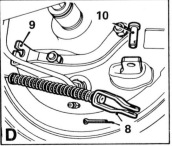

5 · RESTORATION, BODYWORK

INTRODUCTION

Legislation such as the UK MOT roadworthiness test for vehicles is constantly under review, and from time to time extra checks are added which could in the future conflict with advice given in this book.
In the area of bodywork repair standards, the UK test stipulates at the time of writing that any 'structural' bodywork components must equal in strength the original manufacturer's standards. Similarly, the method of joining panels must match the strength which each join possessed when the car was new. Readers are strongly advised to check the current legality of repair methods described throughout this book, but most particularly in the following chapters, before restoring their own car.

You can find the relevant information at approved vehicle testing centres, and it is also worth enquiring whether the information you are given is likely to be superseded in the near future. The standards demanded by the test may be open to interpretation by the individual tester; one tester may accept plug welds in place of spot welds, another might not. Try to address your questions to the person who will carry out the roadworthiness test on your own car when the time comes, to discover how that tester interprets the testing procedures.

The threat of future legislation rendering a recently and perhaps expensively restored car unfit for the public road should encourage every restorer to carry out all work to the highest standards and to use the best components and consumables.

The fact that the Mini is a small car does not necessarily mean that the restoration of its bodywork is any easier than that of far larger vehicles! Some of the jobs can prove very tricky, such as trying to line up the panels at the front of the car, whilst others can

prove infuriating due to the cramped access. However, there will be few individual tasks involved which will be beyond the abilities of the more experienced DIY restorer with welding facilities and abilities.

There are essentially two approaches to bodywork restoration. If you envisage having to substantially rebuild the body and replace not only the sills, but also the floor sections, flitch panels, heel board panel and other structural panels then the best method could prove to be stripping the car to a bare shell and then having it acid dipped, in which the entire body is submerged in acid for several hours. This removes all paint and shows the true condition of the body metal, revealing all traces of rust, the dreaded body filler and GRP repair.

Another advantage to starting the restoration with the car stripped down to a bare shell is that it may be easily rolled on to its side (with suitable support padding). This makes the welding operations on areas such as the floor pans, toe board and sills very much easier than lying on your back underneath in a hail of sparks! If the shell is really weak and you feel that rolling it on to its side might distort it, then it is an easy matter to weld internal brace bars into the shell before rolling it over. Two cross braces cut from lightweight angle iron and running from the top of one door pillar to the bottom of the other, welded together in the middle, would prevent distortion. If the two braces are cut to exactly the same length then you may find that fitting them actually helps to straighten up a twisted shell! In addition to this, you should, where possible, leave the doors in position, because these will help to strengthen the shell.

It is surprisingly easy to be 'fooled' by the skilful use of body filler into thinking that a panel is sound when in fact it is actually scrap. You could strip only those parts of the body which you believe to be in need of attention and subsequently overlook such an area of camouflaged rot. You may not discover it until almost the end of the restoration during paint preparation, and then perhaps find yourself having to remove panels which you recently welded on, in order to gain access to the newly-discovered filler. Having the shell acid dipped prevents this. Furthermore, the complete stripping of mechanicals which precedes acid dipping makes extensive bodywork repair easier by removing weight stresses which could otherwise distort the body, and also by removing inflammable materials which could present a fire hazard during welding operations.

The second approach is to work with the car as intact as possible, which is only possible in certain circumstances and according to the extent of necessary work. Many professional restorers with access to car lifts prefer to keep the car on its road wheels whilst the body is rebuilt, supporting and bracing the body as and when necessary. The car lift allows the car to be raised and lowered at will, to make different areas highly accessible. Anyone contemplating a full bodywork restoration at home is probably best advised to strip the car as far as time allows, then to raise the relatively lightweight bodyshell on to a welded-up stand to bring it to a comfortable working height.

A number of devices which enable a single person to easily manoeurve car body shells have appeared on the market in recent years. Amongst these is a simple pair of linked drive-on ramps which can pivot at their centres on the 'see-saw' principle, to raise the car as it is driven on. Other devices lock on to the wheel hubs, the bumper brackets or some other substantial part of the body assembly and allow the car body to be tipped sideways to give excellent access to the underside for welding. None of these devices will be particularly cheap, and they are unlikely to be bought by the person intending to restore just one car.

The same preparatory tasks usually precede all bodywork restoration. Firstly, the battery must be disconnected and preferably removed (to avoid spillage of corrosive battery acid, accidental electrical fires and shorting of the exposed terminals). If welding at the rear of the car is envisaged then the petrol tank and preferably the electric fuel pump (where fitted to the subframe) and fuel line must be removed.

Before making a start it is as well to remove the seats and all internal panels and carpets, so that the true condition of the floor, inner sill and footwell sections can be assessed. Also, if any areas of the external panels have the slightest rivelling (unevenness) then it is best to strip the paint from them in order to be able to check on their true condition and to reveal any bodyfiller repairs.

All body repair and restoration work follows a certain pattern. Firstly, the full extent of the rot must be determined. It is sometimes necessary to remove some components (such as a subframe) or occasionally a panel (such as the outer A panel on early cars) in order to be able to see and assess the true state of others clearly. When removing larger body panels, it is advisable to firstly provide support for the adjoining panels before metal is cut away in order to prevent the body from distorting.

When the full extent of the rot is apparent, the decision to patch or replace the rotten metal must be made, and will be based on several factors. If a non-structural panel has only a small area of rust, then a patch can easily be cut and welded into position. If the majority of a non-structural panel is rotten then in some circumstances a replacement could be fabricated, although many Mini body panels are available at such reasonable prices that it is more usual to obtain a replacement. When a rotten panel is structurally important, it is usual to replace it completely.

There are degrees of structural importance. The sill ends or subframe mounting areas are of the greatest importance and should not be patched. The entire affected panel must be replaced. Whilst, for instance, the floor panels are strictly speaking of structural importance, their contribution to the overall strength of the car is not so great as that of the sills, and if a rusted area does not adjoin a structurally important panel (such as the welded seam between the floor pan and the toe board), they may generally be patched.

When the extent and severity of rusting has been established, it is as well to order all replacement panels before cutting any existing metal. Ensure that each replacement exactly matches the one which you will be replacing, because different marks of Mini had slight differences in many panels, furthermore, some 'pattern' replacement panels can be a little inaccurate. The new panels are needed so that they can be offered into position and their edges scribed around to save you from inadvertently cutting too

Butt Joint

Lap Joint

Joddled

Corner Joint

LEFT *The main types of welded joint. The gap in the butt joint should be equal to the thickness of the metal being joined. The lap joint can be welded on both sides if required, as can the joddled joint (if you choose to weld the joddled joint only one side, then weld into the gap formed between the flat sheet and the step. A corner joint as shown here would be quite difficult to weld, and it is better if you can fold one side to provide an overlap for plug or seam welding.*

BELOW *When forming a joddled joint, it is important to draw the two sheets tightly together in order that they present a flush face after the surplus weld has been ground down.*

much of the existing adjoining panels away.

Before any rotten metal is cut out, make doubly sure that the shell is properly supported and that no forces are acting upon the body section which is to be worked on. In practice this means either leaving the car on its wheels and providing extra support for individual areas, or supporting solid parts of the body or the subframes on sturdy hardwood or box-section metal runners, and never on axle stands which give so small an area of support that they can act as pivots rather than supports.

Of the forces which can act upon the bodywork, none is so great as that of the weight of the engine. If the weight of the car were to be taken by supports aft of the front subframe (which supports the engine) then they would become pivot points against which the weight of the engine, which falls mainly upon the mountings, could act. If the car is raised for body restoration but the engine is left in place, then be sure to support the car in such a way that full support is given to the front subframe and hence the engine.

There are three main types of welded joint with which the restorer will have to become familiar. The lip joint occurs where two adjoining panels each have a lip set at ninety degrees to them. This is the easiest type of joint to deal with, and ideally these should be spot welded. The lap joint occurs where one panel overlaps another, and the weld is run along the edge of the top panel. In lap joints, it is advantageous to use a joddler. This places a step in the lower of the

two panels, against which the other panel can nestle so that the two panels are flush. Finally, the butt joint occurs where two panels simply butt against each other. A gap equalling the thickness of the panel metal is left between them, and this is filled with weld. The butt joint is very useful when a panel is being patch repaired, because the patch and the panel should be flush after welding.

There are numerous methods of cutting out old panels, including hand shears, chisels and hammers, air chisels, metal 'nibblers' and angle grinders. Each tool and method is best suited to differing panels and according to the ease of access, and often a combination of tools will combine to give the easiest

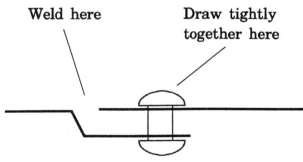

Weld here   Draw tightly together here

The Joddled Joint

These Frost Intergrips are useful for clamping metal prior to butt welding, and they can be used to clamp curved sections (such as a wing front-end), which makes them especially valuable.

This is how the Intergrips work, and the photograph reveals their only drawback: you cannot use them on enclosed sections, because there will be no way to retrieve the pegs.

Intergrips in action. Once the panels are tack welded together, the intergrips are removed and the join can be continuously butt welded. Bear in mind that weld shrinks as it cools, because if you put your tack welds too close to the Intergrips, they will be firmly seized and very difficult to remove. Allow at least 10mm from each intergrip when tack welding (unlike the author when he was setting up this demonstration piece).

and best result. Always be wary of cut metal edges as they can be razor-sharp.

If a welded lip seam or flat join has to be dealt with, it is often permissible to merely cut the old panel at the inner edge of its welded area and then weld the replacement on top to give a multi-layered join. It is neater and stronger (though not necessarily important if the join will be hidden and the panel is not structurally important) to part the old welded seam so that the resultant joint has the correct number of thicknesses.

Before starting to weld up the new panel, ensure that all traces of paint, rust, oil, water and other contaminants have been removed from the two areas which will form the join. You can not achieve a strong weld on contaminated metal, as the contaminants will mix with the weld and weaken it. Furthermore, the existing metal to which you intend to weld must be of sufficient thickness to avoid 'burning through'. Also, ensure that panels being joined are tightly clamped (or temporarily pop-riveted together) and that their 'lines' are correct, taking measurements where necessary.

Finally, remember that all welding generates great heat which can easily distort body panels. When welding a large panel, firstly 'stitch' weld every few inches before joining these up with continuous runs of weld.

Irrespective of how carefully you weld, there will normally be a few slight undulations in large welded panels. These might appear insignificant at this stage, but when the top coat has been applied they will stand out like sore thumbs! They have to be filled prior to priming. The two materials which can be used for this are the traditional lead (also called body solder) and the more modern body fillers.

Use and Abuse of Bodyfiller

Many classic enthusiasts abhor body filler despite the fact that, if properly used, this material can give perfectly acceptable results. Unfortunately, body filler has suffered from a 'bad press' (perhaps including Chapter 2 of this book) because the number of cases of filler misuse easily outnumber cases of proper use.

Body filler is intended and perfectly acceptable for filling shallow dents in external and non-structural car body panels. It is not intended to be used to bridge holes, nor to fill deep dents or cover up areas of bodyrot. Yet those looking for an elderly example of

the Mini will doubtless encounter many cars in which quite large holes and deep dents have been filled with a lump of bodyfiller, in which structurally essential panels have been 'repaired' with a mixture of GRP and bodyfiller.

Bodyfiller should only be used to obtain a smooth surface on metal which has shallow dents, such as might result from heat distortion during welding operations or from minor parking bumps. The filler is the modern equivalent of lead, because bodyshops and car manufacturers for many years treated small undulations in external car body panels by firstly painting on a lead 'paint', melting this to 'tin' (coat) the area in question and to form a strongly-bonded layer to which the lead can adhere, then melting on and spreading with a spatula further lead to build up to the required height. This process is known as 'lead loading' or 'body soldering'. Bodyfiller is far easier to use than near-molten lead, as well as being inherently safer! Lead loading kits and associated equipment are available and widely advertised, although the skill requirement to obtain good results with lead can be understated in advertisements, and for most people, bodyfiller will be the better option. It must be pointed out that lead is highly toxic, so if you do decide to work with it, treat it with the caution you would if dealing with toxic chemicals.

In order to use body filler successfully, it is vital that all traces of rusting, paint (including primers), oils and other contaminants are removed from the surface to be treated. Filler cannot adhere strongly to painted metal, because the join can only be as strong as that between the paint and the metal! If you apply filler over the slightest amount of rust then you can expect it to literally drop out at a later date when the rusting spreads sufficiently underneath. If you apply filler over contaminants then you may find that poor adhesion results, or the filler could chemically react with certain contaminants.

If cleaning the metal renders it very thin then you should not use bodyfiller because it will offer very little strength and furthermore, most types of filler are quite rigid and will be very inclined to loose adhesion to a thin and hence very flexible panel, or even to break up as the panel flexes. The only safe option in this situation is to weld in new metal.

Check the surface carefully for high spots. Whilst you can fill and smooth down low areas, high spots cannot be linished out and must be beaten out before the filling process begins. If there are any deep holes, beat these out as shallow as possible, where access permits. Equipment is available for pulling out dents, and consists of sliding hammer rod to which a number of attachments may be affixed. The attachments can fit through a small hole in the surface of the metal, and the sliding hammer is then used to knock out the dent. If the surface can be made clean and yet remain sound, 'key' the surface with a 36 grit disc (the author uses a cup brush in the angle grinder), then use spirit wipe to remove any grease or oil contamimants.

Most fillers consist of a thick paste and a separate hardener; a chemical catalyst which accelerates the hardening of the filler. The filler itself usually comprises a polyester resin with a mineral-based powder, which forms a thick paste. Alternatives with tiny metal particles instead of the mineral powder can be obtained today. These offer the advantage of not being porous but might not give such good adhesion as the mineral products, which have far smaller particles. Mineral body fillers are porous.

Mix up the smallest quantity of bodyfiller which you feel you can get away with, and always follow the manufacturer's instructions relating to the relative amounts of filler and hardener. Ensure that the filler and hardener are properly mixed and a uniform colour. Cleanliness is vital, because any foreign bodies in the filler will simply 'drag' as you try to smooth off the surface.

Apply bodyfiller in very thin layers, allowing each to fully harden before adding the next, and gradually build up the repair to the required level. Do not be tempted to apply one thick layer of filler, because this may have small air bubbles trapped within it which will only become apparent when you begin to sand down the surface. Also, some resins and hardeners generate heat as they cure, and, if you apply too thick a layer, the extra heat generated by the greater mass might over-accelerate the curing process.

Build up the surface until it is slightly proud of the required level and leave it to fully cure before sanding it down. If sanding by hand, then use a sanding block; electric random orbital sanders and air-powered dual action sanders really come into their own when working with bodyfiller, and can both save much hard work and help to gain better results. The author has found the random orbital electric sander which takes ⅓ of a sheet of paper, gives the best results, since it offers a large contact area and so helps to avoid sanding the filler into a concave section. However you sand down the filler,

always wear a dust mask, because the tiny particles of filler in the air can cause respiratory problems if you inhale enough of them. Before you begin sanding down body filler, ensure that no engine or transmission components are lying out in the open workshop, as the filler dust really does manage to get everywhere!

Most body filler is porous; that is, it can absorb moisture. If the filler is allowed to become wet before it is primed, then the moisture can come into contact with the surface of the metal underneath, and all of your hard work will have been to no avail! Therefore, it pays to spray primer over a filled area as soon as the sanding is completed. This primer can be temporary, and it may be sanded off if necessary at a later stage as the panel is prepared for final spraying.

Lead loading

Lead loading offers one great advantage over body filler because the lead fully seals the surface over which it is applied, and in doing so it prevents future rusting (as long as the metal underneath is bright when coated with lead). In the author's experience, many professional restorers use lead loading for this reason, although obtaining a final smooth finish with lead is not an easy process, and some people use body filler on top of the lead to obtain the best of both worlds!

A combination of lead loading and the use of body filler is especially useful when dealing with welded seams. Clean then de-grease all the area in question (the metal must be perfectly clean), then paint on solder paint, which is obtainable from companies such as Frost Auto Restoration Techniques (address at the back of the book). Apply heat to the solder paint until it melts and coats the metal, then wipe away any flux from the surface using a damp rag. The metal is now sealed, and may be built up using lead then flushed over with body filler.

Lead is applied to the tinned surface by being melted on, heated until it has a buttery consistency and spread using a wood spatula.

It must be pointed out that lead is highly toxic, so if you do decide to work with it, treat it with the caution you would if dealing with any other toxic chemical. Never try to work lead using any sort of sanding device, because this would create a health hazard were you to breathe in lead dust. Use only

This hole was plugged with body filler, and the surrounding paper-thin metal had been flushed over with filler.

Cutting the thin metal away revealed ever more filler!

Drawing onto sheet steel does not do a ballpoint pen much good, but it does result in a clearly visible and thin cutting line. More usually, a scribe would have been used, but the author's was nowhere to be found when it was needed. Note that the actual cutting has been kept to a minimum by aligning the longest straight edge with that of the edge of the steel sheet. After cutting, the section should be trued on an anvil (or similarly flat surface) before bending. A series of 'V' cuts allows the metal to be bent to the complex shape required.

Spot the obvious mistake! The author forgot to drill holes for the pop-rivets and for welding before bending the steel, which made drilling those holes a little more difficult afterwards.

Pop riveted into position and ready for the welding to begin. The author began by welding through the holes, then he finally folded the underside to the correct position and welded this. Finally, the pop rivets were drilled out and their holes welded up. When primed and undersealed, this repair was invisible from the outside yet very strong.

body files when you shape lead.

The author discovered a typical case of filler abuse on his 1275GT. A previous owner or totally unscrupulous 'bodyshop' had moulded a large lump of bodyfiller into a hole in the offside front footwell panel in front of the A post, and had also spread it to cover up the thin metal surrounding this hole within the front wheel arch.

As the author cut away the very thin metal surrounding the hole, the true extent of the weakness became apparent. Eventually, sound and clean metal was reached in all directions, and a cardboard template was made for the replacement panel. This entailed offering up a thin piece of cardboard and drawing the shape of the necessary repair section onto it, marking the lines for the eventual folds and for the 'V' cuts which would prove necessary to get sheet steel to fold as required. The shape was then transferred to a sheet of steel and cut out using aviation cutters.

The next stage was to shape the repair section so that it fitted snugly into position. There are several ways of achieving the necessary folds including proper metal folding machines, a vice and hammer, a hardwood post and a hammer.

The panel was to be MIG 'plug' welded into position. This entails drilling a series of holes in one panel then welding through them onto the underlying metal, before grinding any proud weld flush. A series of holes was drilled into the repair panel for this, then it was offered into position and pop-riveted at regular intervals to keep both surfaces in close contact.

The strength of this repair panel is important, and so in addition to being MIG 'plug' welded it was also continuously MIG welded around its edge. Ideally, the entire area should be rebuilt with new body panels, although as the problem was discovered six months before an engine-out body restoration could commence, the repair was necessary.

Welding

Achieving clean and strong welds is by no means easy (the spot welder excepted). However strong your desire to complete a restoration without outside help, you should honestly appraise your welding abilities and engage the services of an experienced welder if necessary. Practice especially on typically thin repair body panel steel and try to weld this firmly to thicker section steel. You may find that you either fail to achieve sufficient penetration of the thick metal or burn straight through the thinner section steel. If the joins appear sound, try breaking them to ascertain exactly how fit for duty they really are.

You should be able to find a mobile welder in most areas, and because these people charge by the hour (plus a call-out fee) you should carry out all preparation work and have the panels pop-rivetted or clamped in place when the welder arrives to keep the hours and hence the costs down. You can cut costs further by preparing several separate jobs so that they can all be carried out in a single visit. Using a professional welder will add to the overall expense of the restoration, but by an amount which must be considered insignificant when the consequences of doing the welding yourself and making a mess of it are taken into consideration.

Replacement Body Panels

It is always best, if funds permit, to buy 'original' replacement panels rather than 'pattern' alternatives. However, the price differential between the two can sometimes be so great that the pattern is the only affordable choice. In some cases, a pattern panel may be the only option because the original is no longer manufactured. Buy panels from a Mini specialist (preferably one who also has body shop facilities and who will therefore know that the panel will fit) whenever possible rather than from a general car panel supply business. Sometimes it appears better to fabricate your own panels.

In the UK, the MOT test now stipulates that any repair panels for 'structural' parts of the body must be made of the same gauge steel as the originals. Be very careful when ordering panels that if they are structural, they are of the correct thickness. Any MOT testing station will be able to tell you whether a particular panel is deemed structural for MOT purposes.

A heel board repair panel used by the author highlights some of the problems which can be found with pattern panels. When positioned, this was found to be the wrong shape, to be fabricated from too light a gauge of steel and to have captive nuts welded into the wrong positions behind wrongly-positioned holes! The captive nuts (one of which dropped off) were presumably intended to replace those which were held on the author's car in a separate and strong bracket assembly which lies behind the panel. These nuts do not need replacing. Furthermore, the holes around which the nuts were situated on the pattern panel were in the wrong positions. It would have been easier to simply buy a piece of 16g steel sheet and fabricate these panels.

Happily, not all pattern panels are so poorly made, and the majority appear to either fit straight into position or fit after a minimum of tailoring.

Some body panels which are manufactured from GRP (glass reinforced plastic or fibre glass) are available for the Mini. Because this material can not rust, GRP panels appear to offer a huge advantage over panels pressed from steel. In practice, GRP is not without its problems as a material for body panels.

Firstly, it is flammable. If a GRP panel catches fire, it burns fiercely. Secondly, it does not distort on impact and help absorb the energy of a crash like steel, but shatters. Thirdly, it cannot (of course) be welded into position, but must be fixed using screws, bolts or rivets. GRP panels would not normally be used by restorers.

There is an alternative to buying replacement panels or fabricating repair patches which can save a lot of money, time and effort. Many car breakers will have several Minis from which you can cut pre-shaped repair patch panels or even complete panels if desired. From such an establishment you could salvage a roof pillar, an inner rear wing repair section and, of course, complete body panels. The drawback is that you will usually have to resort to hand tools to cut the desired metal work off the body, and you should take a hacksaw, padsaw, hand drill (with a twist bit to make holes large enough to accommodate the padsaw blade), a bolster chisel and lump hammer, perhaps a Monodex panel cutter and aircraft or metal shears. Alternatively, you may possess or know someone who has a petrol-driven angle grinder. Although crude, this will certainly rip through car body metal in double-quick time! It is a good idea to include a magnet in your inventory, to check that the wing you are salvaging is not 90% GRP and body filler!

Always cut away rather more metal than you require, to allow for the distortions which will occur to the edges because of the rather primitive cutting methods employed.

THE MID-SECTION

The sills of a monocoque-bodied car are immensely important and provide much of the structural strength of the shell in addition to being responsible for maintaining the relative positions of the two subframes. Despite the sills' importance, many 'cowboy' restorers and repairers prefer to cover up sill weaknesses than to remedy them. This is a quite ridiculous attitude since it takes almost as much effort to bodge the job as it does to do it correctly!

There are essentially three components in a Mini sill. The door step at the top is the least prone to rot but is often bodged and filled following side impact. The outer sill panel is easily repaired, but is often

When visiting a breaker's yard, do not spend time trying to salvage panels from cars in this sort of condition. However, cars like these can provide very useful low-cost spares, such as the rear light cluster.

fitted after the original and rotten section has been hammered-inwards instead of being removed, which naturally accelerates future rotting of both the new panel and the inner sill. The inner sill is visible from

163

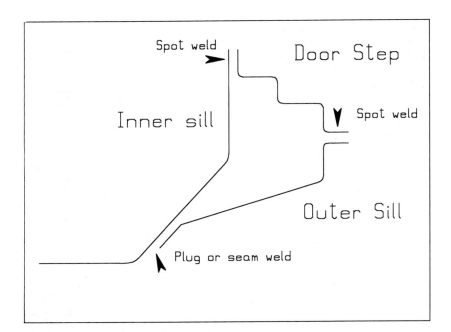

The three panels which make up the sills.

inside the car and any rot should be easily seen by lifting carpets or mats, although it is wise to check clean paintwork with a magnet, just in case a filler 'repair' has at some time been attempted.

When replacing any of the sill members, always firstly trial-fit them using clamps to ensure that they are the correct shape, then tack weld them into position and check that they fit properly by offering up the door before final welding up.

In the case of the outer sill, you may be offered the option of original (narrow) or 'cover' (wide) replacement panels. The original alternative appears to be pressed from considerably thicker steel than that used for the wide cover pattern sill.

Outer sill replacement is a relatively painless job. Firstly, the side of the car must be supported so that no body distortion can occur. This is not very likely, although the consequences of welding a new sill onto a distorted bodyshell are so grave that it pays to take every precaution. The body is best supported by running a sturdy wood or steel beam along the length of the car, and supporting each end of this on axle stands. Be sure to provide full support for the front subframe if the engine is in situ.

With the car firmly supported, either the spot-welded side lip seam has to be parted, or the sill cut immediately underneath the seam using a bolster chisel. The author prefers to part the seam rather than cut underneath it and have a multi-layer seam afterwards as a consequence. The seam can be parted

by using a ⅜″ drill to remove the spot welds (one of the specialised spot weld remover drill attachments is better) then a very sharp bolster chisel to finish off. If the sill has already been replaced at some time in the past, then the seam may be found to be MIG or gas welded along the lip, in which case the welds can be carefully ground down using an angle grinder, then parted with the bolster chisel.

Using a sharp bolster chisel or an angle grinder, cut into the sill about 1″ from its front and rear ends. You may discover that the sill outer section is welded to the outside of the heel board lip along its rear edge. If this proves to be the case, you can simply grind down the bead of weld along rear edge. If the sill end is tucked underneath the heel board lip, the lip may be prised open to allow the remaining portion of the sill to be withdrawn. The main body of the sill can then be folded downwards and back until the bottom welds part, or alternatively grind away or cut around the areas of weld with a sharp bolster chisel, after which the surplus weld may be cleaned up using the angle grinder.

It is by no means uncommon to find a previous sill outer still in position underneath the one you have just removed, and, if so, it is imperative that you remove this too and then clean back all exposed metal inside the structure before covering it with a rust-resistant primer.

Offer up the replacement sill and mark the positions of the edges. The author prefers to tuck the

If the fuel tank and battery are removed and the clutch and brake reservoirs are drained, then one side of the car could be raised quite high to improve access to the sill. With the engine and transmission also removed during a restoration, tipping the car on to its side gives excellent access. Provide plenty of padding for what will be the underside before attempting this. One strong adult can easily tip over a Mini shell.

After drilling out the spot welds, use a sharp bolster chisel to part the seam, taking care not to cut into the door step or lower body side lip. The wearing of stout leather gloves is highly recommended during such processes, because the metal edges left by the bolster chisel can be very sharp. The author, you will note, foolishly does not follow his own advice – and usually has the scars to prove it!

The outer sill may be attached to brackets situated underneath, such as the one being cut around here, which holds the captive nuts into which the rear subframe mounting screws locate.

The sill on this car was welded at its rear edge to the top of the heelboard lip, whereas it might be tucked underneath this lip on other vehicles.

On the author's car, the outer sill had been welded on to the jacking point surround. It was necessary to grind away the welds on the lower edge and ends, then to fold the sill upwards to expose the welds to the jacking point.

The outer sill was welded to the jacking point assembly at these two points. Rather than try to cut or grind away the weld, the author simply bent the panel back and forth until the joints work-hardened and gave way. It was then an easy matter to grind away surplus weld.

In addition to previous outer sill sections, you may well discover sundry pieces of foam rubber lodged in the vicinity. Be sure to remove these plus any other combustible material you may find before you begin welding.

The author decided to tuck the rear end of the outer sill underneath the heelboard lip but, because the replacement sill panel was a wide one, this left the option of either tailoring it around the jacking reinforcer or removing the latter. The easier course of tailoring the outer sill was taken.

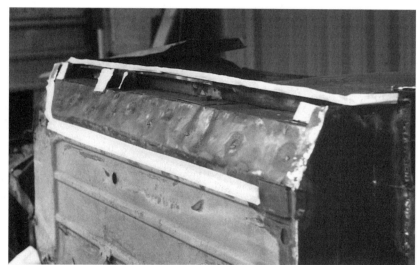

The author uses 'Bonda Prima' within sections which are to be enclosed because of the excellent long-term rust protection it offers. Mask off all surfaces which are to be welded including all brackets and the top and lower lips. At this stage, the author is not concerned about overspray (because the car will eventually be reaprayed and undersealed) and so there is no masking off.

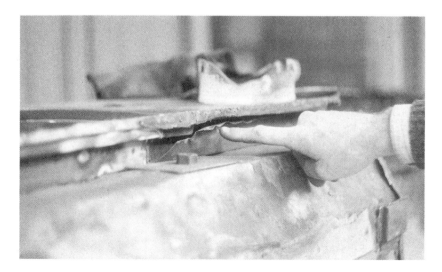

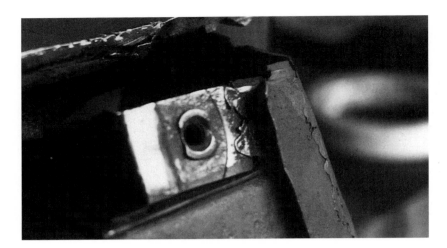

The jacking point bracket surround and the bracket which can be seen ahead of it should both be plug welded to the outer sill for extra strength.

The bracket which contains the captive nuts for the rear subframe mounting bolts should also be welded to the sill. Mask these areas off before applying paint protection to the area which will be covered by the sill.

It is necessary to find the position on the inside of the sill where the various brackets to which it should be plug welded will lie, and there are several methods of achieving this. The cleanest involves lightly sticking the ends of a loop of masking tape on the bracket then offering up the sill. This will hopefully result in the masking tape sticking strongly to the sill. Alternatively, stick masking tape on to the bracket and daub thick paint on this. When the sill is offered up, some of the paint should mark it.

rear edge of the sill underneath the heel board lip for strength and neatness. If a wider sill panel is being fitted, either the rear jacking point reinforcer will have to be removed then refitted (where applicable) or the new section will have to be tailored to fit around it. With the rear of the sill lodged underneath the heel board panel lip, clamp the sill top lip into position and mark the position of the lower edge. The metal to which the sill will join must be clean and sound – rusty metal will not weld properly and thin metal will quickly burn through. Linish bright the metal to which the new sill section will be joined. The author then masks off the steel which is to be welded, and sprays Bonda Prima over the metal which will be contained within the sill structure. It is wise to give

the inside of the structure a thorough cleaning followed by full paint protection if you wish to avoid having to replace the sill again in the not too distant future.

When fitting the new sill it is worth hiring a Spot welder for the side seam, because this will give a stronger join with less chance of burning-through than MIG welding. The lower edge should be MIG or gas welded; in either case, tack the panel into position before joining the tacks up with continuous runs of weld.

The replacement sill may not have a hole for the jacking point, in which case one should be cut. It may be possible to establish the correct position for the hole by placing the old sill on top of the new section

The author drilled three plug weld holes for the jacking point surround, plus another for the bracket adjacent to it. The extra hole in the middle is a pilot hole which can later be enlarged to the square section of the jacking bracket underneath.

The more plug welds you incorporate, the stronger the shell will be. Furthermore, welding the outer sill to these brackets also strengthens them. Practice plug welding on scrap metal before trying it on the car. It is important that you establish the correct Mig settings to achieve proper penetration into the lower surface, otherwise the weld will be very weak and useless.

169

and scribing through, although if the old sill may be too badly damaged for this after removal. The author stuck masking tape to the jacking point surround and daubed old congealed paint on this. When the new sill was offered up, the paint adhered to it and showed the approximate position for the jacking point. Initially, a single ⅜″ hole was drilled into the middle of this, and it was enlarged using needle files after the welding had been carried out. Holes should be drilled around the jacking point area of the sill, so that you can plug weld the sill onto the flat faces of the jacking point structure; many people omit this, despite the fact that doing so must weaken the structure. Using the paint marking method just outlined, the positions for these holes will already be established.

The exact areas to be welded at the sill ends will vary according to whether an original or wide pattern replacement panel has been chosen. It is of course imperative that both ends are welded onto sound metal.

With the door step removed, take the opportunity to clean the newly revealed metal and apply paint protection before going any further. You may discover that the outer sill section was not welded on to the jacking point reinforcer when previously replaced, so take this opportunity to weld the two together.

The old door step was actually in three pieces! A side impact had been hastily 'repaired' by straightening out the two outer sections as far as possible, then by letting in a short middle section. The result was so poorly aligned and bent that filler had been very thickly applied to make it appear respectable. Note that even with spot welding, heat distortion can occur, which the author has had to remedy with a shallow run of filler.

Door step

The door step will not usually have corroded except in the most rotten of shells, and it is most often replaced following either side impact or the discovery of previously bodged attempts at repairing or more usually camouflaging the same!

Repair sections are available, cheap, and fairly easy to fit. Firstly support the car as detailed previously, then, using either a sharp bolster chisel, an angle grinder or preferably a combination of these, cut into the section at each end of the repair, taking care to cut at 90 degrees to the body and firstly offering up the replacement panel to ensure that not too much metal is cut away.

The seams should be spot welded (sometimes a previous repairer will have MIG or gas welded them), and they should be parted using either a drill, a proprietary spot weld remover drill accessory (the recommended tool) and a bolster chisel. When the chisel is used take care not to distort or cut into the top edge of the inner sill. An angle grinder may alternatively be used instead of a spot weld remover or drill twist bit. It can be used to thin the metal within the spot welds on the waste outer sill side, after which the seam is far more easily parted using a bolster chisel.

Door step repair panels are usually longer than necessary, and have to be cut down to suit. Offer the repair section up and then mark and cut it to length. It is best to butt join the old and the new metal using a MIG or gas welder, then to clean up proud weld with an angle grinder. The top and side seams should, if possible, be spot welded for strength, although it is possible to MIG or gas weld these if a spot welder is not available. If MIG or gas has to be used, plug welding will give a stronger and neater result than merely welding along the seam.

An alternative door step panel incorporating an extension which runs to the rear wheelarch is available, and should be used if the body side is damaged through impact or if it is corroded. When fitting these, it is best to use a joddler on the top edge of the extension to disguise the join on the rear body panel.

Inner Sill

The inner sill member is actually the outer edge of the floorpan. Because the inner sill is more difficult to replace than the outer panel, it is often patch repaired. This is simply a matter of cutting out the corroded metal and welding in new, and can give perfectly acceptable results provided that the corrosion is not too extensive and that adjacent rust is removed and the metal properly rust-primed. It is not necessary to remove the outer sill panel if this is sound. It is preferable to cut out a section extending from the centre cross member to either the front inner wing or the B post, and to replace this with either a bought in or home-made panel. As the repair panel will be a plain rectangle with a single fold in the centre and folded flanges for attachment to the cross member, it is easily fabricated.

If the entire panel is rotten, then replacement is necessary. Firstly, remove the outer sill as already described. Then offer the replacement inner sill panel up and mark around its edge before carefully cutting the old metal away, leaving an area of overlap (which can be ground or cut back later if necessary).

A certain amount of tailoring will often prove necessary in order to fit the new inner sill, and the ends may have to be folded to fit, depending on the individual replacement panel. More often than not, the panel will not have a seatbelt mounting, so that the old one must be cut out and welded into the new panel.

When fitting the inner sill, tack weld it to begin with and then tack, pop-rivet or preferably clamp the outer sill panel and door step into position. Check that everything fits correctly (offer the door into position for this) and weld only when you are satisfied that everything aligns correctly.

Heel board panel

The heel board panel which runs across the width of the car is welded to a bracket at each end which contains captive nuts which hold the front end fixings of the rear subframe, and it is vital that the panel is sound. Being covered by the subframe, rust is almost inevitable and also strikes, naturally, from within the sill structure. It is the ends which usually rot out and repair sections are available for this. In order to repair or replace this panel, the subframe must firstly be removed (See Chapter 4).

To examine the panel ends properly, clean them back to bare metal. If they have small rust holes then they may be patched although they should preferably be cut out and replaced. Check current legislation

LEFT *This repair panel did not even fit where it touched. Most importantly, there was no lip to fit over the sills, so that the original lip had to be retained. The panel had to be extensively re-shaped before it would come anywhere close to fitting and the captive nuts had to be removed.*

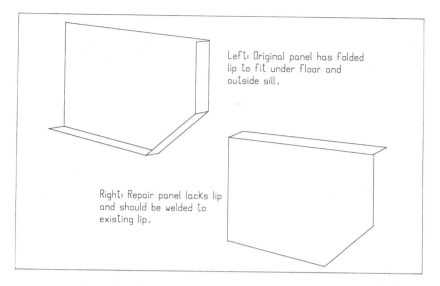

Left: Original panel has folded lip to fit under floor and outside sill.

Right: Repair panel lacks lip and should be welded to existing lip.

RIGHT *The lip at the rear of the jacking point reinforcer was bent up to allow the heelboard repair panel to slide underneath. It was them clamped firmly into position, and welded on to the original heelboard lip, side and the seat base. It is advisable to draw together the seat base and the top lip of the repair panel, using pop rivets, prior to welding.*

before patching.

The repair panel which the author attempted to fit bore scant resemblance to the original. There was no lip to fit underneath the sill, the holes for the subframe mounts were drilled in the wrong places, the captive nuts welded to the panel (which proved superfluous and one of which dropped off anyway) were consequently wrongly positioned, and the general shape was wrong. It would have been far simpler to fabricate a repair panel out of 16g steel sheet! It would in fact have been far better to replace the whole heelboard panel.

The author decided to retain the lip from the original heel board panel, but rather than grind the

edge away and have to perform a tricky weld on the resultant 90 degree joint, he cut into the rear face of the existing panel ½" from the edge, cleaned and painted the metal then hammered this inwards so that the repair panel rested on top of it. The subframe mounting brackets give a clearance between the heel board panel and subframe, so that it does not matter too much if the repair panel sits slightly proud of the position of the original, provided that the actual mounting point part of the panel is in the original position.

If the replacement panels have captive nuts welded on and the original captive nuts are still in situ held within a fabricated bracket (which is not rotten), then it will be better to remove the captive nuts from the new panel and use the existing ones. At the top of the repair panel was a flat lip which ran backwards under the seat base. This may be welded along its edges, although greater strength will result if the seat base has holes drilled into it for plug welding onto the heel board repair panel.

Floor Repairs

Replacement floor panels are generally available for the Mini. The front footwell panels should run from the toe board to the cross member, with a flange for welding to the latter. The inside edge butts against the centre tunnel, and the outer edge may extend far enough to form the inner sill or be shorter and have to be joined to it.

The rear floor panel butts against the centre cross member and the heelboard panel, and should be shaped ahead of the B post in the same profile as the front footwell panel.

Most DIY restorers will be more likely to patch repair floor rust than replace an entire panel, which is arguably the province of the professional body shop. During a complete engine-out body restoration, however, many people will wish to renew entire panels rather than patch repair them. Generally, the work will follow the same basic procedures used in the fitting of any panel, offering the new panel up to find the cutting lines, then cutting out the old and welding in the new. Work on one floor section at a time. The centre tunnel and especially the toe board must be held firmly in the correct positions before any welding takes place. The toe board has the front subframe rear mounting points attached, and its positioning is critical.

Toe Board

It is vital that the toe board of the Mini is strong, because not only the front subframe rear mounts but also the steering column mounts are situated on it.

This is a heavy duty panel which is not particularly prone to rusting to the point at which it is substantially weakened. Most work concerning the toe board will be as a result of impact damage as the car is driven over a rock or similar obstacle.

A dented toe board can be straightened using a hammer and dolly. When attempting this work, take

careful measurements forwards from the heel board to ensure that both subframe mounting points are an equal distance forwards from the heel board.

The toe board is available as a replacement panel, though few amateur restorers are likely to replace this panel because if the toe board has rotted then the more rust-prone flitch panels, floor panels, sills, A posts etc will probably also have rotted and a jig will become a necessity for so major a rebuild.

FRONT END BODYWORK

The construction of the front end of the Mini is extremely simple compared to that of many other cars by virtue of the fact that stresses and weight are taken initially by the subframe, whereas on many other cars they have to be taken by complicated integral chassis member structures. This does not, however, make the business of a total front-end Mini build any easier.

Problems arise in trying to get all the panels lined up correctly. The front end assembly basically consists of the two flitch panels (engine bay sides) and the front panel, to which the flitch panels and wings are joined. The shape of the front end of the car is determined when the flitch and front panels are welded into position.

It is imperative that the front subframe is fitted at its top and rear mounts and that its weight is supported adequately whilst the flitch and front panels are lined up prior to welding, because the front subframe mountings will give the correct position for the front panel. A total front-end rebuild will not always be necessary, however, and the various tasks inherent in this will be tackled separately within this chapter.

Because the front subframe is used to determine the correct positions of panels during a front end rebuild, it is vital that it is itself correctly positioned before any other work commences. Check the measurements detailed in Chapter 2. The rubber subframe mountings used on later cars have a certain amount of 'give'. The main bulkhead cross member mountings can appear to fit properly, even if the rear (toe board) mountings are not true. On the author's car one of the rear mountings was about ⅛" further forwards than the other (over-corrected accident damage), so that the subframe was out of true when

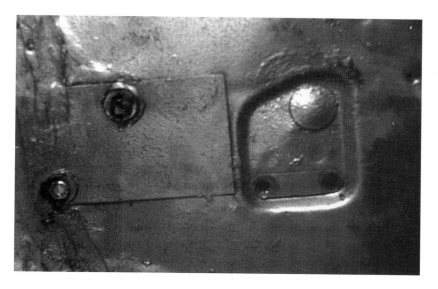

The toe board on the author's car was very obviously crumpled. The car had probably been driven off-road and hit a rock. The front end of the car had been rebuilt using the now misaligned subframe as a guide, and the front was as a consequence out of true.

fitted and one wheel was ⅓″ further forwards relative to the bodywork than the other! The two top mountings had so much 'give' thanks to their rubber inserts that they fitted without any problems to indicate the misalignment of the rear mountings. Although the rear mountings are also rubber and hence have some 'give' in them, they appear to have less potential movement than the top bulkhead cross member mountings.

Front wing removal and replacement

If you are the first person to remove the front wing of a particular Mini, then life can be fairly straightforward, because you will be dealing with neat spot welds which can easily be drilled out. On most older examples of the car, however, the wing will have been replaced at some time in the past, and often it will have been secured in place using plug welds along its joints with the A panel and the flitch panel. In such instances, the plug welds can prove so difficult to deal with that it could prove necessary to scrap the front wing in order to save a perfectly salvagable flitch panel or A panel.

The wing and the A panel are welded together along the visible outer lip seam. Originally this join will have been spot welded, and it can thus quite easily be parted using a spot weld remover. Many of the older examples of Minis which have previously been repaired, however, will have this seam MIG or gas welded, and in this case the join can prove difficult to part without risking damage to the lips of one or both panels. If you are really unlucky then the seam will be plug welded, the difficulties of dealing with which have already been highlighted. Remove the seam trim using a screwdriver or similar to lever it off, then examine the seam. If it is crudely MIG (or even Arc) welded, then it may pay to consider cutting into the A panel, scrapping and replacing this, in order to save the far more expensive to replace wing. It is much easier to part and clean up even the crudest seam or plug welded lip when the panel has been removed from the car.

At the front, the wing is joined to the front panel by an inwards-pointing lip seam. Originally, this will have been spot welded and it can prove difficult to part due to the restricted access, although most previously repaired examples will be gas or MIG welded along the lip and easily ground down then parted. The welds between the headlight surround and wing should be similarly dealt with.

The front wing is joined to the flitch panel along the latter's top edge, and again, the join would have originally have been neatly spot welded and would be easy to part, but may well prove on your car to have been 'plug' welded with a MIG or gas welder. On the author's car it appeared to have been plug welded with an Arc welder! Instead of having a neat circular join to drill out, you can be faced with an irregularly-shaped lump of excess weld which has to be ground right down before the panels can be parted. There is a great deal of difference here between the standard Mini and the Clubman. On the standard shell there is a horizontal lip on the flitch panel and the wing is welded down onto this, giving fair accessibility. On

175

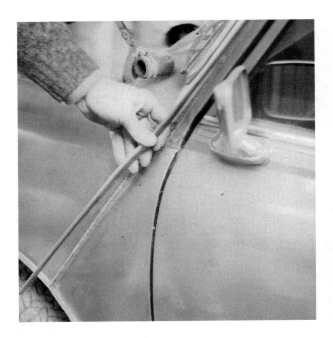

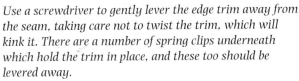

Use a screwdriver to gently lever the edge trim away from the seam, taking care not to twist the trim, which will kink it. There are a number of spring clips underneath which hold the trim in place, and these too should be levered away.

Grinding down a lip welded seam. Take great care not to grind too deeply into the seam, unless, that is, you intend to 'de-seam' the car! This was and still is a very popular modification to the car, which gives it a much softer and more rounded look liked by many. To de-seam the car you simply cut away the various seams and butt join them afterwards. Because looks are of paramount importance in such work, continuous gas or MIG welding is not a good idea because it is liable to buckle the panels. The author has seen flanges simply battered inwards and flushed over with filler.

the Clubman, the joining panels are vertical and much more difficult to get at to the extent that it is not possible to get an angle grinding wheel to a number of these welds, and one or other of the panels may have to be scrapped, or have its lip extensively repaired following removal.

Many restored Minis are spoiled by poorly fitted front wings. The area between the rear concave curve of the wing and the mating convex curve of the top shroud seems to cause the most problems. Begin by clamping the wing so that the line between it and the top shroud is correct. Pay attention to getting the rear of the wing at the correct height; if it is slightly too low then it does not look too bad, although if it is too high (which the author has seen) then it looks awful. Then clamp the front seams and A panel seam, and try the bonnet fit. If the A panel is also being replaced, offer up the two together and keep on adjusting them until the lines are all acceptable before commencing welding.

The usual DIY method of fixing wings along the top (flitch panel) seam, at the front seam and to the A panel is plug welding, which gives a combination of

strength and neatness. Unfortunately, as already stated it can be very difficult to subsequently remove a plug-welded wing because there will be insufficient room to enable an angle grinder to be used, so ensure that full rust-proofing techniques are applied so that the panels do not need replacing for a long time!

A Panel

Two quite different A panel assemblies were fitted to Minis. Early cars with external door hinges had an inner and an outer A panel, whereas later cars with internal hinges were fitted with only the outer panel. With early cars, cut both the inner and outer A panels away from the door frame using a sharp bolster chisel or preferably an air chisel, then clean up

This corner section can be extremely tricky to deal with if it has been seam welded, because there is insufficient room to get an angle grinder to the actual weld. It may prove necessary to resort to a sharp bolster chisel and hammer.

This run of plug welds on a Clubman shell proved very awkward to deal with, even though the engine had been removed from the car by this stage. On the standard Mini, the flitch panel has a horizontal lip welded to the wing and the welds are far easier to get at.

The front wing removed. On the standard Mini shell, the front panel extends the full width of the car, forming, in effect, the bottom sections of the front wings. The ends of the panel and more particularly the curved seam between it and the wing are very prone to rot. Happily, repair end sections are available. Alternatively, smaller repair sections may be fabricated and butt welded in.

In this restoration, both the A panel and the top shroud are receiving attention. The A panel is being replaced and the top shroud is having an end repair section fitted. It is necessary to clamp both of these panels plus the wing into position before any are welded in, to ensure that the lines as a whole will be correct when the job is finished.

the rear edges where the new panels will join. Because the panels house the door hinges, they should be trial fitted with the wings, door and hinges in situ, ensuring that the gaps around the door are even. Clamp both the wing (if removed) and the A panel into position then fit the door and adjust the panels until the door sits correctly. The outer A panel may now be tack welded into the correct position and the inner panel bolted to it.

Few people will have access to the correct spot welder attachments necessary for welding on A panels, and so plug welding is the recommended alternative.

Later cars have just a single outer A panel which wraps around the door post flange at the rear. The panel may be fixed to the flange with spot welds or more commonly with plug welds. The flange may prove to be corroded, so replace it if necessary with a panel cut preferably from 16g steel.

Some pattern A panels are very poorly shaped, and it is vital that trial fitting should be carried out with the wing in position and firmly clamped to the A panel flange, and also with the bonnet in position. The replacement panel should already have a flange, bent at 90 degrees, ready to fold over the door post flange. It is best to begin bending this over a former before attempting to fit it, but do check that its line matches that of the door post flange first. Bending the flange can easily knock the A panel out of shape, so be prepared to have to partially straighten the flange back out and have another go. It is a good idea to use two or three plug welds to firmly secure the A panel to the door post flange.

Top shroud repair

The top shroud rots out at its ends, at the bases of the roof pillars. Repair panels are widely available and are not too difficult to fit, provided that they are reasonably well made. The example which the author purchased naturally left a little to be desired. The flange which should be deep enough to grip the windscreen glazing rubber was just ¼" deep at one end, whereas it should be ⅜" deep to fill the ⅜" groove in the glazing seal. This was acceptable in this case because the inner lip to which the panel was to be welded was of the required depth. The profile of the roof pillar base section did not exactly match that of the car's roof pillar and had to be dressed slightly to fit. Furthermore, the panel appeared to be distorted

(which might have occured during transit and storage), and could only be made to fit under tensioning from four mole wrenches. After being left clamped into position for some time, however, the panel adopted more or less the correct shape.

The windscreen and front wing, plus any flammable trim from the area and the loom (nearside pillar only) have to be removed before the work can commence. Offer the repair panel up, check that it is properly aligned with the existing panels then clamp it very firmly and scribe along its edges to find the cutting lines. Remove the panel, then clamp it into position again to ensure that the cutting lines remain in the same place, if they do not then the panel is probably poorly shaped and could prove difficult to fit. Try forcing and clamping it into the correct position and leaving it there overnight. The old metal should be cut out with a hacksaw and padsaw, and great care has to be taken to ensure that the cuts are really straight. The author found access so restricted for a padsaw that he opted to use the angle grinder with a cutting disc. If the first cuts are made well within the area to be removed, the edges can then carefully be ground back to the correct positions.

The seams along the inside of the pillar and the windscreen lip are spot welded and may be parted easily after the welds have been drilled out; the outer pillar edge is also spot welded, but on the author's car the seam was so badly marked that the actual welds could not be found even after all paintwork was cleaned from the surface. The other seams had by then been parted, and so the author simply bent the panel back and forth until the steel work hardened at the remaining join and parted. Surplus metal was then ground from the pillar. When parting these joins take care not to distort the metal which is to remain.

The closing panel underneath the top shroud end may be replaced at the same time if desired, and is again cut out with a bolster chisel or the angle grinder. Before hacking out metal, make a cardboard template for the replacement closing panel, because its shape is important to the support of the shroud end and thus to the positioning of the wing. If you are able to remove the old closing panel reasonably intact, hammer it flat and use it as a template. There will usually be quite an amount of rust to clean up before the panel can be replaced.

Replacing the closing panel with a panel you fabricate yourself allows you to reshape it very slightly if necessary in order to try and gain a slightly more snug fit between the top shroud and the

179

The roof pillar section of the repair panel had a profile which was slightly different to that of the car's pillar, but in practice it proved an easy matter to dress it carefully to fit. When welded in, there was no discernible step between the two.

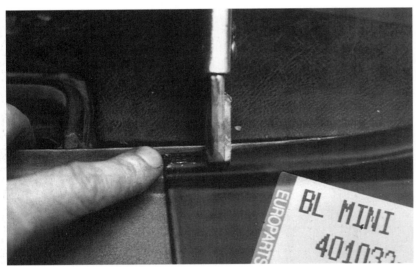

The lip which fits into the glazing rubber on the repair panel was only ¼" deep, whereas it should really have been ⅜" deep. However, the existing inner lip possessed the necessary depth, so no real problems were encountered here.

After being clamped into position overnight, the repair panel had adopted the correct shape, and the author was able to begin marking out cutting lines.

Brutal though it may appear, the angle grinder with a cutting disc fitted saves a lot of tricky and tiring work with hacksaws and pad saws. If you opt to use the angle grinder, do try to avoid cutting into the underlying panels (the author managed to cut two neat slots).

With the old top shroud panel end cut away, expect to find a considerable expanse of rusted steel underneath. The closing panel will normally be rotten and require replacement, but clean up every surface with a cup brush in the angle grinder or electric drill, and probe for thin metal, which should be cut out and patch repaired.

Anticipate finding the worst rot in the metal to which the closing panel was joined.

If you hammer the remains of the old closing panel flat (TOP) then this will serve as a template for the replacement. Cut this from 20g or thicker steel, then shape it as best you can over a block of wood. It may pay to make 'V' cuts in the outer edge to allow it to be folded without distorting the panel too much. Drill holes on the panel (ABOVE) in preparation for plug welding it into position.

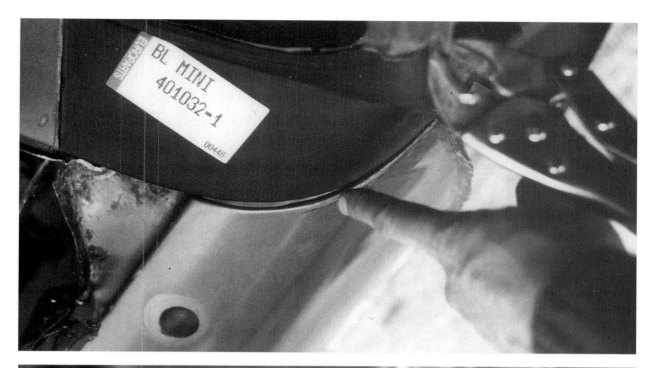

With both the closing panel and shroud repair panel clamped into position, offer up the wing (TOP) and check for a gap in between the two. If too large a gap exists, you can try reshaping the shroud rim (or possibly the wing), or repositioning one or both slightly. When the position has been established and the gap is satisfactory, tack the closing panel into position (ABOVE).

Clamp the top shroud repair panel firmly into position before tack welding the butt joints. Check alignment before further welding whilst you still have the chance to move the panel if necessary.

Plug weld the top and side seams, followed by the join with the closing panel. Then plug weld the closing panel finally into position.

Grind down the excess weld from the plug welds if you wish to at this stage (the job looks a lot better and makes you feel happier!), and run continuous weld between the tack welds at the butt joints.

Very carefully grind down proud weld from the butt joints. One slip at this stage could prove to have dire consequences!

Welding heat had caused the top shroud horizontal surface to buckle slightly, so that it had to be tapped inwards and flushed over with body filler. You can clean off the metal to be filled and also key it for the filler by using a cup brush in an angle grinder.

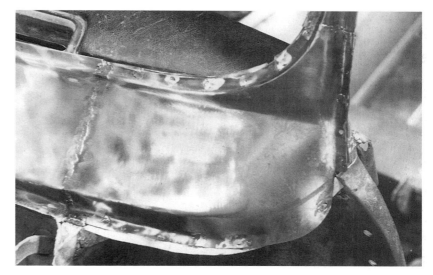

After all this work, it would be a crime to let rusting start again, so prime the metal and filler immediately you have finished sanding the latter. Remember that body filler is porous, and if this is allowed to soak up the slightest amount of moisture then that moisture will remain trapped between the filler and the metal – rusting will be rapid and inevitable.

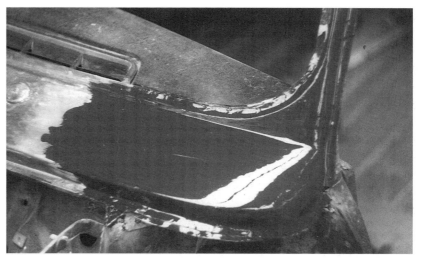

concave face of the wing. This should only prove necessary if the replacement top shroud panel is a poor fit. Clamp both the top shroud panel and the closing panel into position, then temporarily offer the wing into position to check that it fits correctly before welding in the closing panel using plug welds. Clean all metal to be joined and drill holes into the lips of the repair top shroud panel for plug welding.

Clamp the shroud repair panel firmly at the windscreen lip, the side lip and against the closing panel, then check that the edges are in line with those of the top shroud panel and pillar, and that a small gap exists between them for the weld. There is no harm in temporarily offering the wing into position just as a final pre-welding check. Tack the top shroud and pillar butt joints and check alignment before plug welding the panel to the seam lips. The tack welds may now be joined with continuous runs of weld. On the car in the photographs, welding heat caused the top shroud panel and repair panel to buckle upwards. They were carefully tapped down to form a concave surface which was flushed over with body filler.

Flitch panels

Full replacement flitch panels may not be available for your car, so obtain a part panel and measure to find cutting lines. The nearside repair panel will probably not have the radiator shroud fitted, and so this should be cut from the old panel and welded into position before the new panel is fitted.

It is vital that the front subframe is in position when the flitch panels are replaced, because the front subframe mountings give you the position of the flitch panels. Subframes can move, however, so before you cut away the old flitch panels, take diagonal measurements from the bulkhead sides to the subframe front mountings to ensure that it is true.

Remove the damper top mounting bracket. The metal behind this is a key area for rot and, if the repair panel does not extend far enough to cover this, fabricate and weld in a repair panel. If the repair section comes far enough backwards, drill out the spot welds from the cross member to flitch panel bracket. Scribe your cutting line and cut away the old flitch panel, allowing an overlap for the join. The best method of joining on the repair section is to use a joddler to place a step in the edge, then to continuously seam weld it both inside and out. The flitch panels are now regarded as structural for purposes of the UK MOT test, and plug welding, whilst previously acceptable, will probably now fail the test. Before welding in the panel, however, it wise to offer up and clamp the front panel, wing and bonnet, to ensure that the lines are correct.

REAR BODYWORK

The rear suspension and brake components are carried on the subframe. It is hence vital that any areas of bodywork to which the subframe is attached are very sound.

Chapter 4 details the removal of the subframe and other ancilliaries from the rear of the car. In addition to these, major restoration work in this area should be preceded by the removal of the light clusters and any materials which could ignite during welding operations, including, preferably, the rear seat base and back. The battery, fuel tank, line and (where fitted) electric fuel pump MUST be removed.

Battery box replacement

The battery box is very prone to rot out almost completely at the base. This is hardly surprising, given that the interior can suffer acid attack from the battery and that the exterior is slung underneath the car where it is subjected to mud, water, salt from the road and stone chips to help expose bare metal. Some people drop a shelf into the rotten bottom of the battery box in the forlorn hope that this will support the battery even if the base of the compartment is almost rusted out. Do not be tempted to try this, because a good bump in the road can break whatever is left of the original battery box base and your battery is unlikely to survive dropping out of its compartment and being dragged along the road.

This is not a difficult component to replace, as long as a degree of care is taken. Before starting, remove the boot lid and the fuel tank, then push the fuel pipe down and out of the boot compartment. Firstly, remove the old box. This can be achieved by drilling out the spot welds (these may be difficult to locate until the paint is cleared off the top flange), by using a spot weld remover (recommended), by grinding the edge of the flange and welding the new

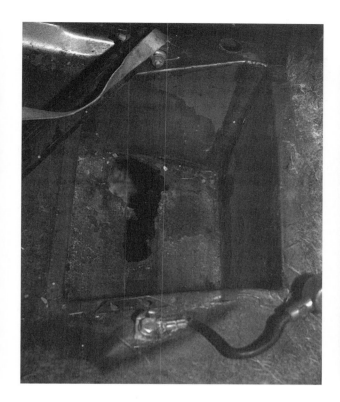

This battery box has not yet reached the stage at which the battery is liable to drop out, yet another winter could see it reach that stage. In the UK, battery security is an MOT test failure and a tester could probably justifiably fail the car to which this battery box is fitted.

Not quite the prettiest way to deal with spot welds, but when access and light are poor this gets the job done and gives far neater results than merely grinding away at the edge of the old box and having a three layered joint as a result.

When the spot welds have been ground down, a sharp bolster chisel and hammer may sometimes prove necessary to part some sections of the original join.

The old battery box may foul the boot edges and be very difficult to lift out. After struggling trying to remove the old battery box for some time, the author hit upon the idea of letting the trolley jack do the hard work for him.

The old battery box may look pitiful in this state, but the four sides are sound metal and will come in very useful for fabricating sundry repair panels. It would have been possible to repair this battery box by welding on a new floor section. Because the car was shortly to be rolled over on to its side for sill repair such work would not be difficult. However, replacement battery boxes cost very little, and most people will opt for replacement.

flange on top to produce a three-layered joint (which can look scruffy) or by grinding down the top flange spot welds and then finally parting them using a sharp bolster chisel.

When all spot welds have been removed, the box may prove difficult to raise, in which case a trolley jack and block of wood can be placed underneath and the battery box easily raised upwards. Using a small hammer and a dolly, true up the edges in the boot floor so that the lip of the new battery box can sit properly for welding.

This is not a structurally important section and in theory it could be pop riveted into position. However, most people will elect to plug weld it. After drilling a series of holes in the battery box lip, clean

Note the paint protection given to the new battery box floor. The boot floor edges have been dressed so that the battery box lip sits correctly. At this stage the two should be held tightly together with pop rivets then plug welded.

the lip underside and the boot floor edge. Use plenty of pop rivets to draw the new battery box lip down firmly onto the boot floor. After plug welding, drill out the pop rivets and weld up their holes.

It makes sense to apply the most thorough rust-proofing techniques to the new battery box if you do not wish to have to carry out the job again in the none-too-distant future.

Body side/Rear wing

The rear side panel, often referred to as the outer rear wing panel, usually rots along its lower edge, and this may be dealt with using a doorstep/lower rear body side panel or half body side repair panel, or a full rear half body side panel. Doorstep replacement is described in the relevant section of this chapter. When fitting the door step repair panel which incorporates the lower body side section, it is simply a matter of offering up the panel to find a cutting line, making the cut just underneath this to allow an overlap and parting the lip along the bottom and rear of the panel, joddling the top edge of the repair section and welding it in. Use pop rivets to hold the two flat areas tightly together during welding.

The half body side (a pattern panel) and full body side (genuine BL) are rather more difficult to fit, and the use of a spot welder is recommended. In the case of the half panel, remove the trim from the rear seam, then offer the panel up to find the cutting lines at the roof pillars. When you make the cuts in the pillars, allow a small overlap which may be ground down at a later stage to ensure a perfect butt fit. The seams at the base and rear of the panel may now be parted, drilling out spot welds or grinding away MIG welds as appropriate.

With the half panel off, take the opportunity to carry out any remedial work to the B post, the inner wing or the base of the storage compartment at the side of the rear seat.

Clamp the new panel into place after grinding the pillar edges to exactly the right level. Fit the door to check that the lines are correct, and ensure that all seams are cleaned before welding. Ideally, a spot welder (with an assortment of extension arms and swan-neck electrodes) should be used for the lip joints. If this is not available, then drill holes in the lip of the new panel and plug weld using a MIG. In either instance, the lips to which the new panel is joined should be clean and very sound.

The roof pillar butt joints must either be MIG or gas welded and the surplus weld ground down and finished off with body filler.

Inner wing

The inner rear wing is joined to the outer wing and the boot floor by welded lip seams, and it is overlap welded to the seat base and back and to the subframe rear mounting strengthening bracket. It is little wonder that many people prefer to patch repair this panel than to replace it.

A patch repair can be very sound, but will usually show within the boot. It is neater to cut a hole around the area of rot and to butt weld in an insert, the shape of which can be very accurately determined using a cardboard template. All traces of underseal should be removed from the vicinity prior to the commencement of welding. There are small clamps commercially available to hold butt joins together during welding operations (Frost Inter-grips); alternatively, use masking tape to hold the repair section in position then tack it to hold it firm, stopping to true it up after each tack is applied. The tacks may eventually be joined with continuous runs.

Inner rear wing replacement is one of those jobs best tackled by a competent professional workshop. If you wish to carry out the work yourself, try to arrange to have an assistant handy to help in aligning the various panels to which the inner rear wing panel is joined. It is vital that the panel is very strongly welded into position, because it holds the top damper fitting and is subjected to great strain when the car is on the move. Your welding skills must thus be first class. Begin by parting the lip joints to the boot floor and the outer wing. Cut into the old panel rather then trying to part the various lap joints straight away. With the bulk of the panel removed thus, access to deal with these joints will be much better.

With all adjoining metal surfaces cleaned and drilled for plug welding, offer up the replacement panel and clamp it at its outer lip join with the body side and carefully check its positioning. The joins with the boot floor, seat back and base will have to be drawn tightly together using pop rivets. Check that the panel sits properly against the heel board panel top, and that it is not trying to pull the body side out of shape.

In most instances, it will prove best to plug weld most of the joints, seam welding where appropriate.

189

Valance

The rear valance is available as a complete repair panel. Rusting, however, is usually localised in the area immediately above the exhaust tail pipe and in the closing panels at either end. You can therefore usually preserve the existing valance by dealing with

The closing panel has been cut out and the previously enclosed metal treated with rust-resistant primer. The edges now have to be cleaned bright for welding.
The closing panel is very easy to fabricate out of 20g steel. Be sure to apply plenty of paint protection before welding it in position.

just these specific areas.

The closing panels are spot welded into position, and if possible, the spot welds should be drilled out and the seams parted. If the welds cannot be located because the panel is too badly rusted, use an angle grinder. The enclosed area under the closing panel is prone to rust, so take the opportunity to clean the metal and treat with a rust-resistant primer. The closing panel is easy to fabricate. Trace the shape of the curved edge onto sheet steel, then measure to find exact locations of the edges. The top edge can be bent over at 90 degrees as in the photograph. Drill holes around the edge for plug welding if a spot welder is not available.

INTERIOR AND FITTINGS

The following assumes that the engine/gearbox unit has been removed from the car. If not, then certain wires and cables will have to be removed before some of the interior fixtures and fittings can be removed.

Carpets

The carpets fitted in many older examples of the Mini will often be found to be glued into position. This is a quick and convenient method of fixing carpets but it is also an extremely convenient method of hiding both rot and GRP/bodyfiller repair from the prying eyes of the potential purchaser and/or MOT tester! Removal of glued-in cheap carpeting will normally result in its destruction.

It is not too difficult to tailor carpet from the roll to fit the Mini, although kits of pre-shaped carpet pieces are available, often with bound edging which prevents the edges from fraying. In addition, the carpet kits should also have heel pads, which prevent your carpet from wearing out in next to no time. Rather than glue these down, it is better to obtain a number of proper stud-type fixings, which hold the carpet in place but which also allow it to be removed if necessary for drying out or to allow access for various repair jobs to be carried out. The studs are fitted to the panelling by self-tapping screws, and the female components are pressed into the carpet and their teeth bent over to hold them in place.

Sound deadening material is usually found on the rear faces of the wheelarch panel and bulkhead, where they protrude into the interior of the car. This should be held by a number of folding metal tabs, although some people again prefer to use glue. Worse, many glue the carpet on top of the sound deadening material. If the removal of glued-in carpets rips the sound deadening material to pieces then it is well worth replacing, because it does cut down on tyre and engine/transmission noise within the car.

Headlining and Windscreens

The headlining fits underneath the front and rear windscreen glazing rubbers, so that the windscreens must be removed before the headlining can come out. For this reason they are both dealt with in the same section, starting with the windscreens.

It helps to have an assistant during windscreen removal, although one person can accomplish it alone, with care. To remove either the front or the rear screen, begin by lifting one of the ends of the filler strip gently using a screwdriver, then place the screwdriver shaft under the strip at ninety degrees to

it and push it gently forwards to force the strip out of the groove in the glazing strip. Take care not to buckle the strip as it comes out of the screen corners.

Place plenty of padding on the bonnet (just in case the screen pops out suddenly) and carefully ease one of the top corners of the screen out of the glazing strip. Push the screen gently from inside the car whilst easing the glazing rubber lip away from the edge of the glass on the outside. When the corner is free, place a small wooden wedge or similar behind the glass to prevent it from popping back in, then gently work your way along the top of the glass, easing back the glazing rubber lip then pulling a thin wooden wedge behind it to free the glass from the rubber.

Take great care when dealing with the opposite top corner of the glazing rubber, because laminated glass and even toughened glass can crack if subjected to twisting forces (laminated glass is more prone to this). When the entire top of the glass is free of the glazing strip, repeat the process down each side, then carefully lift the glass from the bottom channel of the glazing rubber. The rubber may stick to the glass, but

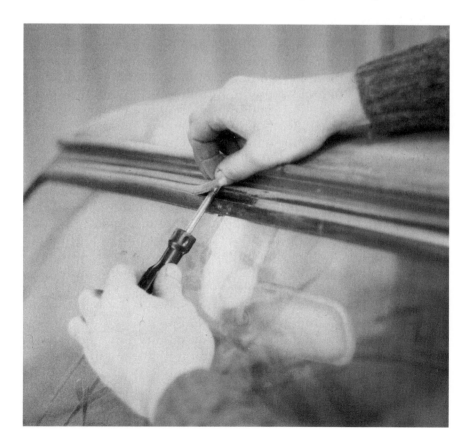

It is probably easier to refit the existing glazing rubber trim than to fit a new length of trim. Using a screwdriver as shown, or alternatively a length of ⅜" rod, to lift the trim will enable it to be removed without getting kinked.

191

An old continental quilt is ideal for padding the bonnet prior to windscreen removal. Should you drop the screen, this will give it a (hopefully) soft landing, and if everything goes according to plan, you can lay the screen down on the quilt.

Considering how difficult it can be to fit a windscreen, the things can be very reluctant to come out and if you do not use a wooden wedge as photographed or something similar you can find the glass popping back in to the glazing seal rubber of its own accord.

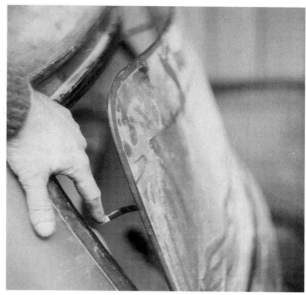

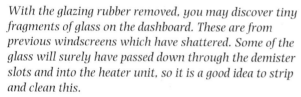

With the glazing rubber removed, you may discover tiny fragments of glass on the dashboard. These are from previous windscreens which have shattered. Some of the glass will surely have passed down through the demister slots and into the heater unit, so it is a good idea to strip and clean this.

Be sure to disconnect the wires if your rear screen is fitted with a demister. The glazing rubber on this car was badly perished and so the lip over the screen was cut away rather than eased over the glass. This makes removal much easier.

it may be gently eased off and the glass lifted away.

Removal of the rear screen is basically the same, although the wires to the heater element must of course be removed firstly, and you cannot arrange a 'safety net' by placing padded material on the bonnet for obvious reasons!

The glazing strips should be examined and, if they are perished, replaced. If a glazing strip is known to be perished before the window is removed, then the securing lip can be cut away and the window simply lifted out with no danger of cracking it.

Whilst the glass is removed, take the opportunity to deal with any rusting in the aperture metal edge or the surrounding bodywork, such as roof pillars and top shroud panels.

When replacing the screens, use plenty of sealant in the glazing channel to prevent leakage. Replace the glazing rubber into the windscreen aperture, taking care to correctly position but not to crease the headlining material. Then fit the glass, starting with a lower corner and easing the glazing rubber over it, running along the lower edge, then moving up one side and along the top, then finally back down the

other side. Alternatively, fit the rubber to the screen and lay a length of strong string in the outer channel. Fit one corner of the assembly into place, then pull on the string slowly right around the perimeter of the screen to ease the lip over the aperture metal.

The finishing strip spreads the glazing rubber so that it grips both the glass and the aperture metal tightly. There is a special tool with a diamond-shaped bent wire edge which makes replacement of the strip easier, although a blunt screwdriver (or two, if you can find an assistant) may alternatively be used if you possess sufficient patience.

The opening side windows are easily removed. The rear bracket is held by two self-tapping screws, and each front hinge is held by a single self tapping screw. Undo these, and the window and trim may be removed.

The author likes to hold these small screws in place using masking tape before placing the window into storage; there are so many of them on the Mini that sorting the correct one for each job during reassembly could double the time requirement for the whole operation.

Headlining removal

With the windscreens removed, the front and rear
edges of the headlining can be carefully eased away
from the metal of the screen surrounds, to which they
are glued. Remove the door surround trims, the side
opening window rear catch and the trim surround
from the top of the side windows. The headlining is
held by several steel rods which locate at either end
into holes in the side members, and which are fed
through loops sewn into the topside of the roof lining.
Carefully ease the lining material from the sides
(where it will again be glued) and, as you reach one
of the rods, 'spring' one end out from the panel, then
free the other end.

If the headlining is to be re-used, fold it so that
the underside (which can be seen from within the
car) does not touch the topside, because this could
have the sticky remains of roof sound deadening
material attached to it. The trim over the 'C' posts is
gripped by the parcel shelf cover, but can be eased out
past this.

Seats

The front seats are held by two nuts and bolts each, at
the front hinges. The rear seat base may simply be
lifted out from the car. The rear seat back is affixed
from underneath the parcel shelf by two self-tapping
screws. Access to one of these (both on Cooper S cars)
is restricted by the fuel tank, and a shortened cross-
head screwdriver will be needed.

Original seat covers for some early cars are now
becoming available again. With other examples, it
will be necessary to have new seat covers made up by
a specialist, which is an expensive business. Owners
of later cars can, of course, often find seats of the
correct type and colour at a general breaker's yard or
from one of the growing number of specialist Mini
breakers. Seat vinyl may alternatively be repaired
using one of the many available kits.

Heater Unit

Thread the heater hoses back through the bulkhead,
then allow the lower of the two to drain into a
suitable receptacle. If you have previously removed
the remote gear change and its gaiter, then you could
simply push the end of the heater hose out through
the floor to let it drain. The heater unit is secured by
two self-tapping screws at the front. Remove these,
then lift the unit from its rear hinges and remove it
from the car.

The heater unit comprises a fan and a small
radiator. Poor heater performance could be due to an
internally blocked radiator or possibly to a build-up of
debris which clogs up the external fins of the radiator
and prevents sufficient air from passing through.

Each side panel of the heater housing is held by a
number of small self-tapping screws. Remove the
screws from either side and gently prise the panel
away. The radiator may now be lifted from the heater
unit. On the author's car the radiator proved to be
clogged externally by masses of dead insects, which
he cleared out easily using an air gun attached to the
compressor. If the radiator appears in poor condition
or is suspected of being clogged internally then it is
best replaced.

Switch panel and instruments

The switch/choke/heater control panel is secured by
two nuts at the rear and to the sides of the unit. The
heater valve cable and choke cable will have to be
freed and fed back through the bulkhead before the
switch panel can be removed.

The offset nacelle is supposed (according to the
repair manuals) to simply pull away from its
mountings, although its fixing lugs are held by sharp
spring clips which are designed to dig further into the
lugs the harder you pull! If the nacelle will not come
away, then you have to use brute force, and hope
that the instrument surround mouldings are not
broken in the process.

With the nacelle removed, undo the four self-
tapping screws which hold the two separate
instrument surrounds, then pull the two together
partially out. Pull out the electrical plugs and remove
the speedometer drive by pressing on its lever as it is
pulled away (Clubman including 1275GT) or by
undoing the knurled nut fixing (other Minis). Take
care not to damage the printed circuit which
connects the instruments.

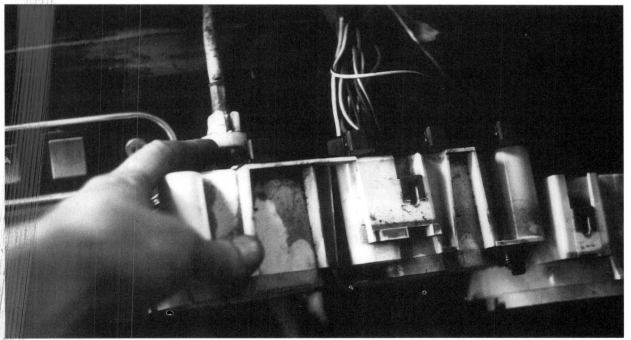

TOP *It is necessary to undo the heater and choke cable ends, then to feed the cables back before the switch panel can be removed.*

ABOVE *The speedometer cable on the Clubman is released by pressing on the side lever whilst gently pulling the cable end. Take care not to damage the printed circuit which joins the tachometer (1275GT and Special) to the other instruments.*

PROFESSIONAL RESTORATION

If you wish a professional restorer to carry out just a number of specific tasks or a full restoration, the problem remains of finding the right business for the job. Restoration businesses which will undertake work on the Mini range from the very worst examples of ill-equipped and unskilled backstreet general car body repairers to the most highly reputable and competent restoration companies. The price of sending your car to a poor restorer or body shop will not be apparent from some months or even a year or two after the completion of the work, because it will probably take this long for the new paintwork to rust through!

The Mini does not enjoy the large dedicated restoration trade which many other classic cars (especially sports cars such as MGs, Triumphs and Jaguars) seem to spawn. Because the car is, unlike other classics, still in production, the mainstream motor body repair trade will contain many competent businesses which will be able and willing to undertake restoration work on old Minis. Alternatively, there are a large number of general classic restoration businesses to choose from.

The majority of the classic car restoration trade does not produce truly concours cars but rather sound, roadworthy cars which will not require any bodywork attention for many years. This is not because they cannot produce concours cars, but rather because so few of their clients wish to incur the immense expense involved in rebuilding a car to 'as new' condition.

In car restoration the law of diminishing returns applies insofar as the basic restoration to roadworthy condition requires a certain amount of work which we could quantify as 100 hours. Beyond that point, each extra hour necessary to take the car to ever-higher standards brings a much smaller improvement than did the previous hour, to the point at which you might commission the final 10 hours worth of work and find it difficult to see where your money went!

It is usual, therefore, for the person who employs a restoration business and who wishes to end up with a concours car to have the basic restoration work professionally carried out, and to undertake the time-consuming extra work necessary to bring the car to concours standards himself.

The very best way to find a restorer for your car is by personal recommendation from a satisfied previous customer of the business. A person whose car has been well restored will usually be only too happy to make such recommendations and will miss few opportunities to show off the car. It can be difficult, however, when looking at a newly restored car to determine whether the work was carried out by a cowboy and will require repair in the not too distant future, or whether it was the work of a competent bodyshop and will be sound for many years. This is because the worst element of the trade are highly adept at covering up their shoddy workmanship and making the car appear excellent with the application of a few pounds of body filler.

Nevertheless, the best way to judge the competence of a restoration business is by a car which was restored by them, but an example which was restored a year or preferably more ago. A competent restorer who has nothing to hide should be pleased to show you or send you to see a car which he restored even three or more years previously. Looking at a car straight from the paint booth will tell you nothing.

You can also gauge a restoration business by its workshop. A neat and tidy workshop indicates a neat and tidy approach to work and will usually be reflected in the quality of workmanship. A scruffy workshop which has tools scattered liberally and seemingly at random is not a good recommendation, if for no other reason then because the workforce will waste a lot of time (which you will be paying for) looking for misplaced tools.

A good restoration business will use high quality tools. If you see an incomplete socket set of dubious and mixed origins then it will probably be of poor quality and it will be incomplete because the missing sockets either burst or rounded. You cannot obtain good quality results using poor quality tools. Similarly, you should be able to see a proper spray booth (although many restorers take their charges to a spraying specialist, so if you cannot see a booth ask where the cars are sprayed).

When you first visit a workshop, take a look at the work in progress. Ascertain whether short cuts such as welding a new panel on top of a rusted one or cutting off part of an expensive bolt-on panel rather than carefully removing it are being taken. Gauge the extent of rustproofing techniques which are being applied, for example, if such work happens to be in progress. See whether panels such as the inner front wing side of the flitch panel are cleaned and repainted before being covered by the outer wing.

Best of all, take a knowledgeable friend when you first visit a restoration business, to gain a valuable second opinion. Although not really fair to the business, turning up without an appointment will ensure that you see the business as it actually is, rather than allowing a more dubious restorer time to tidy up the workshop and remove anything which he does not wish you to see!

Before visiting a professional restorer, you should ascertain as precisely as possible the extent of work which will be necessary. This will prevent rogues from giving you a low cost estimate which suddenly rises when further rot is 'discovered' half-way through the job. It will also guard against the quick turn-around body repair business which advertises an attractive flat rate for perhaps sill replacement, only to again 'discover' that far more than the sills is in need of replacement part-way through the job. When this happens the customer is helpless because his car, divested of a sill, cannot be removed from the premises without suffering serious body distortion! In such circumstances, there is no practical option to sanctioning further, unbudgeted work at whatever huge cost the business elects.

Carrying out your own pre-restoration inspection will also guard against the company which replaces easily salvageable body panels. They may otherwise do this because they can save a few minutes' work by cutting off a panel rather than drilling out a few spot welds to remove it without damaging it.

There are many restoration companies which will happily take on the restoration of a Mini on your behalf, even though they may specialise in another vehicle. The only real drawback with such companies is that they will inevitably take longer to produce a certain standard of Mini restoration than will one of the few true Mini specialists, simply because they do not know the car as well as the real specialist. The very best Mini restoration business will be one which is combined with a spares sales operation, because all likely spares will already be held in stock and so there should be no irritating delays while spares are on order. What is more, these businesses will be buying spares at trade prices with full quantity discounts, and they should be able to pass on some of the cost benefits of this to the customer. The price for a full restoration from such a company could be substantially less than the retail value of spares plus labour.

An alternative to finding a restoration company is to engage the services of a company which can handle one element of the restoration and which can oversee the other parts. For instance, Export Services of Redditch limit in-house operations to the mechanical aspects of restoration, but often undertake the overall management of complete restorations. Bodywork and painting are both undertaken by separate companies, which work regularly and closely with Export Services. This approach can give the best of all worlds, because every aspect of the restoration is undertaken by a specialist, and restorations of the highest standards are possible.

The Estimate

An honest restorer will provide a written estimate which lists parts and itemises labour costs throughout the job, but will always point out that there is a chance that further work may be found to be necessary. This is because some problems only come to light after adjoining metalwork has been removed. A rogue may hold back such information as a surprise for later on when the car is immobile.

A written estimate can tell you much about the business. Labour should be totalled in hours and priced, allowing you to find the hourly rate. If this appears unduly high (or low) then the probable explanation is that the business is run by a person who is either avaricious or incompetent. New body panels should be listed and priced, allowing you to compare the prices with those advertised widely by mail order businesses. If the prices are very high then the business owner might be greedy, if the prices appear low then the business probably uses panels of dubious quality.

An estimate should give some indication of when the work might commence. A good restorer is always in demand, and will often have a waiting list ranging from two months to the best part of a year. A business which can take your car for a full restoration within a month is obviously unpopular. It should be said, however, that there are times of the year when work does slow down; for instance, most people commission restorations in the Autumn, Winter or Spring, preferring to have the car in use on the road for Summer. High Summer is a good time to commission a restoration to commence, because not only is the workshop likely to be free but there is also the benefit of hot dry weather which will help to ensure that panels do not develop surface rusting

197

before they are painted. Workshop time can also become available if a planned restoration is for some reason cancelled, so if a business offers to take your car at short notice then an explanation should perhaps be sought.

It usually pays to obtain more than one and perhaps three or more estimates for the work, so that in assessing any of them you have comparisons which take account of current overheads and material costs.

Attitudes

A good restorer who has nothing to hide will show you around the whole work area and answer any questions you might dream up. Furthermore, he will (or should) invite you to visit the premises at any time during the restoration to inspect the car. If a verbal invitation to visit is not forthcoming, then ask whether you will be made welcome should you 'happen to be passing' and drop in to take a look at the car. A restorer who utilises short-cuts and dubious methods will not wish to have customers visiting without appointments and consequently witnessing what goes on.

Be aware that all car restoration companies spend a lot of time talking to time-wasters. Some people will ask endless questions of the restorer and never actually commission work. When visiting a restorer, therefore, ask your questions by all means but do remember that the restorer has a business to run and a living to make; do not overstay your welcome.

A readiness to comply with requests from customers for work which could leave a car in a dangerous condition is a hallmark of the rogue restorer. If your first question to a restorer is how much he would charge to weld cover sections over rotten structural members on your car then the good restorer will refuse point-blank to do the job and the poor restorer will volunteer a price without issuing the strongest warning that the 'repair' could leave the car in a weak state, and that it will almost certainly accelerate future rusting.

Payment

You will normally be expected to pay a proportion of the bill in advance. In the case of a good restorer, a small sum will be necessary as insurance in case you suddenly change your mind just before the job is due to start and leave him with an empty workshop and a wages bill plus other overheads; remember that the work-load will be planned ahead for many months. This deposit may also cover the costs of any components which have to be bought in prior to the commencement of the job.

An advance payment on acceptance of the estimate and commissioning of the work of 10% of the written estimate should be sufficient in most cases. Never part with much more than this as a deposit. Rogue businessmen in all trades and callings who realise that their business is becoming or is insolvent sometimes try to raise as much cash as possible as quickly as possible by taking deposits and even full advance payment from customers. When the liquidator is called in by a creditor, the poor customer is at the very end of the line when it comes to getting money back!

On commencement of the work, a further sum may be payable to cover the costs of bought-in panels and other materials. Thereafter, percentage payments linked to the portion of work carried out may also be requested ie., a third payment a third of the way through the job.

One must have sympathy with the restorer whose customer becomes 'financially embarrassed' part-way through a restoration: the car might be in a state whereby it cannot be moved (with the sills off) and he might not be able to spare the workshop space to leave the car where it is until the customer's own cash-flow improves. There can be, despite this risk, no justification for charging very high deposits.

Cost Cutting

It is possible greatly to reduce the costs of a truly professional standard restoration by undertaking some of the work at home. The extent of work which may be undertaken will vary according to the experience, ability and facilities enjoyed by the individual, although most people will be able to carry out sufficient work to almost halve total body restoration costs.

The car should be delivered to the restorer as a bare bodyshell, which entails the removal of all mechanical components, trim and electrics. Dry, clean storage should be arranged for the components which are to be removed from the car. Firstly, as ever, the battery should be disconnected, then removed. The fuel tank should be drained and removed, followed by the fuel pump. These two jobs ensure that the remainder of the task may be carried out in safety, without fear of electrical fires or explosions.

All windows, exterior trim and interior trim should be removed. It is as well to keep all fixings with the relevant components so that the purpose of each is clear when the time comes to rebuild the car. Screws, nuts and bolts can be temporarily fixed to their respective brackets or components using masking tape. Throughout the stripping procedure, make a list of all components which have to be replaced so that these may be ordered in time for the rebuild.

Electrical connections may be parted, and labels (masking tape is ideal) attached explaining where each connector goes. Electrical fitments may then be removed, including lights, wiper motor, the coil and so on.

It may prove useful to leave the two subframes in situ so that the shell may be pushed around on its road wheels, although generally it is better to remove both subframes along with all items of suspension and braking, and to place the bodyshell on some sort of stand (which could be fabricated from angle iron) for the final stripping. The recommended order is to remove all fittings from the underside of the car (handbrake cable, brake pipes, wiring etc.) then the engine, transmission and front subframe as a unit, then to remove the rear subframe. The near-bare bodyshell will be reasonably easy to manoeuvre due to its relatively light weight. Four strong adults should be able to pick up and move the Mini shell, so that it can be carried out from the workshop and placed on a trailer.

There is no virtue in beginning to remove rotted body panels at this stage. Even thoroughly rotten panels may be contributing in some small way to the strength of the shell and to remove any before transporting the shell to the restorers could be to invite distortion to occur. The paintwork may be removed if desired, although because the underlying body panels will begin to rust immediately the practice is not recommended.

Whilst the bodyshell restoration is in process there will be plenty of work to carry on with, inspecting components, cleaning those which are to be retained and ordering replacements where necessary so that the eventual rebuild can proceed without hitch.

It is a good idea to request that the bodyshell is returned to you with the subframes and suspension already fitted, to minimise the chances of the newly-restored and possibly repainted underbody being damaged through contact with the ground or the trailer.

You could request that only welding work is carried out, leaving the finishing work (filling, sanding and painting) to be carried out at home or elsewhere. It is more usual to request that the car is returned with all new bodywork finished in primer. The attraction of the former is that you will be able to see exactly what work has been carried out and to what standard; the drawback is that the areas of bare metal will already be rusting by the time you receive the car. The attraction of the latter is that rusting should not have occurred by the time the car is back with you; the drawback is that shoddy practices could be concealed underneath layers of primer.

Not all restoration businesses enjoy first-class painting facilities; many use a corner of their workshop, which must rank as one of the worst possible places for a respray, because the air will be full of dust from the flatting process plus sundry oils and silicones from polishing operations. You may choose to prime the car (or have it primed by the restorer) and then take the car to a professional spray booth for the final finish to be applied. In this case it is essential that the primered finish is as near perfect as possible, because the finish of the primered car will show in the finish of the paintwork.

PAINTWORK

There is greater potential for things to go seriously and expensively wrong during the painting of the car than there is at any other time during the restoration. The whole process involves a considerable investment in paint, and all this outlay can be wasted due to mistakes during preparation, due to there being the tiniest particles of silicon in the atmosphere or dust blowing through a gap in the door, or to the paint being contaminated by water and/or oil from the compressor. There is thus a strong case for having the spraying and paint preparation of your Mini carried out professionally, and the majority of people who do restore their own cars would appear to take this option.

Some people prefer to carry out the preparation work themselves and to have just the topcoats sprayed by professionals. This approach is fine as long as the preparation is of the highest standards, for any shortcomings in the preparation are equally as serious as problems with the application of the topcoats. If you chose to prepare the car for spraying yourself and have the topcoats sprayed at a professional spray shop, it is worth asking the person who will be doing the work to carry out the final preparation for you.

The primary object of painting a car is to prevent the steel of the bodywork from corroding, which paint achieves by insulating the metal surface from the atmosphere. In order for the paint to achieve this result, it must be applied on to corrosion-free, clean, dry and grease free metal. If paint is applied on to metal which has started to corrode, however slightly, then that corrosion will spread under the surface of the paint. If paint is applied on to a contaminated surface, then one of two things can happen. Either the contaminant can react with the chemicals in the paint to cause blistering or one of a dozen different problems, or the paint can fail to adhere properly to the metal. In both cases the paint will sooner or later lift from the surface of the metal and allow corrosion to begin.

The first stage of paint preparation is thus to remove all traces of ferrous oxide (rust) from exposed metal, and to remove any contaminants (including earlier paint of types which are incompatible with the paint which you now wish to spray). In other words, the shell should be taken back to clean, bright metal. This can be achieved using emery paper and much energy, although the modern dual action and orbital sanding devices speed and ease the process so much that there can be few who would nowadays carry out this work by hand.

Previous layers of paint and primer do not necessarily have to be removed, so long as they are sanded down to provide a key for the new paint and to remove totally any traces of silicons or other contaminants which may lie on the surface. Also, the previous paint and primer must be of a type which will not chemically react with the paint which you intend to use. Problems can arise if you attempt to spray cellulose over other types of paint, because the powerful cellulose thinners will soften and possibly lift the underlying paint.

Before buying your paint, therefore, ascertain which type of paint has previously been used and ask the paint mixing specialist which paint type can be used over this without any ill effects.

Equipment and Facilities

There are three types of equipment which could be considered suitable for painting cars. Small electric sprayers have a very low output and although they might prove ideal for re-touching a small area of damaged paint, they will prove inadequate for spraying whole cars or even whole body panels. The recently introduced warm air sprayers offer a high volume of low pressure air, and are claimed to reduce paint wastage (high pressure compressed air wastes a lot of paint in the atmosphere) and give good results. Unfortunately, no example was made available for testing whilst this book was being prepared.

The traditional equipment consists of an air compressor and spray gun. Air compressors for spraying range from tiny units which have so short a duty cycle (the period of continuous operation) that a roof panel might have to be sprayed in two goes to giant floor standing units with huge air tanks. In between there are a number of compressors which are popular with DIY restorers. The minimum acceptable compressor for serious work would have a 25 litre air tank, although 50 litres is far better and a 100 litre tank would be by far the best option. Small air tanks rapidly run out of 'puff' when the air pressure drops and this has to be replenished by the air pump. This places warmed air into the tank, which can dry the paint in the air before it ever reaches the panel!

In addition to the compressor, you will need at least one and preferably two water/oil traps for the outlet connection. When air is compressed, water droplets form in the tank and can be blown through the spray gun to mix with your paint and ruin the painted finish. Also, tiny droplets of oil from the pump will contaminate the air within the cylinder, and both this and the water will have to be filtered out before the air reaches the paint gun.

Most spray guns work rather like the SU carburettor, because as air is forced past a jet of sorts at high velocities (and hence at low pressure) paint is drawn up to mix with the air in exactly the same was that petrol mixes with air in the SU. Other guns have a gravity paint feed and are characterised, not unsurprisingly, by the paint container being mounted on top of the gun. You should buy the best spray gun and compressor that you can afford, or alternatively, hire them.

You will also need a mask. Paint which dries in the air forms a fine dust which you should avoid breathing in, and because the fumes from thinners are also to be avoided, a respiratory mask is needed rather than a simple dust mask which cannot provide sufficient protection.

It is possible to spray a car out of doors given favourable conditions. The weather should not be too hot nor too cold, it must not be wet or windy. A still day is essential, and the temperature should be somewhere in the range 10-20 degree celsius. A warmer day may appear a better prospect, but warmed days see greater activity from winged insects, which appear to be fatally attracted to wet paint! However, it is far better to apply paint indoors if this is possible, because it allows you some control over the conditions.

The paint should be applied in a clean dry atmosphere which has reasonable ventilation. The corner of the workshop in which you recently rubbed down body filler is no place unless it is scrupulously cleaned firstly. The floor should also be lightly damped down with water to prevent dust from being kicked into the atmosphere by your own movements. You will require good, even lighting so that you can see which areas you have covered and which you have not.

The temperature and humidity at the time of spraying are important factors. If the temperature is too high, much of the paint can dry in the air before it ever reaches the panel, giving what is known as 'dry spray'. If the humidity is too high then water contamination will be apparent as 'bloom'. The surface will be very dull. Avoid very windy days if your workshop has a lot of ventilation.

Types of Paint

Earlier Minis would have been finished in cellulose paint. This is quite a good choice for the novice to use, because it dries fairly rapidly and so lessens the chances of dust falling on to the still wet fresh paint surface and spoiling it. Another advantage is that the thinners used will soften existing paint, so helping blend in any future touching-up. Against these advantages, with cellulose there is rather a lot of wastage. The paint has a low pigment content and so a fair thickness of it is required to produce a finish.

Most body shops today use either synthetic or two-pack paints. Synthetic paints can give an excellent finish but they tend to look a little 'plastic' if used on an older Mini.

Synthetic paints have a fairly long drying time, and so there is a greater chance of air-borne dust being able to settle on the surface before it dries. Only two coats of the paint are necessary to produce a gloss finish.

Two pack paints have a high pigment content and so produce a deep finish. Unfortunately, some of the ingredients of the paints are highly toxic and so they should only be used with proper breathing apparatus, which in practice really means an external air supply. The two pack paints are therefore used in the main by well equipped professional spray shops only.

Preparation

The quality of the paint finish is wholly dependent on the quality of the preparation. The entire area which is to be sprayed should be flatted using increasingly fine grades of wet 'n dry, used wet (except on body filler, which would absorb the water). Begin using a coarse grade of 400 then progress through to 1200 grade for the final finish. The surface to be sprayed should be perfectly smooth with no ripples. Use a flexible straight edge to check for unevenness in filled areas. When the finish is acceptable, begin masking off. Masking tape and newspaper is quite acceptable. Avoid using plastic sheeting, because the paint will not adhere strongly to this and will quickly dry to a powdery dust which can be blown around the workshop on to the painted area before it has dried. Large plastic bags are, however, ideal for quickly masking off wheels.

When the masking off is complete, damp down the floor. Clean the metal using a tack cloth, which will remove all traces of paint and filler dust, then finally use spirit wipe to remove any traces of oils or greases.

All types of paint have to be thinned before they can be sprayed. The paint manufacturers produce data sheets which will give the correct concentration for the paint being used. Strain the primer before thinning it, because even 'new' paint can contain stringy lumps which clog the paint spray gun. An old stocking can be used to strain the paint. After adding the appropriate amount of thinner, stir the mixture

Because body filler cannot adhere strongly to paint, it is necessary to carry out all operations involving the use of filler before you begin spraying. The orbital sander in the photograph makes sanding down excess filler very much easier. At this stage it can be difficult to see just how smooth the filled area is and whether it blends in with the surrounding metal. A coat of primer helps to highlight any undulations.

The roof of this Mini is to be primed following the application of body filler. This is a simple area to mask off using masking tape and newspaper. When the area to be sprayed has been masked off, use the air compressor followed by a tack cloth to remove all traces of dust from the surface, then clean it using spirit wipe and a lint-free cloth.

well before pouring it into the spray gun. You can obtain special cups which you can use to gauge the paint/thinner solution viscosity by allowing a set amount to drain from a hole in the base of the cup and timing it, and one of these could prove worthwhile for checking the paint/thinner mixture, because the viscosity of the mixture will vary according to temperature.

You can now set the spray gun controls. There should be one for controlling the air flow and one for the paint needle. Set the output pressure from the compressor tank firstly to 30psi, then open the paint and air controls fully on the spray gun. Make a rapid pass with the gun over a test surface. If large spots of paint can be seen, increase the air pressure at the tank in 5 psi increments until the rapid pass produces a suitably fine and even spray. Now adjust the spray gun air and paint controls until the correct sized pattern is achieved.

When using the spray gun, the technique is to keep the gun at a constant distance from the surface. Too close and the paint will go on so thickly that runs will develop immediately, too far away, and some of the paint will be air dry before it reaches the surface. Keeping the gun at a constant distance also gives a even spray band width. The gun should have a two-stage 'trigger pull', where stage one allows air to pass through and stage two opens the paint needle and allows paint into the airflow. The two stages can

The gun should be between six and nine inches from the surface. Note that the coiled air feed hose is being held away from the car, because it is easy to accidentally drag this across the freshly painted surface.

usually be felt through the trigger, and at the end of the first stage of travel there will be a discernible stop. Further movement of the trigger introduces the paint.

The technique which is preferred by the author is as follows. When making a pass over a panel, begin to one side of it and start moving the gun with the trigger at stage one, then press it fully home just before the edge of the panel is reached. Move the gun over the panel in a single, clean movement, and release the trigger back to the first stage when the far end of the panel is reached, to clear paint from the nozzle. Then repeat the exercise until the panel is covered.

Beware the 'dry edge'. This is when a band of sprayed paint is allowed to dry before the next band is applied. It could occur if, for instance, you were to begin in the middle of the roof panel and work your way outwards. By the time you came to spray the other half, the first paint to be applied would be thoroughly dry and a visible edge would result. Always begin spraying the roof at an edge, and do not spend too much time moving around the car when you have reached the middle.

203

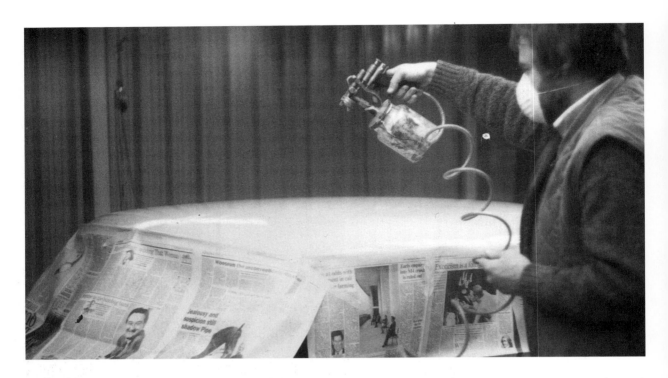

Problems. If the gun is held too far away from the surface as shown here, the paint particles could dry before they reach the surface. If the gun is too close, runs will result. The gun should be kept at an even distance from the sprayed surface to achieve an even spray band width.

The roof is now primed, and the author can progress to deal with other bodywork repairs safe in the knowledge that the roof is protected against moisture to prevent the steel from rusting and the porous body filler from absorbing water.

Masked off ready for a professional respray. A large, well-lit space with plenty of room for manoeuvre and ventilation.

When you have sprayed your first panel, allow it to dry and inspect it. You are looking especially for signs of contamination. Small dark spots surrounded by lighter circles of up to ¼" in diameter are caused by oil/water contamination from the compressor, and another oil and water filter will have to be placed in line. If the surface has paint runs then you could be moving the gun too slowly, the air pressure could be too high or the paint could be too thin. If the paint begins to wrinkle before it dries then the underlying surface is contaminated, and the primer will have to be removed completely and the surface properly cleaned.

Look closely for scratches, dents and hollows which are in the underlying surface but which the primer may highlight. The problem with matt primer paints is that they can make a rough surface look quite acceptable, even though the final gloss will make every little blemish stand out like a sore thumb.

When it has hardened, the primer may be flatted down with very fine wet 'n dry. Small scratches in the surface which now become apparent may be filled using body stopper, which should be allowed to cure then primed. Not even the tiniest scratch should remain if the car is to be painted in cellulose, because this paint shrinks, and the final gloss will show every little flaw in the preparation. The author prefers to remove all masking materials and re-mask the car at this stage, because over-spray on the masking materials can enter the air as a fine dust which will contaminate the final finish.

Clean the entire surface again, using a tack cloth to pick up any paint and filler dust which lies on the surface. The topcoat paint should be strained and thinned, then the surface should be given a last wipe over with spirit wipe before the first of the topcoats is applied. The number of topcoats will vary according to the type of paint being used. With synthetic paint, two coats will be sufficient to give a good gloss. With cellulose, you could almost add as many coats as you wish although three coats should give sufficient depth. Each extra coat should be applied around twenty minutes after the preceding one with cellulose, to allow the thinners to evaporate. You can obtain slow or fast thinners for use in warmer or cooler conditions.

Remove the masking materials as soon as the paint has dried. If you remove them too soon then dry paint dust which is unsettled will land on the still wet surface of the paint. If you remove them too late then the paint could have cured to the point at which the paint which has settled on the masking material rips at the paint on the car.

The preferred order for spraying the car is to do the roof first, followed by the roof pillars, then the bonnet and finally the sides. If the interior, engine bay and boot are also being sprayed, then complete these before starting on the outside of the car.

Car spraying is too vast a subject to be covered comprehensively in a book like this, and so the reader is advised to seek out further reading material such as 'How To Restore Paintwork', published by Osprey Automotive. It is also worth seeking specialised advice from your paint supplier when you buy.

The best advice for the person who is restoring just the one Mini and who does not intend to make restoration into an on-going hobby is to have at least the final stages of preparation and the application of the topcoats carried out professionally. The costs of purchasing paint and reasonably competent equipment can by a wide margin exceed that of a reasonable quality professional respray, and the potential for things to go badly wrong for the first-time DIY car sprayer is immense. Even if you cut the overall outlay by hiring good equipment, you could still spend almost as much as a reasonable professional respray would cost, but with all the attendant risks of DIY.

6 · MODIFICATIONS

The Mini has undergone almost every conceivable modification during its thirty year production life, ranging from minor engine 'tweaks' to the most fantastic examples of bodyshell modifications. The car has been given six wheels, three wheels, two engines, big engines; it has been made into a convertible, into many attractive (and some less attractive) component or 'kit' cars, it has been lowered, raised, squashed and stretched.

This book will deal only with three broad types of modification. It will deal with those moderate performance modifications which the 'classic enthusiast' who does not wish to substantially alter the character of his car might contemplate, which will always be quite mild and usually discreet. Secondly, it will deal with performance modifications ranging from cheap and simple ways to make the standard Mini 1000 a bit quicker to full engine and suspension modifications which are guaranteed to seriously annoy GTi drivers! Finally, it will delve into the wonderful world of Mini-based kit cars.

Classic Car Modifications

There can be no rules to govern what is and what is not appropriate in the way of modifications to classic cars. If your wish is to customise a 1959 Austin Seven with velour trim, walnut dashboard and lots of chromework then that is entirely your own affair and this chapter has not been written for you. This section is written, however, firmly from the viewpoint of the person for whom an early Mini is a classic car with a very special character which can be destroyed by what is perceived by like-minded enthusiasts as thoughtless modification, and it reflects the values of such enthusiasts.

However, the decision to modify any car is in the hands of the owner, and those who do choose to do so are by no means alone; owners of many '60s classics – most notably the Volkswagen Beetle and some (British) Ford models – gain a lot of pleasure from customising and driving their cars.

In general, it will be deemed acceptable by many enthusiasts only to fit 'period' accessories to an aged Mini. That is, a 1960s style radio might be considered appropriate for a '60s car whilst fitting a quadraphonic tape/CD player with graphic equalizer would most certainly be considered infra dig by many people for a car with collector's value. Such modifications are inarguably at odds with the character of an early Mini.

Other non-production but period accessories may be widely accepted as appropriate for a classic Mini. A small sports steering wheel, Cooper wheels and wider tyres, long stemmed dashboard switches and so on all contribute to the 'character' of the car, which may well have been fitted with such adornments more than two decades ago by its first owner! Do not, incidentally, be tempted to fit very wide wheels and tyres or wide wheel spacers to the car (competition cars excepted), because the effect on overall roadholding will not be too marked and this does place great strain on the wheel bearings. Furthermore, wheel arch extension will have to be fitted to comply with current UK law, and these are not entirely appropriate on a very early car.

From the Mini Coopers' first Monte Carlo winning year of 1964, it became the fashion for younger owners of Minis to heavily patronise the car accessory shops which sold 'go-faster' items. Some turned standard 850cc cars into Cooper lookalikes just as many youthful owners of Ford Cortinas turned them into bogus Lotus Cortinas, and the few surviving examples (victims?) cannot today be considered any the less collectable. In fact, the author would dearly love to be able to find one of the genuine '60s customised Minis still fitted with all of the period accessories. Those 60s accessories so beloved of the boy racer are probably themselves nowadays considered collectable items of motoring memorabilia.

There are few performance enhancing modifications which the owner of a early standard 850cc Mini or one of the 1960s variants can undertake without compromising its originality and, in fact, its very character. The cylinder head may be swapped for one from a 1000cc or larger car to give a discreet (sometimes barely perceptible) increase in bhp and a slightly more marked and useful increase in torque. The not too efficient brakes (along with their backplates) from very early cars may be exchanged for more effective alternatives from later cars. This is arguably the only aspect of the entire braking/suspension system which can benefit from alteration without affecting the originality of the car to a great extent.

Some owners of early cars fitted with the Hydrolastic suspension system may care to add dampers as fitted to cars with the dry rubber cone suspension, which will improve the ride greatly.

Modifications to the engines of early cars can give so little improvement in bhp (even swapping to a 1000cc engine will only give another 4bhp) that not many people will consider the exercise really worthwhile. The tuning potential of the 850cc engine is limited, especially because the majority of performance components have been developed for the 1000, 1100 and 1275cc versions. However, performance cylinder heads are now available for this engine, and should give a rather larger power increase than would swapping the unit for a standard 1000cc.

Alternatively, some pancake air filters are claimed and generally accepted to give a small power boost, and the same is true of some special exhaust systems.

The beauty of fitting the performance cylinder head rather than a pancake air filter and a performance exhaust system is that the alteration is practically 'invisible' and can not detract from the classic aspect of the car's appeal. People who are worried about fitting such a cylinder head to their otherwise original Mini can always opt for outright purchase rather than exchange, keeping the original

head so that the car can be returned to original specification at a later date if desired. A car fitted with such a cylinder head might develop an extra 10bhp at the flywheel. It will not by any stretch of the imagination be a 'fast' car, but simply a classic car which has been made more pleasing to drive on today's roads.

Further engine modification arguably brings a danger of losing the character of the car insofar as the tickover becomes necessarily higher and less smooth as the engine is progressively modified. (At the time of writing, many modified cars are reportedly failing the new UK exhaust emission tests purely because they are ticking over at such high rpm). Further modification also narrows the power band so that, although extra brake horse power is achieved, usable power only becomes available between a narrow revolutions band.

If you improve your engine BHP then it can safely be assumed that you intend to travel faster, in which case the braking system should also be upgraded.

Classic Coopers, naturally, are another matter. The brakes on early Coopers were not really a match for the enhanced performance, and so a switch to later twin leading shoe brakes (including later hubs) or even front disc brakes (including CV joint, hub, caliper etc) will give a marked improvement.

The full range of performance add-ons appear to be available 'off the shelf' for the Coopers, although the Cooper 1275S naturally attracts the greatest number of options.

However, the Mini Cooper is now firmly established as a highly desirable collector's cars and, whilst cars used in competitions will undoubtedly continue to be modified in order to increase performance, many owners of the remaining 'road use only' examples will undoubtedly view originality as becoming an ever-more desirable trait of their cars.

Whilst many enthusiast owners of eary Minis nowadays believe them to be sacrosanct and would never alter them, the owner of perhaps a mid to late 1970s Mini might have a diferent outlook. As ever, Coopers and showroom condition examples excepted, few cars of this period appear to currently have high collector's values, and so there seems to be no value to be jeopardised by carrying out whatever modifications the owners can dream up.

There is certainly no shortage of add-on goodies for Minis, and accessories both cosmetic and performance-improving can be found in many motorist's shops as well as specialist mail order catalogues published by companies such as Ripspeed.

MODIFICATIONS TO SUSPENSION/ BRAKES

Even in standard form, the Mini is a superbly handling car and modifications to the suspension do not really become necessary unless the power of the engine is raised considerably for high-speed use, unless the car is used off the road or unless it is to be used in competition. However, many people like the looks of lowered cars which are fitted with wider wheels or perhaps with spacers, and cars with some suspension modifications, applied sensibly, can be very pleasing to drive even if the power unit is only a standard 1000cc.

Always take advice before fitting any special suspension components to your Mini, because it is essential that the suspension as a whole is balanced and that the components complement each other. Merely bolting on a full set of 'goodies' is no guarantee of better roadholding.

Lowering the Mini is in theory (see Chapter 4 to become acquainted with the difficulties of stripping the suspension) simplicity itself and entails shortening the tapered ends of the aluminium suspension trumpets. This lowers the car in roughly the ratio of 5:1, that is, for every 1mm you take off the trumpet the car will sit 5mm lower, although the ratio is not the same for the front and rear suspension. If you take too much away then the standard damper will not fit and shorter ones will have to be substituted; it may pay to obtain spare trumpets from a breaker's yard to experiment with before shortening your own too much! However, the obvious problem with lowering the already low-slung Mini is that it will 'ground' much more easily and frequently. You could fit a sump guard to prevent the sump from hitting a bump at speed, but this will reduce the already minimal ground clearance further. If any off-road driving is anticipated, you will be better advised to consider slightly raising the suspension if anything AND fitting a sump guard.

Alternatively, adjustable height kits are widely available, and allow you to set the suspension high or low as and when required. This does, however, not enable the driver to alter the height of the suspension at will whilst the car is being driven in the same way as can the driver of a Citroen. The kits comprise alternatives for the aluminium suspension cones, and in order to alter the ride height the driver must stop the car, get out and use a long key to alter each corner of the car independently. The ability to raise the suspension for driving over rougher surfaces might save you from looking in your rear view mirror and seeing your exhaust system lying on the ground behind you! When lowering suspension, always avoid placing strain on brake pipes.

Another (and a very worthwhile) modification is to fit adjustable dampers. These enable you to set a hard suspension for fast driving and softer for normal road progress. With both adjustable suspension height and adjustable dampers you could have almost competition-grade suspension for either track or off-road yet still be able to set up the suspension for normal road use.

Many owners broaden the wheeltrack by fitting wheel spacers. Whilst this undeniably improves roadholding in dry conditions it can place a very high strain on the wheel bearings. As a more expensive alternative, wider wheels and tyres may be fitted to better effect. It is best to avoid second-hand alloy wheels because the actual strength of even perfect-looking alloys is impossible to determine, and the material does deteriorate in time.

When fitting spacers or wider wheels, bear in mind that wheelarch extensions may also have to be fitted because it is illegal (and an MOT failure point) for the wheels to protrude outside the bodywork. Wheelarch extensions are available in alloy or in plastic materials. The author found that extensions made from High Impact Polystyrene (HIPS) material split when he attempted to fit them in cold weather. Furthermore, they were only really suitable for use on de-seamed cars. Do not fit wide wheelarch extensions unless you can properly fill them with your new wheels and tyres, because little looks sillier than a widened Mini with apparently inboard tyres. Narrow wheelarch extensions are available from better accessory shops, so fit these where appropriate.

If the wrong sized wheels are fitted then they can foul the bodywork or suspension components, so make doubly sure that the wheels you buy are suitable for your car. Owners of later 1275GTs which were originally fitted with Denovo run-flat tyres and wheels often replace these with wheels from the Hillman Imp, although these are nowadays becoming quite rare because 1275GT owners have bought them all.

At the rear of the car, both fixed and adjustable rear camber plates and anti roll bars will be of interest to those contemplating competition work. The anti roll bar is manufactured from spring steel, and is fitted to the subframe in the middle and to the suspension at each end. If the suspension is compressed on one side of the car, the anti roll bar transmits a smaller force to the other side, so slightly compressing this also and so keeping the car more upright. This helps prevent the wheel on the inside of a tight bend from lifting.

In order to work well, anti roll bars must match the suspension to which they are fitted. Some people fit the thickest anti roll bars they can find, and this is always a mistake because it can ruin the handling and roadholding of the car rather than improve it. The anti roll bars should match the springing and suspension. Buy anti roll bars from an accredited specialist, seek their advice to build a balanced suspension, and do not even consider trying to adapt bars from other vehicles.

Hydrolastic Suspension

Many people believe that the dry rubber suspension system is superior to the Hydrolastic alternative fitted to Mini saloons between 1964 and 1969 (1971 in the case of the Clubman). You can fit dampers to the hydrolastic-equipped car by sourcing the necessary brackets from a scrap yard Mini and bolting them into place. This gives a far better ride from a Hydrolastic car.

You can convert a Mini from Hydrolastic to dry suspension, but there is a considerable amount of work involved and it would be far more advisable to sell the car and buy one with dry suspension.

Brakes

If your intention is to make a car faster then you should always ensure that it will be capable of stopping safely from higher speeds. The standard drum brakes of the Mini, whilst more than adequate in the standard car (early examples excepted), will often be found seriously wanting if the car is driven to the limit or given performance modifications.

Early cars will benefit from a swap to later brake components, because these are far more effective and both widely and cheaply available from breakers'

yards. It is worth having brake drums checked over; if they are scored or have worn out of true (they can become oval) then braking efficiency will be seriously reduced. Braking efficiency can be improved by fitting finned brake drums. These are made from alloy and allow the heat to dissipate much more quickly than do the standard iron drums, so improving their performance.

For serious work, it may prove worth fitting Cooper S or 1275GT disc assemblies. These used to be easy to obtain from breakers' yards, although nowadays they are increasingly difficult to track down. Complete assemblies (which must include the CV joints) are available from specialists but are very expensive.

For the ultimate in performance and for competition work, companies such as Ripspeed offer almost every conceivable engine/suspension modification and they will also give technical assistance. Any rally car preparation business will have experts on hand able to advise you regarding which combination of modifications to pick for your chosen purpose.

ENGINE MODIFICATIONS

The A series engine offers many possibilities to those who wish to make their Mini faster. A visit to a breaker's yard could furnish a larger capacity engine or perhaps just the cylinder head from one at far less than the cost of an exchange reconditioned unit. At the other end of the pricing scale, high performance versions of just about all Mini engine components are available, so that you could build or have built an engine suitable for the race track, albeit at huge cost.

The very simplest way in which to obtain more power from a car fitted with an 850cc or 1000cc Mini engine is to fit a larger capacity engine, which offers the advantage of increasing power whilst retaining tractability by increasing torque along with power. All A-series integral gearbox units from the Mini and Austin 1100/1300 range can easily be fitted into your 850 or 1000cc Mini and, as long as the unit in question is in good condition (and larger than the existing unit), an immediately power increase should result.

Fitting a larger capacity engine, of course, means that you will have to inform your insurers of the change and perhaps pay higher insurance premiums as a result. You should actually inform your insurers of any modifications to the car's engine.

Rather than fitting a larger capacity engine, it is possible to raise the power of your own engine in a number of ways. In some circumstances, the engine can remain in the car and a component or combination of components at the top end changed to give a power increase. If much more than a modest increase is aimed at, however, you will be well advised to remove the engine/gearbox unit from the car and begin by overhauling both the engine bottom end and the gearbox.

Before trying any power increasing modifications to your car, you should check the compression on all cylinders, the ignition timing, and overhaul and set the carburettors.

Mild increases

You can generally gain a few bhp simply by allowing your engine to breathe more freely. This is achieved firstly by replacing the air filter(s) with performance variants which offer less restricted air flow, such as those manufactured by K&N, coupled with fitting a long centre branch exhaust manifold and larger bore exhaust system. If the engine is in good condition and the timing and mixture are correctly set, these modifications might show an increase from 5% upwards, although far higher increases in the order of 16% have been claimed in advertising for a performance exhaust manifold and system alone. These modifications should have no adverse effects on the smooth running and tractability of the engine.

If all that you did was to replace the filters and exhaust as described above, then to take the car for proper setting up and jetting on a rolling road, the power increase could be substantial enough to transform the performance of your car, especially if it (like most cars on the roads) was not previously operating at 100% efficiency.

The next stage (because it is the easiest) is to fit a higher performance cylinder head. Those with the standard 1000cc engine could fit a standard cylinder head from another variant of the engine, such as that fitted to the Austin 1100/1300 range. Before fitting another cylinder head, compare it minutely with your own, to ensure that the coolant passages will correctly align, because there is no guarantee that the cylinder head was the correct one for the car from

which it was sourced, and some 1275cc units are not suitable for other variants of the engine.

Alternatively, you could opt for one of the modified performance cylinder heads, which may be fitted with larger valves, which may be gas-flowed, or both. If you do decide to swap the cylinder head on your car (and this precludes very high performance heads and Cooper S heads which have very large valves) then you could consider fitting one which has been specially modified to operate safely and effectively with unleaded fuel.

The lead in leaded petrol is there to control (slow down) the burn rate of the air/fuel mixture, which allows the ignition to be advanced with a consequent increase in performance. Unleaded fuel burns very much more quickly than leaded (so that the ignition timing has to be retarded) and generates very high temperatures. In addition to controlling the burn rate of the fuel, the lead also has the effect of coating the exhaust valve and its seat with a sacrificial layer of lead. The prevents both the exhaust valve and its seat from burning away due to the very high temperatures of burnt fuel mixture which leave the cylinder. The cylinder head which is converted to tolerate unleaded fuel will be fitted with hard valve seat inserts and exhaust valves manufactured from harder material, because the exhaust valve seats of cast heads burn away very quickly when used with unleaded fuel, and could erode at the rate of .001" per hour at high engine revolutions. The Cooper S has large valves and some experts feel that there is not sufficient 'meat' left for inserts to be fitted safely – they will go in, but there appears a strong possibility that they may just pop out again at some stage.

There is a possibility that, at some time in the future, leaded petrol will be all but phased out from most world markets. This leaves the owners of cars unable to use unleaded fuel with two options. The first is to gamble with a fuel additive or with one of the 'miracle' sacrificial metal systems which are supposed to release a metal compound into the fuel, either by being dropped into the fuel tank or placed in an in-line fuel pipe canister. The second option is to fit a cylinder head which has been altered to make it compatible with unleaded fuel. The second option is recommended.

Many companies will supply performance cylinder heads on an exchange basis at quite reasonable cost, although as the degree of performance claimed for the head increases, so does the price. The alternative is to strip your own cylinder head down and (if it is not cracked) to take it to a company which can carry out the desired work. You could, for instance, have larger valve seats cut and larger valves lapped in, have the head gas flowed and the ports/manifolds 'blueprinted' (matched so that they are in perfect alignment – many will not be). This option will be more expensive than merely fitting an exchange performance cylinder head which has been modified in a cost-effective manner on almost a production line basis, but if you go to a company which possesses a rolling road, you can hand the whole job, including final setting up, over to them, and be guaranteed good results. If you obtained your 'go-faster' components from one company and had the car set up by another, then each could blame the other if the results were not satisfactory!

A performance gain is to be had with sensible carburettor swapping. An HS2 could be swapped for an HS4, and an HS4 swapped for twin HS4s on the appropriate manifold, etc. In all cases of carburettor swapping (certainly within the UK) your insurers should be informed. If you do change carburettors, then the car will most definitely require setting up on a rolling road if the full potential benefits of the exercise are to be felt.

Higher States of Tune

There is an old adage that engine tuning should begin at the bottom end. The author likes to interpret this as meaning the brakes and suspension of the car, because higher performance levels require substantial improvements in the braking efficiency of the Mini. However, the proper implied meaning of the expression is that the work should begin with a bottom-end engine rebuild.

At the very least (unless the engine is in truly excellent condition) the crankshaft journals and crankpins should be examined for scoring, reground if necessary and new bearings fitted, the crankshaft and flywheel should be balanced (to reduce wear at higher rpm), and preferably the cylinder block should be rebored and new pistons and rings fitted. The timing gear and the transfer gears should be checked and replaced if necessary. Because the gearbox is now fully accessible it makes sense to strip and examine this also.

Building a performance engine from scratch could be a very interesting and absorbing project, but it could also prove an expensive mistake. Working

conditions must be scrupulously clean, because a tiny piece of grit which finds it way into the engine at this stage could quickly wreck a bearing! The rust and dust conditions which are typical of the restorer's workshop make it no place in which to rebuild an engine.

You have the choice of overboring the cylinder block or fitting a longer-stroke crankshaft to increase the capacity of the engine, fitting performance pistons and a performance camshaft, using lightened connecting rods and so on. You can even obtain a cross-flow cylinder head (which positions the carburettors at the front of the engine). With a cross-flowed head and other modifications, you could extract around 130 bhp from a 1275cc unit for 0-60mph times of between six and seven seconds and a top speed of over 120mph. However, each extra bhp costs much more than the preceding one. The potential to spend money on making your Mini faster are enormous.

The camshaft controls the operation of the valves. It determines the timing, duration and amount of their opening, and so can have a fundamental effect on the characteristics of the engine. The type of camshaft chosen will reflect the likely use to which the car will be put. An out-and-out racing camshaft will give absolute maximum bhp from the engine but it can make the engine run so poorly at normal road revolutions that the car will be anything but a pleasure to drive. Camshafts are available which raise torque, raise bhp, or more usually give a permutation of these but still result in a tractable engine which is almost as happy around town as a standard Mini. Choose carefully.

Gearbox

Obviously, all components of the gearbox should at the very least be in good condition for a speeded-up Mini. Remember that any minor problems with the unit when used in the standard car are going to be amplified greatly when more power and higher revolutions are being fed through it.

Restoring a gearbox is by no means an economical exercise. If, for instance, you replaced third gear to stop an annoying whine (which is caused by worn gear teeth), then you should also replace the laygear, because the gear teeth to which third gear meshes will also have worn out of true. This means that the other gears which will have to mesh with the new laygear should also be changed, and you end up replacing just about everything! Unless you wish to in some way modify the gearbox then the most cost-effective option can be the exchange unit.

However, a straight-cut close-ratio gearbox with a limited slip differential and competition drive shafts may be more to your liking. The necessary components are widely available (if very expensive) so there is no impediment to carrying out the work yourself. The amounts of money which you will be parting with for these components will be so great that most people will consider it wise to pay that little bit extra and have the work carried out professionally.

On a more down to earth note, the gearbox could simply be swapped for one in better condition or one from another car which uses the transverse A series engine. The gearbox fitted to the Austin 1300 GT offers close ratios and synchromesh in all four gears, and is probably the most popular straight replacement.

The differential may be swapped for one from a different version of the Mini or the Austin 1100 range to alter the final drive ratio. The limited slip differential offers a rather expensive modification which will usually only be considered by those who are preparing a competition car.

MINI-BASED KIT CARS

Originally, the modifications section of this book was not intended to include any mention of the many Mini-based kit cars. This chapter has been included for the benefit of those who own later 1970s and 1980s Minis which are in need of full restoration. These cars can have very low collector's values irrespective of how superbly they are restored. If such cars were restored, their eventual worth would be but a fraction of their restoration costs. The exercise is financially so unsound that these Minis continue to be scrapped in their thousands as rusting takes its toll.

The beauty of the kit car is that it can, sometimes at relatively low cost, give a new lease of life to a Mini which has little or no collector's value and which would otherwise be destined for the scrap yard. Perhaps more importantly than 'saving the life' of the individual Mini, kit cars allow the owner of such a car the opportunity to turn it into a vehicle which will, in its own way, give every bit as much pleasure as the old favourite itself. What is more, this can not be considered to be robbing the World of a future classic, because many early kit cars are now becoming considered every bit as much classic cars as the donor cars they are based upon. If the Mini ever became a rare car then no doubt these remarks would be regarded as heresy. In 1992, it is difficult to believe that the Mini could ever become a rare car.

Given that the handling and roadholding of the Mini has always been considered exemplary by any standards, it is little wonder that for years, companies have been producing alternative sports bodies to mount on the Mini's sub-frames, usually to be powered by the larger variants of its engine. Such vehicles are commonly known as 'kit cars', although enthusiasts much prefer to use the more up-market term of 'Component Cars'.

Buying cars in component form became very popular during the late 1950s and early 1960s within the UK because the vehicles in this form were exempt from purchase tax. When, in 1962, Lotus unveiled their new Elan in component form, the kit car became perfectly socially acceptable. Although a number of kit cars were available before this period, it was the advent of GRP which enabled the industry to really grow. Previously, car bodies could be manufactured from plywood (also a relatively new material) steel or aluminium; in the case of the metal body, the individual panels could either be pressed (which incurred massive tooling-up costs) or hand rolled (which required many hours of skilled craftsman's time and thus made the cars expensive). With plywood, the kit car enthusiast usually ended up building his own bodyshell from plain sheets of the material. In contrast, with GRP the manufacturer can simply make a 'plug' (a full-sized model of the body), take a 'female' GRP moulding off this, brace the mould and then lay up bodies as fast as he likes! If demand for the bodyshells outgrows manufacturing capacity, new moulds can easily be made from the original plug, and extra unskilled labour quickly trained in the unbelievably messy but quite easily learnt art of laying up GRP.

Probably the best known and most highly regarded Mini kit car is the Mini Marcos, which was first introduced in 1966. This highly attractive diminutive fastback is considerably lighter in weight than the standard Mini, and so it will go considerably faster than the standard car for a given size of engine.

The Mini Marcos was first introduced back in 1966 and was very highly regarded as an economy sports car able to hold its head high amongst the production sports cars of the day.

The Mini Marcos also boasted a lower centre of gravity than the standard Minis', and so it actually improved on the already superb handling of the Mini. In the mid-1960s, a well set-up example of the car with a pokey engine could run rings around just about anything else on the road. Also launched in 1966, the Mini Miura was a kit car which was years ahead of its time. This car had its Mini engine/gearbox mounted behind the seats (mid-engined), benefited from disc brakes all round, offered the option of five speed transmission and had a right hand 'racing car style' gearchange. The Mini Miura must have been one of the best-handling rear wheel drive cars of its time.

There are essentially four vastly different designs of Mini kit car. Following in the Mini Marcos mould (pun not intended) are true sports cars which retain the front wheel drive layout of the Mini. The body shells of these shapely cars are almost universaly constructed from GRP. Secondly, there are sports car designs which utilise the engine and drive train of the Mini, but in a mid-engined configuration like the Mini Miura kit car already referred to and the Fiat X1/9 and Toyota MR2 sports cars. Thirdly, the Mini Moke was always bound to be flattered by imitators, but has in fact spawned a whole class of utility/fun vehicles which range from the straightforward Moke lookalikes to superb utility estates and pickups. Some of these are manufactured with GRP bodyshells, although a number have shells which are constructed entirely from steel and/or aluminium. Lastly, there are Mini kit cars which look like – Minis! These cars can appear at first sight to be customized Minis, but in reality they have completely new GRP bodyshells.

The Mini is an excellent donor vehicle on which to base kit cars. Its mechanics are easy to work with, robust and in plentiful supply due to the large numbers of 1970s and early 1980s cars which are bodily rotten and not worth restoring, but mechanically sound and able to supply a good engine, drive train and subframes. The Minis two subframes can be bridged by a simple to produce and hence low cost chassis, giving in effect a three-piece chassis which already has all the necessary mounting points for the engine, transmission and suspension. This form of construction helps to cut production costs, and some of the Mini-based kits are thus very attractively priced when compared to kits with other donor cars.

Some of the more recent kits do away with steel altogether, and bolt components directly onto the GRP monocoque bodyshell. Others retain the subframes, but bridge them with an entirely GRP shell.

Building a Kit Car

Some kit cars require more than one donor vehicle, that is, they may need the running gear and engine from a Mini but many other components sourced from quite different cars. For instance, the Moke styled kit cars usually require an under-floor fuel tank, which may in some cases be a custom-made special supplied by the kit manufacturer, or which in other cases may be salvaged from another type of car or van. Happily, most Mini-based kit cars seem to rely largely upon the Mini for their components, which keeps the building costs down.

The first step is obviously to decide on which kit car you intend to build. It is highly recommended that you see an example of the completed vehicle 'in the flesh' (and preferably have a test drive) before making a decision, rather than trying to judge the car from a catalogue or magazine photograph. Very often, a car which looks lovely from the angles photographed looks hideous (beauty being in the eye of the beholder) when viewed from the 'wrong' angle, and it would be a great shame to discover that you were unable to live with the car only after you had built it! When you have made a choice, you will be asked for a holding deposit against which your kit will be manufactured. The amount of this can vary, although 10% of the total bill seems a not unreasonable figure from both parties' viewpoints. The delivery time also varies greatly from manufacturer to manufacturer.

Sadly, a small number of kit car manufacturers seem to go out of business every year. Usually, the moulds find a buyer and the car continues in production with its new manufacturer. If the original company is liquidated and holds your deposit, then under UK law that money is counted as a part of the assets of the business by the liquidator. In other words, you may lose it. For this reason, it is as well to deal only with well established manufacturers and never to pay an unusually large deposit. It is also a good idea to collect the kit in person, so that you can inspect it before paying the balance of the money.

Some manufacturers appear rather coy with regard to the total build cost of their kits, and they advertise attractively low prices for 'starter kits' which exclude many necessary and often expensive components which can only be sourced from the manufacturer. It is by no means unusual to discover that you will have to spend up to three times the advertised starter kit price with the manufacturer if you opt for all the 'accessories' which in reality are essentials.

Obtain a total listing of necessary components and all extras (such as a windscreen, hood, special fuel tank or anything which cannot be sourced cheaply from the Mini or from another production car). Do ensure that everything you will require is included in the final price before placing your order. List those components which you will not be able to source from a single Mini, and set about collecting these at once. When costing the exercise, do allow for the replacement of many of the components from the donor car. Many components will not appear unsound until they have been stripped from the car and can be viewed properly or stripped and inspected, others (especially nuts, bolts and screws) may be damaged during removal.

Your choice of donor vehicle will have a great bearing on the final cost of the completed car. You could opt to buy a real wreck or a car which has been standing idle for a long period of time. In both cases the car will certainly come cheaply, but the costs of replacing or exchanging mechanical and other components from such cars will rapidly mount up during the build. An 'MOT failure' car could also be bought cheaply, and again, this could prove a false economy. If you spend more on the donor car and buy one in roadworthy condition and with an MOT, then you have the ideal opportunity to thoroughly test all of the mechanical and electrical components before you begin work, simply by running the car for a month or so. Any latent problems which are highlighted during this period can be dealt with before the build-up gets under way. If they are discovered part-way through the build-up then they will delay the work. If they are discovered after the build is completed, then your kit car will prove a constant source of frustration, breaking down every time another tired old component gives up the ghost.

The very best donor car is one on which the owner has spent much money on mechanical repair, only to then discover that the body is in need of extensive restoration. The use of such cars will enable the build up to be completed far more cheaply than using a real wreck with a large number of dubious mechanical components.

There are two ways to strip the donor car. The first is using a big hammer, stilson wrench and cold chisel. The recommended way is to strip the car as though you intended to fully restore it. This will not only lessen the chances of necessary donor parts being damaged during removal, but it will also furnish you with a stock of saleable commodities in the form of the unwanted Mini spares (including the bodyshell), which you can later sell to help defray the costs of the kit.

Read the chapters dealing with mechanical restoration and deal with suspect components accordingly, bearing in mind at all times that if you refit a part-worn component within the engine bottom end or within the gearbox, the entire unit will have to come out again in the future when said part fails! Removing the engine unit from some GRP-bodied kit cars brings a risk of damaging the gel coat or even the GRP itself should the engine scratch, hit or drop onto it. It is a risk best avoided by building the car properly in the first place!

Kit Car Materials

GRP (Glass Reinforced Plastic) consists of many strands of glass which are contained within a resin (usually polyester resin). The glass starts off effectively in a 'cloth' of sorts. Chopped Strand Mat (CSM) is formed by dropping short lengths of glass filament at random onto a type of glue base on a moving conveyor belt to produce a flat cloth, whereas Woven Rovings is actually a woven cloth of glass filaments which have been spun into a thread, and gives stronger results than CSM at higher costs. The shells are manufactured by polishing the inside of the mould with a release agent which prevents the

shell from sticking to its mould. On to this the gel coat (the smooth outer surface) is painted and allowed to harden. Then the CSM or woven roving 'cloth' is laid on the inside of the gel coat and 'wetted out' with polyester resin and a hardening agent, until the desired thickness is reached. When it has cured, the shell is removed from the mould.

The weight of GRP is expressed in ounces, where the figure given represents the total weight per square foot (or metre) of the glass cloth. If the shell had two layers of 4oz. CSM, then it would said to have been laid up to 8 ounces. One of the great beauties of GRP construction is that stress points can easily have extra CSM laid up into them, so that the shell can be thick in its stress areas yet light in non-stress areas.

The greatest advantage which GRP offers over steel as a material for car bodyshells is that it does not rust. Some repairs to GRP can be easier than with steel, and, of course, there is no welding involved. Other GRP repairs can be a nightmare. If the shell comprises a single moulding or perhaps just a few large mouldings and one wing is shattered, then there are no visible seams to cut to, and lining up the repair section accurately is a matter for great skill.

GRP has two great drawbacks when compared to steel as a car body material. Firstly, it cannot, unlike steel, bend to absorb the energy from a hefty impact. It simply shatters. Secondly, some of the resins used in GRP manufacture are highly flammable. The author can remember seeing a GRP-bodied vehicle go up in flames in the mid-1960s, and it is not a comforting sight. However, flame-resistant resins are now available and appear to be widely used by the reputable trade.

From the builder's viewpoint, GRP bodyshells can be moulded to the most beautiful shapes, and the work can be carried out by workers who are low-skilled in comparison with the panel beaters who are needed to manufacture steel bodied specials.

The Kit Car Alternatives

With new designs being introduced at frequent intervals and kits passing from one manufacturer to another, it is essential to begin your search for one by scouring the kit car magazines. The publishers of these magazines often produce guides of the kit car market place, listing the majority of kits which are available at the time. These guides are extremely valuable in helping track down manufacturers. There are a growing number (some believe too many) kit car shows, at which manufacturers display their cars. These are good places to hunt for the car of your dreams, because many kit car owners take their own completed kits there and are usually pleased to discuss the merits of their car and any problems encountered during the build up.

The Moke style is probably the most prolific Mini-based kit car type. At the time of writing, there was a choice of five of these.

The Cub bears probably the closest resemblance to the original Moke. This all-steel kit includes a monocoque shell to which the engine is mounted directly, so that the subframe of the donor can be sold to help defray costs. The shell consists of a steel spaceframe chassis and zinc-coated panelling, so that rusting should not be a problem. The manufacturers recommend that a 1275cc or 1300cc A-Plus engine is fitted.

The kit is comprehensive and includes the special under-floor fuel tank usually needed for Moke-type kits although it does not include the soft top nor side curtains. Build up time is quoted at '10 days', to achieve which you would have to begin with cleaned and tested donor parts.

The Nomad is a quite remarkable vehicle and comes in four varieties, Convertible, Van, Estate or Variant. The Convertible is a simple, Moke-style open vehicle with only the option of a soft top to shield the occupants from the weather. The Van has a fixed hard top, as does the five seater Estate. The Variant is perhaps the most exciting, for it may be used as an open top or cab top pickup with the option of a soft top (which unusually for a kit car, looks good), or as a van or estate with removable hard tops.

The Nomad is based around a space frame chassis, to which aluminium and hot-dip galvanised steel panels are fitted. The main chassis can also be hot-dipped at extra cost. The Mini subframes are utilised, and although Hydrolastic suspension and subframes may be used, dry suspension is generally preferred. The manufacturers recommend that the 998cc engine gives the greatest economy, but that a rather more satisfactory performance will result from the fitting of an 1100cc or preferably a 1275cc unit.

The final 'all metal' Moke-type kit is the Scamp which, after a production life of 21 years, is now available in Mark Three form. Like the Nomad, the Scamp comprises a strong steel chassis, with aluminium panelling. The manufacturers can supply the Scamp in a number of formats, including a longer wheelbase and six-wheeler versions for load carrying.

The Scamp utilises the front subframe (only from cars with 'dry' suspension), so that the engine, suspension and hubs/wheels could be built onto the subframe and the bodyshell lifted over and on to this for easy assembly. The rear subframe is not used, and any A series engine may be used.

There are two Moke-type kits which utilise GRP for some of the bodywork. The Gecko possesses what appears to be a massively constructed steel chassis which is clad with aluminium panels and finished with a GRP bonnet and wheel arches. The Gecko utilises the Mini front subframe but not the rear one, and it will take any A series power unit. The basic design of the Gecko makes it easy for the factory to supply specials with long or short wheelbase to customer's order.

The Jimini appears to be the only all-GRP kit in the Moke tradition. The basic design was originally built in steel as a more modern Moke, and it is now offered in all-GRP monocoque construction. As with all kits of this type, the manufacturers do not recommend Hydrolastic equipped donor cars, but, that apart, any Mini will serve as the donor. The kit is said to be very comprehensive.

Some manufacturers offer very attractive open or coupe sports car style kits which take advantage of the excellent roadholding of the Mini and the relative low cost at which the A series engine can be uprated, to give a good looking, fast and beautifully handling sports car at low cost.

The Wynes (previously the Birchill) McCoy uses the standard Mini subframes front and rear, bolted directly on to a sporty GRP monocoque bodyshell. Best described as a roomy sports saloon with a capacious boot, the McCoy is capable of very rapid progress when fitted with one of the larger Mini engines, and 50mpg economy is also claimed by the manufacturers.

The McCoy is also available as a very practical, attractive and unusual sports estate, which might perhaps be considered a smaller and far more economical alternative to the Reliant Scimitar.

The open top GTM Rossa and fixed head Coupe are out and out sports cars which use the Mini engine but situated behind the seats to give the mid-engined layout which first appeared in a Mini-based kit car (the Miura) way back in 1966. These cars are billed as 'the affordable alternative to the latest (1991) Lotus, Mazda and BMW soft top cars' and there could

This fascinating special was reputedly made by Jaguar apprentices during the early 1960s; the plate dates it at 1964 – if correct, pre-dating the obviously similar-looking Mini Marcos by two years. The special is based on a Mini van floorpan, and has a number of components from other cars of the period. Those rear lamp clusters look like Mk.1 Cortina issue, and the bonnet (not shown in these photographs) is cut-down from a Morris 1000 bonnet (and obscures the view of the driver to such an extent when fitted that it is probably a later addition). This car was photographed at the premises of Export Services of Redditch, and the company will oversee its full restoration. If the car was made at Jaguar, they can expect to find plenty of evidence of lead loading in that interesting bodywork!

ABOVE *The Nomad must rate as one of the most versatile vehicles of all time, because it can be built as a van, estate, cab pickup or open 'Moke' as pictured. The Nomad is especially worthy of note for its lines with the hood raised. Many otherwise very nice-looking kit cars are spoiled by cheap and utilitarian hoods. With a construction of galvanised steel and aluminium, the Nomad should be rust-free but offer the extra safety benefits of metal over GRP.*

RIGHT *These mid-engined cars from GTM not only look good, they should be able to show a clean pair of heels to many a production sports car. What is more, they enable the reasonably good DIY mechanic to turn a rotted Mini into a quite stunning sports car for a fraction of the price of the new wave of small sports cars of the early 1990s. People who have driven mid-engined cars will be aware that, correctly set-up and well shod, they seem to go around bends as though they were on rails!*

be few better uses to which you could put a badly rusted '70s or '80s Mini.

The last group of Mini-based kit cars are those which look like very well customized and de-seamed Mini saloons. The Minus is a well-established design which uses almost every component of the donor Mini (save the bodyshell itself) including seats, windscreens, lights and doors. The GRP monocoque bodyshell is reinforced with steel around the door apertures and a roll over bar connects these. Obviously, like all GRP monocoque-bodied cars, the standard loom has to be supplemented with individual earth return wires from electrical components.

The Pimlico Premier HT also resembles a tastefully customized Mini and is based on a steel reinforced monocoque GRP bodyshell. From the same company, open 'T' top versions called the

If you want to go topless, then you could do a lot worse than considering the conversion from Auto Services of Redditch, England. This is not only smart, but the kit provides a safe and proven route to a Mini convertible, and a full range of luxury interior trim is also available.

Pimlico and Pimlico Premier are available. These practical and stylish four seater convertibles can be built from any post 1976 Mini.

Bodywork Modifications

The Mini has been subjected to just about every bodywork modification conceivable during its long production life. It is imperative when contemplating such work to ensure that the final shell be at least as strong as the original and that it will still be street legal. What constitutes 'street legal' varies from country to country, and so it is important to check up on local legislation before attempting any drastic surgery to your Mini.

One of the most exciting Mini modifications is to turn the car into a convertible. The strength of the car would be severely reduced if you were merely to chop off the roof without substantially strengthening the sills and building in bracing, both to the top of the flitch panels and main scuttle crossmember in order to strengthen the top subframe mounting areas, and to the rear subframe mounting points. Some people have simply chopped down the doors a little and then weld them into position to brace the shell.

The recommended way to acquire a convertible is to buy a kit which is specially designed for the purpose, and to either carry out the necessary welding yourself or, preferably, to have it carried out professionally. Auto Services of Redditch market such a kit, which comprises not only extra body panels but a sturdy roll bar and trim – including a quality

folding hood. The kit is attractively priced, so that even if you elect to have the conversion carried out professionally, it will be relatively economical.

As far as street legality is concerned, in the UK, an MOT tester is permitted to fail a car if he considers that any part of the bodywork might pose a danger to other road users. If you were to, for instance, make up your own wheel arch extensions and leave a sharp corner or edge on them, this would surely be a potential MOT failure point.

If you wish to substantially alter the bodywork of your Mini, then the author suggests that you attend one of the many Mini special events which are held around the UK summer months and also in some other countries. At such events, you can normally see many examples of customized Minis and talk to the owners who actually carried out the work on the cars. The experiences of these people will be invaluable in helping you decide exactly which modifications you wish to perpetrate upon your own car, and in supplying invaluable background information on the problems found along the way.

Recent Mini History

In the last twelve years a number of Limited Edition Minis have been manufactured and, because these will inevitably in future become more sought-after by classic car enthusiasts than the standard saloon, they are described here as an aid to authenticity and as a reference for the future.

The most recent limited edition cars make sound economic sense for the buyer who wants a 'nearly new' car with character, with some degree of exclusivity and – most importantly – with sound bodywork and reliable mechanical components. Few of these limited edition cars have as yet grabbed the attention of the classic car press and, perhaps partially as a result, their second-hand prices are largely unaffected by the hype and nonsense which has driven the prices of so many great cars beyond the reach of the enthusiast. At the time of writing, most of the limited edition cars may be obtained for a little more than the book prices for the Mayfair of the same year – if the interest in classic cars continues to rise in the future, however, expect the values of all limited edition cars to rise accordingly.

Interestingly, some of the limited edition cars today seem to be quite a rare sight on the roads of the UK in proportion to their (limited) production figures, and it appears that enthusiasts may already have been buying up bargain-priced examples to keep for posterity – perhaps to be fully restored in the years ahead. The history of the Mini special begins outside the factory. Many limited edition and 'special' Minis (usually featuring more luxurious interiors and sometimes with special coachwork) were made by outside companies, such as Wood & Pickett (whose mid-1960s Margrave special was particularly successful, and who are still producing custom Minis today), when the Mini was *the* small car to be seen in and when the fashion conscious were consequently

prepared to pay up-market prices for very up-market Minis.

The story of factory specials really began during the early to mid 1970s with a limited edition Mini in 1974 and a special 1000 in 1976. In August of 1979 (the Mini's 20th anniversary), the company launched the limited edition 1100cc Special, which had metallic paintwork, better interior trim and a centre instrument console complete with a clock. Costing £3,300, 5000 examples were manufactured. The 1100 Special (like the two earlier limited edition cars) is quite a rare car in 1992, but so far it has escaped the classic car price boom and may still be acquired (for those who are prepared to spend enough time looking for one) at low prices. This is to a large extent true of most of the specials covered here.

The Mini Sprite was launched in October of 1983. Priced at £3,334, the Sprite featured side decals with a Sprite logo, alloy wheels and a special interior, and was powered by the 1 litre engine as fitted in the Austin Metro. Production ran to just

ABOVE RIGHT *It is difficult to believe that this 1988/9 Mayfair could ever truly aspire to the rank of coveted 'classic' car because it is a mainstream production model, yet who can predict what sort of fond memories it could conjure up in the year 2000 for the teenager who might have learned to drive in one when new. Furthermore, it is an example of one of the last Minis to be fitted with a carburettor. If you have one of these or any other recent Mini, look after the bodywork! (courtesy Rover Cars)*

RIGHT *The 1991 Mini Neon Special Edition. With just 1500 examples built, undoubtedly destined to be a classic. (courtesy Rover Cars)*

2,500 examples, and so this (the first Mini Sprite – not to be confused with the 1992 Mini Sprite) is quite a rare car today.

To celebrate the Mini's 25th anniversary, the company introduced a limited edition 'Silver Jubilee' model in July of 1984. Named the Mini 25 and priced at £3,865, it featured silver paintwork, tinted glass and door mirrors, reclining seats fitted with head-rests and velvet upholstery. Although fitted with only the standard 998cc engine, the brakes were uprated to discs at the front and more efficient drums at the rear. A total of 5,000 Mini 25s were manufactured.

The company then took the Mini special concept up-market, and endowed a series which lasted until 1987 with a number of names taken from the 'better' London addresses. Although the City and Mayfair models were to be the regular production versions of the Mini, they should be included in this list because the earlier versions will probably one day become sought-after. The City and Mayfair were initially introduced in September 1980 and October 1982 respectively. The City E (economy) and HLE were launched in 1982, fitted with 'A Plus' economy engine from the Metro 1000. Both the City and the Mayfair were upgraded in October of 1984 to include 12″ wheels and wheelarch spats, plus disc brakes (the same as those fitted to the Mini 25). The interior was sawtooth design fabric for the city and for the Mayfair, chalk stripe velvet.

The limited edition Mini Ritz was introduced in June of 1985. The car was fitted with 12″ alloy wheels and wheelarch spats, plus a three spoke steering wheel, radio and rear seat belts. The metallic silver leaf paintwork featured a side coachline and the 'Ritz' logo, the red, white and blue interior was colour coordinated. A total of 3,725 Ritz cars were built, priced at £3,798.

Based on the 998cc Mini City, the Chelsea was a limited special launched in January 1986, featured

ABOVE LEFT *The 1992 Mini 1.3 Mayfair. A mixture of 1960s style (chrome bumpers, grille and door handles) and opulent (as opulent as the Mini has ever been) interior. (courtesy Rover Cars)*

LEFT *The 1992 Mini 1.3 Sprite. The name is evocative of one of the illustrious periods in the company's history – the 1950s – when sports cars like the Austin Healey 'Frogeye' Sprite conquered the world. (courtesy Rover Cars)*

Targa red paintwork with twin side coachlines (with Chelsea logo) and Osprey grey cloth trimmed reclining front seats. As with previous special editions, the Chelsea had 12″ alloy wheels and wheelarch spats. A total of just 1,500 were produced, making this quite a rare variant. At just £2 under £4,000, it was also the most expensive Mini to date. The limited edition Piccadilly followed the Chelsea in June 1986, and differed mainly in the paintwork (gold, with Piccadilly logo on seats, coachline and boot) and interior trim (claret, chocolate and coffee). A total of 2,500 were produced, priced at £3,928.

The up-market limited edition Park Lane (£4,193) was introduced in January 1987. This featured black paintwork with Park Lane decals, full width wheel trims, tinted glass, seates trimmed in coffee/beige velvet and a stereo radio cassette player. Only 1,500 Park Lane models were produced, making this – the last of the series of more luxurious, limited edition 'London address' cars – a rarer variant.

In May 1987 (to coincide with the French tennis Open – the UK launch came in June of that year to coincide with Wimbledon), the Mini Advantage was introduced. The paintwork was Diamond white with matching wheel trims, and there were 'tennis net' side stripes with the Advantage logo. The interior was grey with jade green pin-stripes and a tennis ball logo(!), and came complete with radio and tachometer. 2,500 of these cars – priced at £4,286 – were sold in the UK. More than any previous special Mini, the fully colour-coordinated Advantage reflected modern fashion trends, in this case, the 'designer' cult of the 1980s. The Advantage marked a change in the approach of the company to Mini specials; preceding models were based around the smart London district theme, whereas most later specials adopted a new and then very fashionable theme – nostalgia for the 1960s.

In February 1988 two limited edition specials were launched, the 'Jet Black' and 'Red Hot'. With paintwork (obviously) in black or red, the interior was black velour with red piping and with badges on the front seats. These cars also had tinted glass and a push button radio, and 2,000 were sold on the UK market at a price of £4,382. The next in the growing list of limited edition cars was the Mini Designer, launched in June of 1988, with designs taken from Mary Quant. Paintwork was either black or diamond white, and the interior had black and white striped seat covers. The radiator and headlight surrounds

ABOVE *The Mini's engine bay has always been a crowded place, but that of the 1.3i Cooper is especially so. (courtesy Rover Cars)*

ABOVE LEFT *Taking one of the most powerful icons of the 'Swinging '60s' – the Mini Cooper, and re-creating it thirty years on shows a degree of commercial commonsense which the company often appeared to lack during its much-critcised BMC/BL phases. The Mini Cooper is currently (1992) accounting for 40% of Mini sales worldwide. (courtesy Rover Cars)*

LEFT *A motor manufacturer in the 1990s cannot afford to neglect the interior comforts offered by a car, no matter how strongly nostalgia contributes to its sales. The 1.3 Mini Cooper interior. (courtesy Rover Cars)*

were grey. 2,000 of these £4,654 cars were sold in the UK. Revived 1960s style became of increasing importance in its influence of the design of Mini specials. In January 1989 the company introduced not one but four limited edition Minis – the two-tone Flame (red) and Racing (British racing green) were to celebrate the Mini's 30 years of motor competition success, and 2,000 of these were sold at a price of £4,795, whilst the Rose and Sky (white with pink or pastel blue roof panels respectively) were a continuation of the 'designer' theme of Mini specials; just 1,000 of these were produced to sell at £4,695. All have special interior trim and a stereo radio/cassette player. The Flame and Racing variants were marginally more expensive than the Rose and Sky, suggesting perhaps that nostalgia for the racing heritage of the Mini can be sold at a higher price than nostalgia for general '60s style!

229

In June 1989 the Mini Thirty was launched in recognition of the car's thirty years of production. To celebrate this milestone, a party was held at Silverstone and attended by an incredible 130,000 Mini enthusiasts. The car was fitted with 8 spoke alloy wheels and leather faced black seats. Some 3000 Mini Thirty models were manufactured, to sell at £5,599.

Presumably encouraged (delighted might be a more accurate description) by the success of its limited edition Minis, the company re-introduced the Racing and Flame variants in February of 1990 and, along with the Checkmate (black with a white roof), sold a further 2,500 at a price of £5,455.

In June of 1990 the Mini 'Studio 2' – based on the City – was launched. Apart from the Studio 2 decals on the sides and seats, the car had a more traditional chrome grille, opening rear quarter lights and doeskin seat covers. Priced at £5,375, 2,000 of this special were manufactured.

Probably the most important new Mini variant for years was launched in July 1990 when the Mini

ABOVE *The Range Rovers and Land Rover Discoveries in the background are of course completely out-numbered by the Cooper and other Minis waiting to be loaded onto this strange looking vessel – the 'Jinsei Maru' – whose port of registration tells us that the cars are destined for Tokyo. Strange to think that the Mini was around before the Japanese car invasion of Europe started, that it has constantly been in manufacture throughout, and that it is finally emerging as the only British car to seriously challenge it! (courtesy Rover Cars)*

RIGHT *An almost unbearably trendy publicity photograph of the Racing, Flame, Rose and Sky in their first – 1989 – incarnation. (courtesy Rover Cars)*

Cooper name again adorned a production car. The last Mini Cooper had been built nineteen years earlier in 1971! The manufacturer, in conjunction with John Copper Garages, had in fact been offering a 'Mini Copper' performance conversion kit for the Mini since February of the same year, but the July launch was a

limited production run of 1,000 cars (priced at £6,995 – at the time some 'collectors' were immediately re-advertising their Coopers for sale at prices nearer £10,000 when good 1960s Coopers were fetching far less. Presumably these people were selling the cars at such prices as 'instant classics') with white bonnet stripes and the John Cooper signature. Thereafter, the new Mini Cooper continued in normal production. Especially notable was the fact that the car was the first production vehicle for ten years to be fitted with the 1275cc engine.

The new Cooper boasted a reasonable turn of speed, with a 0–60mph time of just 11.5 seconds and a top speed of 92mph. The 1275cc engine produced 78BHP at the flywheel, which gives it more urge than the non-S Coopers and the 1275GT, but less than the original 1275cc Cooper S. The performance figures, however, show the car to be more than adequate for 1990s traffic.

The limited edition Cooper was fitted with black leather trim, a glass sun-roof, tinted glass, auxiliary driving lamps set against a chrome Cooper grille, and with alloy wheels.

The still current Mini Cooper 1.3i comes with a catalytic converter as standard and a fuel injection system. Fuel consumption should work out at around 36mpg during urban driving, stretching towards around 48mpg or so, on longer runs.

In February 1991 the special edition Neon (like so many recent specials, based on the City) was introduced, with Caribbean Blue paintwork. Chrome bumpers and door handles were another link to the Mini's past, but the full width wheel trims, chevron velour upholstery trim and digital stereo radio/cassette player were concessions to modern tastes. Priced at £5,570, production was limited to 1,500 examples.

A convertible Mini was announced in June 1991. This conversion was carried out by Rover's German dealership LAMM Autohaus, and was based on the new 1.3i Mini Cooper to give the benefits of enhanced performance. Just 75 examples were offered and, despite the £12,250 price tag, sold out days after the model was first announced.

The Mini Racing Green of February 1990. (courtesy Rover Cars)

The Mini Today

A the time of writing, the current range comprises three models (the City was discontinued during 1992); these are the Mayfair, Sprite and Cooper 1.3i. The base model is the Sprite, although this stylish treatment looks anything but a base model. The exterior perspective is improved greatly by wheelarch spats and attractive wheel trim, chrome bumpers and a side decal. The long-serving Mayfair takes style even more seriously with a chrome grille, door handles and bumpers, plus tinted glass throughout.

The Mini Cooper has become an established and very important part of the current range, accounting for no less than 40% of all Mini sales during 1990/1991. It is popular in export markets, particularly in Germany, Switzerland and Japan.

From October 1991 the Mini Cooper has been fitted with the 1.3i engine and has had a closed loop catalytic converter as standard, so allowing the car to sell on markets where exhaust emissions regulations are stringent. The new Mini Sprite and the latest version of the Mayfair also share the Cooper engine/catalytic converter. At the ripe old age of 33, the Mini is still going strong and, in fact, has in recent years notched up yet more accolades as Britain's best selling car in Japan and – little short of astounding – as Britain's best selling export car overall!

Exactly why so old a design should sell more strongly in some markets than the sometimes faster, more efficient and more comfortable cars of the 1990s is open to debate. Certainly a large part of the attraction of Mini ownership is connected with the car's undoubted 'cult' status, which appears particularly strong in Japan; but something as intangible as cult status cannot on its own turn any old car into a modern sales success – the Mini has to have something extra.

New Minis continue to sell well in the UK; the Mini is one of those cars which gain such driver loyalty that many long-term owners continuously replace their Minis every few years with brand new ones. The Mini also gains its fair share of new converts in the UK, probably in the main people who started out looking at economical modern hatchbacks but who came to realise that the Mini offered something extra.

A brand new Mini is a very sound purchase for a variety of reasons. The main reason for the car's continuing sales success is undoubtedly that in recent years it has in all respects been a thoroughly competent small car for the 1990s. Fitted firstly with the new cylinder head and thus able to run on unleaded fuel, and with the option of a catalytic converter for the green at heart, the little car would regularly return around 45 miles to the gallon overall, rising to roughly 60 mpg on longer runs. Now with its 1.3i injection engine and cat, the Mini meets the most stringent environmental requirements.

True, acceleration of the recently discontinued carburettor-equipped models was slightly short of staggering, with a 0–60mph time of 17 seconds and a

If the Mini Cooper is good enough for this gentleman, it's good enough for anyone! (courtesy Rover Cars)

top speed of 80 mph, but these Minis were able to get from A to B as quickly and to keep up with traffic as well as the Minis of yesteryear by virtue of their superb roadholding and handling. Pure paper figures belie the eagerness of the standard 998cc engine, anyway, and the overall performance of the car should enable it to easily keep up today. Now fitted with the same 1.3i power plant as the Cooper, the most recent Minis are thoroughly competent road cars.

The factors which made the Mini a great car at its 1959 launch are still relevant today. No other manufacturer has managed to provide true four adult seating in so small a car, which makes the Mini ideally suited to town and city work, where parking is always at a premium and where there can usually be found small vacant parking spaces which so few other vehicles could possibly squeeze into.

What really separates the Mini from all its competitors is the ease and low cost of maintenance procedures and spares purchase, low insurance premiums, the very low depreciation, and the fact that every cared-for Mini should one day have depreciated to the point at which collectors' values takes over from straightforward 'book' value. Then this remarkable car ceases to be (as is every new car) a depreciating liability and becomes instead an asset.

If you take the long-term view, the Mini is the most sensible buy in small cars today, just as it has always been.

SPECIALISTS' ADDRESSES

CLUB ADDRESSES

Mini Owners' Club
15 Birchwood Road, Lichfield, Staffordshire WS14 9UN,
England

Mini Seven Racing Club
345 Clay Lane, South Yardley, Birmingham B26 1ES,
England

Mini Moke Club
13 Ashdene Close, Hartlebury, Worcestershire DY11 7TN,
England

Mini Marcos Owners' Club
28 Meadows Road, Claines, Worcester WR3 7PP, England

Mini Cooper Club
1, Weavers Cottages, Church Hill, West Hoathly, West
Sussex RH19 4PW, England

Mini Cooper Register
14 Gaveston Road, Leamington Spa, Warwickshire CV32
6EU, England

MINI SPECIALIST SPARES SUPPLIERS

Mini Spares Centre Limited
29-31, Friern Barnet Road, Southgate, London N11 1NE,
England. Tel. 081 368 6292
(All Mini Spares)

Ripspeed International Ltd
54 Upper Fore Street, Edmunton, London N18 2SS,
England.
(Body styling kits, performance components)

Merryhill Mini Centre
Unit 7, Stour Vale Road, Lye, West Midlands England
(New and Used Mini spares)

Discount Mini Centre
New Road, Rainham, Essex RN13 8SH, England
(Mini Spares, Repairs)

Minimail
Dymock, Gloucestershire, England Tel. 0531 85 325.
(Mail order Mini spares)

Westford Mini and Metro Centre
4, Bath Place, The Octagon, Plymouth, Devon England
(Spares and Restoration services)

Mini Sprint
295 Avenue Road Extension, Welford Road, Leicester
England
(Mechanical spares and services)

Midland Mini Centre
317 Highfield Road, Hall Green, Birmingham B28 0BX
England
(All Mini Spares)

Minispeed
5 Oak Street, Elworth, Sandbach, Cheshire, England
(Mini dismantlers)

Penarth Mini Centre
Cornerswell Road, Penarth, South Glamorgan CF6 1XQ,
Wales
(Original and replacement Mini Spares)

JT Restorations
979 Oldham Road, Newton Heath, Manchester M10 6FE,
England
(Performance and accessories retail)

Downton
The Old Works, Crookhill, Braishfield, Romsey, Hampshire
SO5 0QB, England
(Stage One conversions for Mini Coopers retail)

Mini Machine
Unit 2, North Road Industrial Estate, Darlington DL3 0OR,
England
(Parts and restorations)

Minifare
8-10 Rectory Lane, Ashtead, Surrey KT21 2BB, England
(All spares and accessories for all Minis. Retail)

Chequered Flag
71 Eastfields Road, Mitcham, Surrey CR4 2LS, England
(All mechanical spares for all Minis. Retail)

Auto Services
Unit 9, Meadow Road, Lakeside, Redditch, Worcestershire,
England
(Mini convertible kits, custom trim and upholstery)

APPENDICES

TORQUE WRENCH SETTINGS

	Foot pounds	Kg/metres
Camshaft nut	65	8.9
Clutch spring set screws	16	2.2
Water temperature sender	16	2.2
Connecting rod big end nuts	33	4.6
bolts	37	5.1
Crankshaft pulley bolt	75	10.3
Flywheel driving strap set screw	16	2.2
Flywheel bolt	112	15.5
Flywheel housing nuts/bolts	18	2.5
Main bearing bolts	63	8.7
Manifold nuts	14	1.9
Oil filter centre bolt	14	1.9
Oil pump bolts	8	1.1
Oil pipe banjo	38	5.3
Oil relief valve nut	43	5.9
Cylinder head nuts	50	6.9
Extra nuts 1275GT	25	3.5
Rocker cover	3.5	.5
Rocker shaft bracket nuts	24	3.2
Spark plugs	18	3.5
Oil sump drain plug	25	3.5
Timing cover/front plate bolts ¼"	5	.7
⁵⁄₁₆"	12	1.7
Cylinder side cover 1000cc	3.5	.5
Water pump bolts	16	2.2
Water outlet elbow nuts	8	1.1

LUBRICANTS AND FLUIDS

Engine/gearbox oil. Multigrade 20W/50, 10W/30 or 10W/40 engine oil. 10W/40 for all cars after 1983. Capacity 8.5 pints, 4.83 litres, 10.2 US pints. Automatic 9 pints, 5 litres.

Carburettor dashpot oil. As above.

Grease points. Lithium multi-purpose grease.

Brake and clutch hydraulic system. Hydraulic fluid to SAE J1703.

Anti freeze. To BS3151 or 3152. To −19 degrees C 33%. To −36 degrees C 50%. Coolant capacity 6.25 pints, 3.55 litres.

TOOLS AND EQUIPMENT SUPPLIERS

Note: companies listed as Manufacturers will not usually supply directly, but will be pleased to advise of your nearest stockist

Frost Auto Restoration Techniques Ltd
Crawford Street, Rochdale. OL16 5NU, England
(Wide range of traditional and modern tools and equipment for bodywork restoration. Includes metal stretchers, metal shaping equipment, lead loading, etc. Retail and Mail Order)

Mr. Fast'ner
Units 1 and 2, Warwick House Industrial Park, Benbury Road, Southam, Warwickshire. CV33 0HL, England
(Nuts, bolts, self tappers, split pins etc. Retail and Mail Order)

SIP (Industrial Products) Ltd
Gelders Hall Road, Shepshed, Loughborough, Leicestershire. LE12 9NH, England
(Compressors, welding equipment and accessories. Manufacturer)

Machine Mart
Lower Parliament Street, Nottingham. England Tel. 0602 411200
(Extensive range of compressors, welders, general garage equipment and hand tools. 20 showrooms within UK. Retail and Mail Order)

Bondaglass-Voss Ltd
158-164 Ravenscroft Road, Beckenham, Kent, England
(Paint and paint-related products, including Bonda-Prima rust-resistant primer paint. Manufacturer)

Transpeed Mail Order Ltd
211 Portland Road, Hove, Sussex BN3 5JA England
(Wide range of compressors and accessories, welders and hand tools. Mail Order)

Kellers
24 Cattle Market Street, Norwich NR1 3DY, England
(Wide range of specialised hand tools, plus various welding accessories. Retail and Mail Order)

Apollo Sprayers Ltd
48 Eyre Street, Birmingham B18 7AA, England
(Low pressure paint spraying equipment. Manufacturer)

Sykes Pickavant Ltd
Warwick Works, Kilnhouse Lane, Lytham St. Annes, Lancashire FY8 3DU, England
(Quality hand tools. Manufacturer)

PUBLICATIONS

Practical Classics
EMAP National Publications Ltd., Bushfield House, Orton Centre, Peterborough PE2 0UX, England
(Minis featured from time to time. This magazine always has excellent mechanical repair/bodywork restoration articles of interest to the DIY restorer)

Popular Classics
EMAP National Publications Ltd., Bushfield House, Orton Centre, Peterborough PE2 0UX, England
(Minis featured from time to time. Covers most classic cars with profiles, buyer's guides etc)

Which Kit?
Filby Publishing Ltd. 1 Howard Road, Reigate, Surrey RH2 7JE, England
(All Kit cars in monthly magazine. Special buyer's guides also published)

Kit Car
Redalpha Ltd. Old Run Road, Leeds LS10 2AA, England
(All Kit cars in monthly magazine. Special buyer's guides also published)

Mini World
Link House, Dingwall Avenue, Croydon, CR9 2TA, England
The only UK magazine devoted to the Mini is, sadly, a quarterly. The chances of finding a quarterly publication on the shelf at a newsagent's are slim, so interested parties should either place an order with their newsagent or write to the subscriptions department of the publishers.

INDEX

Page references in *italics* refer to captions.